THE
PORTABLE MBA
IN ECONOMICS

The Portable MBA Series

The Portable MBA Series provides managers, executives, professionals, and students with a "hands-on," easy-to-access overview of the ideas and information covered in a typical Masters of Business Administration program. The published and forthcoming books in the program are:

Published

The Portable MBA (0-471-61997-3, cloth; 0-471-54895-2, paper) Eliza G. C. Collins and Mary Anne Devanna

The Portable MBA Desk Reference (0-471-57681-6) Paul A. Argenti

The Portable MBA in Finance and Accounting (0-471-53226-6) John Leslie Livingstone

The Portable MBA in Management (0-471-57379-5) Allan R. Cohen

The Portable MBA in Marketing (0-471-54728-X) Alexander Hiam and Charles Schewe

New Product Development: Managing and Forecasting for Strategic Success (0-471-57226-8) Robert J. Thomas

Real-Time Strategy: Improving Team-Based Planning for a Fast-Changing World (0-471-58564-5) Lee Tom Perry, Randall G. Stott, and W. Norman Smallwood

The Portable MBA in Economics (0-471-59526-8) Philip K. Y. Young and John McCauley

The Portable MBA in Entrepreneurship (0-471-57780-4) William Bygrave

The Portable MBA in Strategy (0-471-58498-3) Liam Fahey and Robert M. Randall

The New Marketing Concept (0-471-59576-4) Frederick E. Webster

Total Quality Management: Strategies and Techniques Proven at Today's Most Successful Companies (0-471-54538-1) Arnold Weimerskirch and Stephen George

Market-Driven Management: Using the New Market Concept to Create a Customer-Oriented Company (0-471-5976-4) Frederick E. Webster

Forthcoming

The Portable MBA in Global Business Leadership (0-471-30410-7) Noel Tichy, Michael Brimm, and Hiro Takeuchi

Analyzing the Balance Sheet (0-471-59191-2) John Leslie Livingstone

Information Technology and Business Strategy (0-471-59659-0) N. Venkatraman and James E. Short

Negotiating Strategically (0-471-1321-8) Roy Lewicki and Alexander Hiam

Psychology for Leaders (0-471-59538-1) Dean Tjosvold and Mary Tjosvold

THE
PORTABLE MBA
IN ECONOMICS

Philip K. Y. Young
John J. McAuley

John Wiley & Sons, Inc.

New York • Chichester • Brisbane • Toronto • Singapore

This text is printed on acid-free paper.

Copyright © 1994 by Philip K. Y. Young & John J. McAuley
Published by John Wiley & Sons, Inc.

This publication is designed to provide accurate and
authoritative information in regard to the subject
matter covered. It is sold with the understanding that
the publisher is not engaged in rendering legal, accounting,
or other professional services. If legal advice or other
expert assistance is required, the services of a competent
professional person should be sought. *From a Declaration
of Principles jointly adopted by a Committee of the
American Bar Association and a Committee of Publishers.*

Library of Congress Cataloging-in-Publication Data:

Young, Philip K. Y.
    The portable MBA in economics / Philip K. Y. Young, John J.
McAuley.
        p.   cm.
    Includes index.
    ISBN 0-471-59526-8
    1. Economics.   2. Decision-making.   3. Business forecasting.
I. McAuley, John J., 1947–   . II. Title.
HB71.Y68   1994
330—dc20   93-41321

Printed in the United States of America

10 9 8 7 6 5 4 3 2 1

THE
PORTABLE MBA
IN ECONOMICS

Philip K. Y. Young
John J. McAuley

John Wiley & Sons, Inc.

New York • Chichester • Brisbane • Toronto • Singapore

Copyright © 1994 by Philip K. Y. Young & John J. McAuley
Published by John Wiley & Sons, Inc.

Library of Congress Cataloging-in-Publication Data:

Young, Philip K. Y.
    The portable MBA in economics / Philip K. Y. Young, John J.
McAuley.
        p.   cm.
    Includes index.
    ISBN 0-471-59526-8
    1. Economics.   2. Decision-making.   3. Business forecasting.
I. McAuley, John J., 1947–   . II. Title.
HB71.Y68   1994
330—dc20   93-41321

Printed in the United States of America

10 9 8 7 6 5 4 3 2 1

To my parents, Kenneth and Frances

PKYY

To the memories of my parents,
Joseph and Evelyn
and my father-in-law,
Arthur Felton

JJM

To my parents, Kenneth and Frances

PKYY

To the memories of my parents,
Joseph and Evelyn
and my father-in-law,
Arthur Felton

JJM

PREFACE

This book is written for managers and professionals who wish to gain a better understanding of how economic analysis can be used to shape and guide business decisions. It is based on macro- and microeconomic theory but concentrates heavily on the application of these theories to business decision making.

Part One of the book deals with macroeconomic analysis. It seeks to highlight the importance of macroeconomics by showing how people in different business positions, such as an assistant treasurer of a public utility and a buyer for a retail store, can benefit by understanding the forces that affect the level of economic activity. The use of equations and graphs is kept to a minimum. Instead, the workings of the aggregate economy are explained primarily by defining and tracking actual economic data and by carefully describing the workings of such key economic institutions as the Federal Reserve System. Much of the content of the macroeconomic chapters is based on the experiences of John McAuley, who has 20 years of experience as a business economist—first for a major commercial bank and now as a consultant for the bond trading divisions of a number of private financial companies.

Part Two deals with applied microeconomics. To illustrate how this aspect of economic theory is used, a number of recent examples involving companies in the Fortune 500 are presented. The explanation of microeconomics requires a slightly greater use of graphs and numerical examples, but here again they are kept to a minimum. The emphasis is on how the concepts illustrated by these graphs and numbers can be applied to business decisions. The way in which microeconomics is linked to actual business decisions is based on the teaching and consulting experiences of Philip Young. In addition to teaching for 20 years in undergraduate and graduate business programs, he has considerable experience developing and presenting seminars and workshops in applied economics for a number of major corporations. Many of the specific examples cited in the text are based on the corporate education programs that he has been involved in, as well as on the material that he has prepared for his MBA students.

CONTENTS

1 BUSINESS AND ECONOMICS

Economic news is pervasive across all media. The business world exists within an economic environment that shapes business conditions, which is itself shaped by business decisions, and these business decisions are often made on the basis of economic principles. This book is intended to bring the economic influences on business decision making—management—out of the dimly lit background into the spotlight.

The influence of overall economic effects on business conditions, as well as the feedback from businesses to the overall economy, stems from one of the two main branches of economics, *macroeconomics,* which focuses on aggregate economic conditions. These conditions set the environment within which a business operates. Consequently, a full understanding of these conditions enhances the ability of a manager to make sound business decisions and to avoid surprises.

The other branch of economics, *microeconomics,* focuses on the economic forces that influence the decisions made by individual consumers, firms, and industries. These decisions are often made in an instinctive way, yet consistent economic forces underlie them. Thus, an explicit recognition and understanding of the forces that influence these decisions is a vital part of a manager's intellectual equipment.

The book begins with the widest, most aggregate issues—the macroeconomic—and then proceeds to the more specific topics of microeconomics.

MACROECONOMICS

Overall economic activity is measured in a variety of ways. These measurements—the number of people with jobs, the total income of persons, the output of factories, and the amount of total goods and services produced in the economy (GDP)—are regularly reported in newspapers, business periodicals, and television and radio news. These reports often fail to explain the importance of these and other economic indicators. A business manager should be able to put these announcements in perspective in regard to both the relationships among indicators and the manager's own business.

Gross domestic product (GDP) is the most comprehensive measure of economic activity. It can be viewed from either the demand side or the supply side. On the demand side, GDP provides insight into how the various decision-making sectors of the aggregate economy—households, business firms, government entities, and foreigners—interact. These elements constitute the market demand that a firm faces and therefore should be understood by a competent manager.

The supply of goods and services requires firms to bring together the factors of production, particularly labor and capital, to produce output that meets demand. For the aggregate economy, the available supplies of labor and capital, and the additions to the capital stock through investment, limit the amount of production that can take place. Managers need to be aware of these limits and any ongoing changes in them to manage their own resources efficiently.

Unfortunately, economic activity seldom proceeds at a smooth pace that fully utilizes all resources. Instead, the U.S. economy, as well as other economies of the industrialized world, in the post-World War II era usually has shown signs of either inflation or unemployment, and occasionally both at the same time. Such distortions of the economic environment require business managers to adapt their decisions to these forces. Thus an understanding of the factors leading to unemployment and inflation and to the existence of a tradeoff between them is important for a manager in dealing with a variety of business decisions, from hiring to pricing.

Money and credit are the lubricant and fuel that drive the macroeconomy. The demand for money, the supply response of the Federal Reserve and the banking system, and the resulting effect on interest rates are factors that affect all businesses. It is necessary to look at the monetary economy from an entirely fresh perspective to gain the insights that a manager needs to manage the financial aspects of a firm.

Business decisions are increasingly made in an international context. Consideration of the international trade and finance flows that affect business broadens even further the notion of *macro*economics. It is not enough for a manager to take into account the conditions that affect the domestic economy. Even in an economy as large as the United States, economic conditions in foreign economies greatly influence domestic business decisions. This has been even more true since the early 1970s, as the share of total GDP accounted for

by foreign trade has doubled. Along with this increased importance at the aggregate level has been an increasing impact on individual business firms from international economic conditions.

MICROECONOMICS

In Part Two of the book, we turn to a closer focus on the economic forces that influence the decisions made by individual firms.

The most basic economic forces a firm has to address are those that shape the supply and demand for the goods or services it produces. Even as American businesses are undergoing massive management changes, it is increasingly recognized that changing *market* conditions provoke these responses. While supply and demand are among the most basic concepts in economics, an understanding of these forces is nonetheless essential to efficient management.

The conditions that underlie the demand for a product are so important to a firm's price setting that this subject deserves a more detailed discussion. In particular, the notion of *elasticity*—the measure of consumers' responsiveness to price changes—is at the root of a firm's ability to set and change prices. Other factors also influence the intensity of consumer demand for a product and must be considered when setting prices. These considerations go to the core of business management: These techniques are essential to the manager's ability to function.

The other side to pricing in the profit equation is cost. To manage a firm effectively, a manager must have a thorough understanding of the relevant costs of production. This understanding also requires the manager to distinguish between costs that are relevant only in the short run and those that are crucial to the firm's long-run survival. The method for examining cost and determining the optimal level of production is another of the basic applications of microeconomic theory to management.

The crux of the microeconomic influences on business decision making is the answer to the two-part question: How much should the firm produce, and how much should it charge for this output? The book refocuses the prior discussion on demand, supply, and costs into an explicit consideration of this question demonstrating the key economic principles to effective business management.

Our viewpoint starts from the U.S. economy. Most of the concepts, however, are equally true for other developed (and even developing) economies. Just as the MBA approach to business management is gaining adherents elsewhere in the world, we believe the economic influences on business management discussed in this book also have applicability beyond the United States.

PART ONE

MACROECONOMICS

2 MEASURING ECONOMIC ACTIVITY

How to Understand and Use Economic Indicators

Business managers usually make decisions specific to their department or part of the firm. These decisions usually take into account the concerns of the company as a whole and, at times, are subject to wider industry or market conditions. This chapter focuses on the main measures of economic activity. Fluctuations in economic activity set the conditions within which the market, industry, and company must operate, and these measures reflect those fluctuations. Thus, the well equipped manager must understand economic indicators to make informed business decisions. This chapter provides a working knowledge of the main U.S. economic indicators. While the explicit references are to U.S. economic data, the concepts also apply with little modification to other developed economies.

We will use as an example Tim Roberts, who is the assistant treasurer for a utility company. His company has to refinance $15 million of maturing 10-year bonds sometime in the next 3 months. Whether the offering is made immediately or later in the 3-month period depends on the prospects for interest rate movements. (Even slightly higher rates will raise costs over the life of the bonds.) The outlook for interest rates, in turn, depends on two sets of economic activity measures:

1. The economic forces that affect the demand and supply for credit will set the environment within which the utility firm must offer its bonds.

2. Economic conditions also influence the Federal Reserve's monetary policy. The Fed responds to those conditions, and so the timing of the bond offering has to be sensitive to the same factors that influence the Fed.

This situation requires a manager—whose speciality is something other than economics—to evaluate conditions for the macroeconomy as a whole. To do this, Tim Roberts may well seek expert advice from either an in-house economist or an outside consultant. (In a smaller firm, he might simply monitor the reporting on economic conditions in the business press—*Business Week, Fortune, The Wall Street Journal*—much more closely than usual.) Nevertheless, to recommend when to come to market with the bond offering, he will need to be familiar with macroeconomic measurements and concepts.

There are many measures and indicators of overall, or macroeconomic, activity. Regular readers of *The Wall Street Journal* or the business pages of major newspapers will have at least heard of many of these indicators. In fact, measures such as the unemployment rate, the consumer price index, retail sales, and housing starts frequently are featured on the evening news. At a minimum, well-equipped business managers should be thoroughly familiar with just what such indicators actually measure and, more important, what these measures mean. At the least, this reduces the danger that a manager can be bamboozled by some jargon-tongued economist.

To start, we will focus on four key indicators and then widen our examination to outline most of the major economic indicators regularly reported by the U.S. government and its agencies.

FOUR KEY MACROECONOMIC INDICATORS

The four measures described in this section measure economic activities that constitute the core of economic activity: Jobs reflect production and are the main source of income. Thus, the separate measures of employment, industrial production, and personal income are individually important. In combination, they provide a great deal of insight about the behavior of the overall economy. A summary of the behavior of the overall economy—which partly summarizes these other indicators—is the measure known as *gross domestic product* (GDP). There are, thus, four data series that can be examined to get a working impression of the statistical measures of the U.S. economy:

1. Payroll employment.
2. Personal income.

3. Industrial production.
4. Gross domestic product (GDP).

Each of these major economic indicators exerts important influences on business conditions and business decision making. Employment is the most basic measure of how wider economic events affect individuals. The jobs people hold are typically the main source of their income, which is the fuel that enables consumer spending. Production is the act of using labor and other resources to make the goods that consumers buy. GDP measures the total value of goods and services produced (and purchased) in the economy.

Post-World War II annual levels and percent changes for each of these four measures are shown in Table 2–1 and in Figures 2–1 through 2–5. While the exact patterns have varied, an upward trend is common to all four. There is a much sharper rise for personal income because this is the only indicator measured in *current dollar* terms, meaning that personal income still contains the effects of inflation. Employment is a *real* measure because it is in terms of the number of jobs rather than a monetary measure. Industrial production is measured in terms of physical output, while real GDP has the effects of inflation explicitly removed.

Figure 2–5 shows the annual percent changes in each measure. While the trends are not precisely the same, once again the annual percent changes for employment, industrial production, and GDP are more similar because they measure trends for real activity for the same periods. Moreover, the trend for personal income is of the same family, even if once removed by inflation. These four measures present a pretty good picture of the behavior of the U.S. economy over the past 45 years.

The graphs also show lines at the peaks and troughs of business cycles during the postwar era. Most measures of economic activity are classified as either *procyclical* (moving up or down along with the overall economy) or *countercyclical* (moving in an opposite direction to the overall economy). To gain a fuller sense of the cyclical characteristics of each indicator, we will examine the behavior of each of these indicators in the latest recession—which began in July 1990 and bottomed out in March 1991—as well as during the subsequent recovery.

Establishment Employment Data

Given his job, Tim Roberts will almost certainly be aware of, and sensitive to, the monthly employment report. Financial markets pay nearly slavish attention

TABLE 2–1 Employment, personal income, industrial production, and real GDP: Post-World War II levels and annual percent changes.

	Employment (000s)	Personal Income ($ Bil.)	Industrial Production (1987 = 100)	Real GDP (Bil. 1987 $)	Employment (% Change)	Personal Income (% Change)	Industrial Production (% Change)	Real GDP (% Change)
1946	41,652	177.7	20.2	1272.1				
1947	43,857	190.1	22.7	1252.8	5.3	7.0	12.4	−1.5
1948	44,866	209.0	23.6	1300.0	2.3	9.9	4.0	3.8
1949	43,754	206.1	22.3	1305.5	−2.5	−1.4	−5.5	0.4
1950	45,197	227.8	25.8	1418.5	3.3	10.5	15.7	8.7
1951	47,819	256.5	28.0	1558.4	5.8	12.6	8.5	9.9
1952	48,793	273.7	29.1	1624.9	2.0	6.7	3.9	4.3
1953	50,202	290.4	31.6	1685.5	2.9	6.1	8.6	3.7
1954	48,990	293.0	29.9	1673.8	−2.4	0.9	−5.4	−0.7
1955	50,641	314.5	33.7	1768.3	3.4	7.3	12.7	5.6
1956	52,369	337.5	35.1	1803.6	3.4	7.3	4.2	2.0
1957	52,853	356.5	35.6	1838.2	0.9	5.6	1.4	1.9
1958	51,324	367.2	33.3	1829.1	−2.9	3.0	−6.5	−0.5
1959	53,268	391.2	37.3	1928.8	3.8	6.5	12.0	5.5
1960	54,189	409.2	38.1	1970.8	1.7	4.6	2.1	2.2
1961	53,999	428.5	38.4	2023.8	−0.4	4.7	0.8	2.7
1962	55,549	453.4	41.6	2128.1	2.9	5.8	8.3	5.2
1963	56,653	476.4	44.0	2215.6	2.0	5.1	5.8	4.1
1964	58,283	510.7	47.0	2340.6	2.9	7.2	6.8	5.6
1965	60,765	552.9	51.7	2470.5	4.3	8.3	10.0	5.5
1966	63,901	601.7	56.3	2616.2	5.2	8.8	8.9	5.9
1967	65,803	648.5	57.5	2685.2	3.0	7.8	2.1	2.6
1968	67,897	708.9	60.7	2796.9	3.2	9.3	5.6	4.2
1969	70,384	773.7	63.5	2873.0	3.7	9.1	4.6	2.7
1970	70,880	831.0	61.4	2873.9	0.7	7.4	−3.3	0.0
1971	71,214	893.5	62.2	2955.9	0.5	7.5	1.3	2.9

1972	73,675	980.5	68.3	3107.1	3.5	9.7	9.8	5.1
1973	76,790	1098.7	73.8	3268.6	4.2	12.1	8.1	5.2
1974	78,265	1205.7	72.7	3248.1	1.9	9.7	-1.5	-0.6
1975	76,945	1307.3	66.3	3221.7	-1.7	8.4	-8.8	-0.8
1976	79,382	1446.3	72.4	3380.8	3.2	10.6	9.2	4.9
1977	82,471	1601.3	78.2	3533.3	3.9	10.7	8.0	4.5
1978	86,697	1807.9	82.6	3703.5	5.1	12.9	5.6	4.8
1979	89,823	2033.1	85.7	3796.8	3.6	12.5	3.8	2.5
1980	90,406	2265.4	84.1	3776.3	0.6	11.4	-1.9	-0.5
1981	91,156	2534.7	85.7	3843.1	0.8	11.9	1.9	1.8
1982	89,566	2660.9	81.9	3760.3	-1.7	5.0	-4.4	-2.2
1983	90,200	2862.5	84.9	3906.6	0.7	7.6	3.7	3.9
1984	94,496	3154.8	92.8	4148.5	4.8	10.2	9.3	6.2
1985	97,519	3379.8	94.4	4279.8	3.2	7.1	1.7	3.2
1986	99,525	3580.4	95.3	4404.5	2.1	5.9	1.0	2.9
1987	102,200	3802.0	100.0	4540.0	2.7	6.2	4.9	3.1
1988	105,536	4075.9	105.4	4718.6	3.3	7.2	5.4	3.9
1989	108,329	4380.3	108.1	4838.0	2.6	7.5	2.6	2.5
1990	109,782	4673.8	109.2	4897.3	1.3	6.7	1.0	1.2
1991	108,310	4850.9	107.1	4861.4	-1.3	3.8	-1.9	-0.7
1992	108,435	5144.9	108.5	4986.3	0.1	6.1	1.3	2.6

Sources: Employment Bureau of Labor Statistics, U.S. Department of Labor; Personal Income and GDP: Bureau of Economic Analysis, U.S. Department of Commerce; Industrial Production: Board of Governors, Federal Reserve Board.

FIGURE 2–1   Nonfarm employment.

Millions

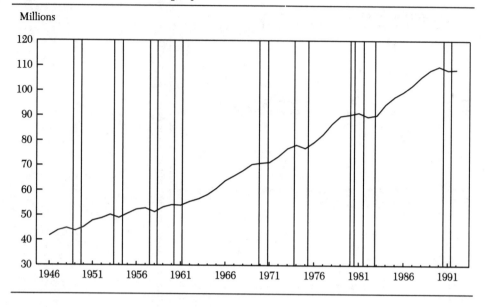

FIGURE 2–2   Personal income.

$ Billions

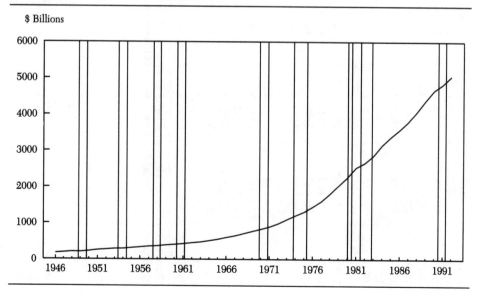

FIGURE 2–3   Industrial production.

1987 = 100

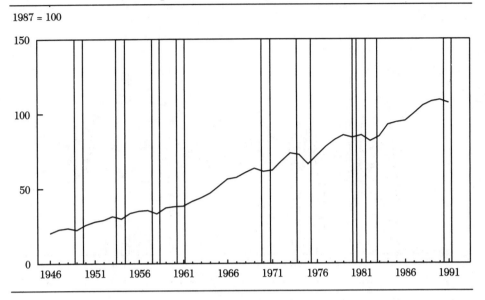

FIGURE 2–4   Gross domestic product.

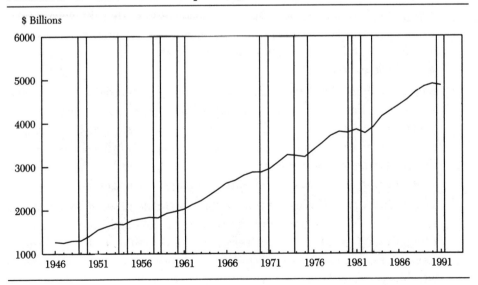

FIGURE 2–5   Post-World War II economic trends.

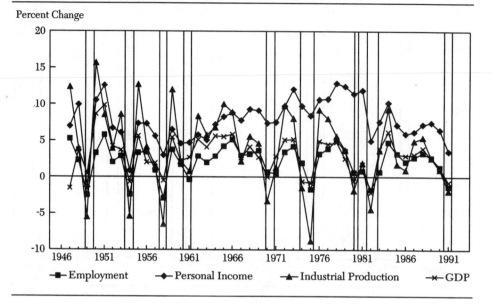

to the monthly changes in payroll employment, as it is popularly known, for three good reasons:

1. *Timeliness.* The *Employment Situation* report, which contains the data on payroll employment, is the first of the major reports that the government statistical agencies (in this case, the Bureau of Labor Statistics) issues each month. Thus, the employment data give an early reading on the near-term state of the economy.

2. *Empirical Value.* The level of employment, along with other measures such as length of the workweek and average hourly wages (see Table 2–2) contained in the report, are used by other government statistical agencies to estimate personal income, industrial production, and other measures. So, the employment report has an empirical importance—as the source for other measures—beyond its reflection of employment conditions.

3. *Theoretical Value.* The use of these data to estimate other economic activity measures is a recognition of the central role of employment in macroeconomics. (Indeed, this was reflected in the title of John Maynard Keynes's book, *The General Theory of Employment, Interest, and Money,* which is the foundation of macroeconomics.)[1]

TABLE 2–2 Establishment survey data on employment, average weekly hours, and average hourly earnings.

	Employment 000s		June 1992 Average Weekly Hours		Average Hourly Earnings
Total	108,423		34.3		$10.58
Goods-producing industries	23,470		n.a.		n.a.
Mining	634		43.4		14.52
Construction	4,600	n.s.a.	38.9		14.20
Manufacturing	18,236		41.0		11.44
Durable goods	10,371		41.5	n.s.a.	12.04
Lumber and wood products	684		40.1	n.s.a.	9.41
Furniture and fixtures	469		39.8	n.s.a.	8.99
Stone, clay, and glass products	521		42.3	n.s.a.	11.66
Primary metal industries	706		43.2	n.s.a.	13.69
Fabricated metal products	1,338		41.6	n.s.a.	11.43
Industrial machinery and equipment	1,954		42.2	n.s.a.	12.44
Electronic and other electrical equipment	1,549		41.1	n.s.a.	11.06
Transportation equipment	1,836		41.9	n.s.a.	15.18
Instruments and related products	946		41.2	n.s.a.	11.90
Miscellaneous manufacturing	368		40.0	n.s.a.	9.12
Nondurable goods	7,865		40.4	n.s.a.	10.69
Food and kindred products	1,671		40.3	n.s.a.	10.21
Tobacco products	49	n.s.a.	39.5	n.s.a.	18.13
Textile mill products	680		41.3	n.s.a.	8.60
Apparel and other textile products	1,023		37.2	n.s.a.	6.97
Paper and allied products	689		43.7	n.s.a.	13.03
Printing and publishing	1,520		38.1	n.s.a.	11.67
Chemicals and allied products	1,073		43.2	n.s.a.	14.38
Petroleum and coal products	155	n.s.a.	43.6	n.s.a.	17.62
Rubber and miscellaneous plastic products	883		41.8	n.s.a.	10.36
Leather and leather products	122		38.0	n.s.a.	7.41
Service-producing industries	84,953		n.a.		n.a.
Transportation and public utilities	5,745		38.6		13.47
Wholesale trade	5,988		38.1		11.38
Retail trade	19,156		28.6		7.11
Finance, insurance, and real estate	6,672	n.s.a.	35.6		10.76
Services	28,854		32.4		10.53
Government	18,538		n.a.		n.a.

Source: Bureau of Labor Statistics, U.S. Department of Labor.
n.a.: not available; n.s.a.: not seasonally adjusted

The Federal Reserve pays close attention to the signals about the state of economic activity that payroll employment emits. This was apparent, for opposite reasons, in July and October 1992:

- On July 2, the *Employment Situation* report for June showed a decline of 117,000 jobs, countering the impression of earlier data that the year-old economic upturn was gathering strength. In fact, the negative aspects of that report were so strong that they suggested the recovery was in danger of faltering. In response, the Fed announced a cut of 50 basis points (one-half of one percentage point) in the discount rate to 3.00 percent within hours of the release of the report. Over the next few days, the Fed made clear that this "easing" had also included a decline of 50 basis points in the Fed funds rate to 3.25 percent—the basic interest rate that banks charge each other to meet their reserve requirements at the Fed.

- On October 2, the *Employment Situation* report for September showed a falloff of 57,000 jobs, but these were all attributed to the end of subsidized government summer jobs programs. Private jobs increased more than the markets had anticipated. In addition, it was barely a month before the Presidential election. Contrary to market expectations, the Fed did nothing to either the discount rate or the Fed funds rate. As a result, money-market-determined interest rates began to rise.

The financial markets, thus, scrutinize the employment data closely to gain insight to the Fed's likely response in terms of monetary policy action. Tim Roberts would have wanted to issue the new bonds in the immediate aftermath of the July 2 report. If instead, he had waited until after the October 2 report, he would have missed the lower interest rates. There is no guarantee that such a result would be avoided, but the more Roberts knows about economic data such as employment, the less likely he will be to make such a misjudgment.

The *Employment Situation* report is usually issued on the first Friday of the following month (the report for September 1992 came out on Friday, October 2) by the Labor Department; the report measures employment conditions using two surveys: a survey of households (discussed later in this chapter) and a survey of establishments. The establishment survey data is referred to as *payroll* data because it uses data derived from the state unemployment insurance tax payments made by employers through payroll deductions. These data include the number of employees, the hours worked per week by production workers, and their average hourly earnings. Table 2–2 presents data for a representative month (June 1992).

The data on employment and earnings trends are useful for managers in nonfinancial firms for, among other things, establishing relative pay scales within industries. For instance, a personnel manager in a fast-food chain may use the data on average earnings within its industry (the "eating and drinking establishments" category, found within the detailed breakdown for the retail sector) for setting wages. Alternatively, a marketing company might find these data a useful source of emerging income trends.

Personal Income

The financial markets are less attuned to the personal income report than to employment. This is largely because the data are reported much later in the reporting cycle than employment, usually not until the fourth week of the following month (for instance, the personal income data for September 1992 were reported on October 28, nearly four weeks after the employment data were released). Nevertheless, financial managers and other managers have an interest in these data because they translate the employment data into spending power, which drives the economy. This is clear when we look at the two ways in which the personal income data are presented:

1. The *composition* of personal income shows the income received by persons from all sources. As Table 2–3 shows, the major sources of income are wages and salaries, other labor income, proprietor's income, rental income, personal dividend income, personal interest income, and net transfer payments (transfer payments less personal contributions for social insurance). These income sources represent payments to the factors of production.

2. The *disposition* of personal income shows the ways in which income is spent. There are three main categories: (1) personal tax payments (when this is subtracted, we are left with *disposable* personal income), (2) outlays (consisting of personal consumption spending, interest paid by persons, and personal gifts to foreigners), and (3) personal saving. Consumption spending, as can be seen from Table 2–4 is by far the largest of these components and represents—in a real sense—the end of economic activity.

Tim Roberts would be interested in the personal income and consumption data as a measure of the actual and potential strength of consumer demand. Oddly enough, the financial markets view signs of economic strength adversely: the stronger the demand, the more the upward pressure on inflation and in turn the greater the upward pressure on interest rates. The personal income and consumption data for September 1992 each showed increases of 0.7 percent following declines of 0.2 percent in each case for August. Interpretation of the data for both months was complicated—the hurricane that hit south Florida and the Gulf Coast depressed rental income and spending in August but led to a bounce-back in September. The two months taken together,

TABLE 2–3 Personal income components.

	1991 (Billions)	Share of Total (%)	1992 (Billions)	Share of Total (%)
Wage and salary disbursements	2815.0	58.0	2973.1	57.8
Other labor income	296.9	6.1	322.7	6.3
Proprietor's income	376.4	7.8	414.3	8.1
Rental income	−12.8	−0.8	−8.9	−0.2
Dividend income	127.9	2.6	140.4	2.7
Interest income	715.6	14.8	694.3	13.5
Transfer payments	769.9	15.9	858.4	16.7
Less: Personal contributions for social insurance	237.8	−4.9	249.3	−4.9
Equals: Personal income	4850.9	100.0	5144.9	100.0

Source: Bureau of Economic Analysis, U.S. Department of Commerce.

however, suggested moderate gains in income and spending and added to the emerging impression of a firming economy.

Managers outside the financial markets, especially those in retailing or marketing, would have a completely different reaction to personal income and consumer spending data. Strengthening spending power would be viewed as a positive signal of higher spending in the future, while signs that actual spending had picked up would be welcomed as evidence that the consumer sector was growing. Such information is also of great use to managers in industries that service retailing. Advertising agencies gear their business plans to the expected sales of their customers. Thus, recent consumer income and spending

TABLE 2–4 Disposition of personal income.

	1991 (Billions)	Share of Personal Income (%)	1992 (Billions)	Share of Personal Income (%)
Personal income	4850.9	100.0	5144.9	100.0
Less: Personal taxes	620.4	12.8	644.8	12.5
Equals: Disposable personal income	4230.5	87.2	4500.1	87.5
Less:				
Personal outlays	4029.0	83.1	4261.5	82.8
Personal consumption expenditures	3906.4	80.5	4139.9	80.5
Interest paid by consumers to business	112.2	2.3	111.1	2.2
Personal transfer payments to foreigners	10.4	0.2	10.5	0.2
Equals: Personal saving	201.5	4.2	238.6	4.6

Source: Bureau of Economic Analysis, U.S. Department of Commerce.

patterns would be a useful input to this planning. Even consumer banking—both credit card operations and the more traditional consumer lending areas—are geared to consumer demand, so a consumer banking manager would be extremely interested in recent consumer income and spending trends.

Industrial Production

Things—the "goods" part of "goods and services"—are produced in factories, mines, or utility companies (electricity, natural gas, and water are regarded as "goods"). The Federal Reserve Board has measured the production of the nation's factories, mines, and utilities since the 1920s. In fact, industrial production is an older measure of U.S. output than the national income and product account measures, such as GDP.

Without question, Tim Roberts will be interested in industrial production. For one thing, the output of his industry—electric utilities—is included in industrial production. More important, much of the demand for electricity is by manufacturing industries, the output of which accounts for nearly 85 percent of industrial production. Most important to Tim, industrial production directly reflects output and so is a key measure of economic activity. Consequently, increases in production represent a strengthening of economic activity and impart upward pressure on interest rates. (Moreover, since the industrial production index is compiled by the Board of Governors of the Federal Reserve, the Fed is especially sensitive to industrial production in its regulation of monetary policy to economic activity.)

Since industrial production measures the output of goods ("things"), a recent criticism has been that it ignores the output of services, which have accounted for an increasing share of total U.S. output in recent years (see Table 2–5 and Figure 2–6). Most services, however, exist either to distribute the goods produced in the industrial sector or to facilitate goods production. For instance, the transportation, wholesale, and retail sectors distribute the goods

TABLE 2–5 Shares of U.S. output by industry sector (percent).

	1950	1960	1970	1980	1990
Agriculture, forestry, and fisheries	7.5	4.2	3.1	2.7	2.2
Mining	2.2	1.3	1.0	1.9	0.8
Construction	5.1	5.3	5.7	5.6	5.0
Manufacturing	31.1	29.2	25.8	23.5	19.0
Private services	43.9	46.7	47.7	49.9	57.9
Government	9.7	12.5	15.9	14.2	14.7
Rest of the world	0.6	0.8	0.9	2.1	0.5

Source: Bureau of Economic Analysis, U.S. Department of Commerce, derived from National Income Without Capital Consumption Allowance by Industry.

FIGURE 2-6 Shares of U.S. output by industry.

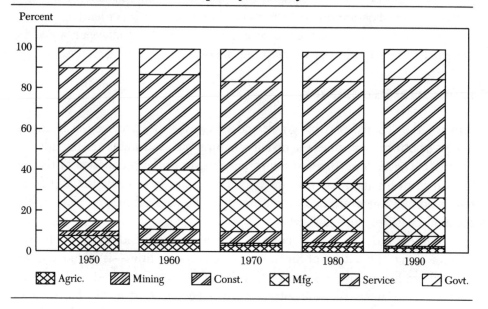

produced in manufacturing (contrasting the number of jobs in Table 2–2 for transportation, wholesaling, and retailing with manufacturing shows a ratio of 1.7 to 1.) In addition, the categories of finance, insurance, and real estate, and other services (including business services, such as advertising and accounting) exist largely to facilitate manufacturing. So, while manufacturing his slipped from representing nearly a third of U.S. output in 1950 to just under a fifth in 1990, industrial production still affects most of the U.S. economy.

Industrial production looks at the *supply* side of the economy. This can be seen by examining the first column in Table 2–6, which presents the share of key manufacturing, mining, and utility sectors in total industrial production. For instance, Tim Roberts's industry—electric utilities—accounts for 6.3 percent of industrial production. Many of the other industries, however, are large-scale users of electric power (such as primary metals, which use one-sixth of all electric power consumed in the United States), while other major industries use comparatively little electricity (apparel production and furniture production, combined, account for less than 1.5 percent of electric power used). In his longer-term planning for financing needed generating capacity, Roberts would be keenly interested in the prospects for these industries.

Roberts, however, like anyone sensitive to movements in interest rates, is going to be most interested in the reaction of the Fed to the industrial production data. During the summer (third quarter) of 1992, the industrial production

TABLE 2–6   Industrial production trends for selected industry sectors (percent).

	Share	Average Annual Growth Rates			
		1950–60	1960–70	1970–80	1980–90
Manufacturing	84.7	3.8	4.8	3.4	3.4
Durable goods	47.3	3.8	4.8	3.6	4.0
Lumber and products	1.8	1.3	3.1	1.4	2.8
Furniture and fixtures	1.3				
Stone, clay, and glass products	2.2				
Primary metals	3.1	0.4	3.7	−0.4	−0.2
Fabricated metal products	5.0	2.4	3.6	2.0	1.4
Nonelectrical machinery	9.9	4.3	6.4	6.3	7.6
Office machines and computers	3.6				
Electrical machinery	8.9				
Transportation equipment	9.0	4.6	3.3	2.7	3.9
Motor vehicles and parts	3.9	0.5	2.6	2.3	3.7
Instruments	3.6				
Miscellaneous	1.4				
Nondurable goods	37.5	4.0	4.9	3.1	2.6
Foods	8.9	3.1	3.2	2.8	2.4
Tobacco products	1.0				
Textile mill products	1.7	1.4	5.0	2.2	0.9
Apparel products	2.1	2.4	2.1	1.7	1.0
Paper and products	3.5				
Printing and publishing	6.7	3.8	3.8	2.9	4.8
Chemicals and products	8.9				
Petroleum products	1.3				
Rubber and plastics products	3.1				
Leather and products	0.2				
Mining	7.5	2.3	3.3	0.9	−0.7
Metal mining	0.4				
Coal	1.2				
Oil and gas extraction	5.1				
Stone and earth minerals	0.7				
Utilities	7.8	8.9	7.0	2.8	1.2
Electric	6.3				
Gas	1.5				

Source: Board of Governors, Federal Reserve System.

index showed a strong increase (+0.8%) in July but then declined for two straight months (−0.2% in August, and −0.3% in September). This reinforced the impression held in the financial markets of a faltering economic·recovery and contributed to a decline in interest rates during the summer quarter. These signals might well have encouraged Roberts to recommend an earlier, rather than a later refinancing.

Gross Domestic Product

When business managers want to get an overview of how total economic activity is faring, they turn to gross domestic product, or GDP, the broadest measure of U.S. economic activity. Prior to December 1991, gross national product (GNP) was the main measure. The small differences between the two are in the details. GDP measures only output produced within the United States (although exports are still shown on a net basis, with imports subtracted), while GNP also includes earnings by U.S. residents from foreign production (mainly the repatriated overseas profits of businesses) net of payments to foreigners of earnings from their production in the United States. GDP measures economic activity using two approaches, which arrive at the same total:

1. The *income* accounts measure the various income payments to the factors of production.
2. The *product* (expenditure) accounts measure the value of the goods and services produced in a year.

The two approaches have to equal: The payments to the factors of production equal the costs of production, the value of output. The two approaches are summarized in Tables 2–7 and 2–8.

The *income* approach is presented in Table 2–7—beginning with personal income and ending with gross domestic product. It is simply an allocation of total output among households (personal income) and corporations (profits) that

TABLE 2–7 Relation of gross domestic product, gross national product, net national product, national income, and personal income.

	1991 (Billions)	Share of GDP	1992 (Billions)	Share of GDP
Personal income	4850.9	84.8	5144.9	85.2
Less: Items either included in profits or transfers	1613.4	28.2	1693.1	28.0
Plus: Corporate profits, net interest, and social insurance contributions	1347.7	23.5	1374.4	22.8
Equals: National income	4585.2	80.1	4826.2	79.9
Plus: Indirect business taxes and other payments	525.7	9.2	570.9	9.5
Equals: Net national product	5110.9	89.3	5397.1	89.4
Plus: Depreciation	626.2	10.9	648.7	10.7
Equals: Gross national product	5737.1	100.2	6045.8	100.1
Plus: Net factor income payments to foreigners	−14.2	−0.2	−7.3	−0.1
Equals: Gross domestic product	5722.9	100.0	6038.5	100.0

Source: Bureau of Economic Analysis, U.S. Department of Commerce.

TABLE 2–8 GDP in current and constant dollars, and implicit price deflators.

	1991			1992		
	Billions of Dollars	Billions of 1987 Dollars	Deflator 1987 = 100	Billions of Dollars	Billions of 1987 Dollars	Deflator 1987 = 100
Gross domestic product	5722.9	4861.4	117.7	6038.5	4986.3	121.1
Personal consumption	3906.4	3258.6	119.9	4139.9	3341.8	123.9
Durable goods	457.8	426.6	107.3	497.3	456.6	108.9
Nondurable goods	1257.9	1048.2	120.0	1300.9	1062.9	122.4
Services	2190.7	1783.8	122.8	2341.6	1822.3	128.5
Residential construction	189.6	169.5	111.9	223.6	197.1	113.4
Nonresidential fixed investment	555.9	514.5	108.0	565.5	529.2	106.9
Structures	182.6	160.2	114.0	172.6	150.6	114.6
Producers durable equipment	373.3	354.3	105.4	392.9	378.6	103.8
Change in business inventories	−8.6	−8.4		7.3	6.5	
Net exports	−19.6	−19.1		−29.6	−33.6	
Exports	601.5	543.4	110.7	640.5	578.0	110.8
Imports	621.1	562.5	110.4	670.1	611.6	109.6
Government purchases	1099.3	946.3	116.2	1131.8	945.2	119.7
Federal	445.9	386.5	115.4	448.8	373.0	120.3
State and local	653.4	559.7	116.7	683.0	572.2	119.4

Source: Bureau of Economic Analysis, U.S. Department of Commerce.

shows how the output is allocated among the factors used to produce it. Thus, personal income is adjusted to remove payments that are either mixed between households and businesses (for instance, dividends are part of corporate profits) or unrelated to current production (transfer payments are excluded from both GDP and GNP). Corporate (before-tax) profits are then added to arrive at national income. Indirect business taxes and business transfer payments (mainly pensions) are added to arrive at net national product, while the addition of depreciation—the charges for capital stock consumed in producing the output— yields *gross* national product (GNP). The appropriate adjustments for factor income paid to foreigners (added back in) and received from foreigners (subtracted out) are then made to derive GDP, the main measure of the nation's economic activity.

The *production* or *expenditure* approach, shown in Table 2–8, is the more familiar aggregate demand approach (examined in more detail in Chapter 3) that forms the core of macroeconomic analysis. It is represented by the familiar equation:

$$GDP = C + I + (X - M) + G$$

This approach sums the expenditures on consumer goods (C), investment goods (I), net exports ($X - M$), and government spending (G). One difference from the income approach, however, is that GDP is presented both in current (market) price terms and in constant (1987 = 100) terms. As a result, the change in GDP can be separated into its *real* (constant dollar) and *inflation* (price deflator, or any of the price index measures that are compiled) components.

While it is often only partly understood, GDP is one of the most often-cited economic indicators by business managers in their discussions of the economic environment. This is a recognition of the fact that real GDP growth is a summary of the economy's general condition. At its most basic, increasing real GDP suggests an expanding economy, while declining real GDP signifies recession.

Tim Roberts would view the data in more detail. In particular, Roberts—like most financial managers—would be sensitive to the implications of the pace of economic activity on inflation and interest rates. As a rough rule of thumb, a rapidly growing economy utilizes existing capacity, signals strengthening demand relative to supply, and suggests increasing inflation and upward pressures on interest rates (stemming from both financial market reactions and the possible policy response of the Fed). Slowing growth or an outright decline in real GDP, however, suggests lessening demand pressure on supply, less inflationary momentum, and thus falling interest rates.

Someone in Tim Roberts's situation has to consider more factors than does a financial market participant. A financial manager is concerned at getting the lowest interest rates on any financing. However, the projects that have to be financed are, themselves, related to the state of economic activity. Plans for expanding capacity may be put on hold if the economy appears to be heading into a recession. GDP is, thus, a crucial business indicator. Indeed, other managers in a range of industries may follow GDP and its components even more closely:

- A manager of a furniture store will be sensitive to the strength of consumer demand for durable goods, which is strongest when GDP growth is strongest.
- A sales manager for an office computer equipment supplier will look on a string of increases in GDP as a signal that the business demand for desktop computers will rise.
- A production manager for a carpet manufacturer will look at increased homebuilding as a sign of increased demand for carpets in subsequent periods.

The importance of GDP will be emphasized in the next two chapters, which look at aggregate demand and supply concepts. Many other less aggregate economic indicators also are discussed in the remainder of this chapter.

OTHER ECONOMIC INDICATORS

The four indicators discussed so far in this chapter are important measures of overall activity. Official government agencies, private organizations, and international agencies, however, compile and report many other economic indicators each month. These reports provide additional background information for business decision making.

To get a feel for the regular flow of economic information that managers are exposed to each month, we have used October 1992 as a representative month. Figure 2–7 shows a *Calendar of Economic Indicators* that one of the authors prepared for clients on October 2, 1992 (after the release of the *Employment Situation* report for September). We will use this as a guide to the information flow in the month. A key point to keep in mind is that, since this was the month prior to the 1992 Presidential election, other forces were at work on short-term business and financial market psychology. However, there is probably no such thing as a "normal" month, devoid of "special" factors. In addition, this discussion will only touch on the impact of these data *"as they were reported"*; subsequent revisions may have changed these impressions. (Some of the forecasts were off the mark, but not badly, and so the record stands.)

In the week leading up to the release of the *Employment Situation* report each month, a number of indicators provide either more complete readings on past economic activity or pointers to future activity. The *index of leading indicators,* or "leaders," is a composite of 11, mostly previously released, indicators that have been found to have a good track record at giving early warnings—2 to 15 months—of turning points in economic activity. The index for August 1992, which was reported on Tuesday September 29, showed a decline of 0.2 percent, after an increase of 0.1 percent for July, and a decrease of 0.3 percent in June. As a rule of thumb, changes of plus or minus 0.3 percent are considered insignificant: For one thing, the index is subject to considerable revision since many of the component series are still subject to revision. The financial markets reacted to the August report with a shrug, since it left in place the previous impression of economic sluggishness.

The Conference Board's *consumer confidence* index for September was reported on the same day (it is usually reported on the last Tuesday of the month). This is a more timely measure and one that has widespread interest both for those who want to know how the consumer sector, the economy's main engine, is behaving and for those businesses closely related to consumer spending. The decline reported for September was the third in a row and brought the index back nearly to its low point in the 1990–1991 recession. This partly reflected the effect on consumers of a spate of sluggish economic reports released during the summer months. In addition, the election campaign had focused on the

FIGURE 2–7 Calendar of key economic indicators.

SEPTEMBER 28–OCTOBER 30

MONDAY	TUESDAY	WEDNESDAY	THURSDAY	FRIDAY
28	29 **Consumer Confidence** July: 61.2 Aug: 59.0 Sep: 56.4 Leaders June: −0.3% July: +0.1 Aug: −0.2	30 New Home Sales June: 581,000 July: 607,000 Aug: 570,000	1 Construction June: −0.3% July: +0.2 Aug: −0.8 NAPM Index July: 54.2 Aug: 53.7 Sep: 49.0	2 Payroll Employment July: +171,000 Aug: −128,000 Sep: − 57,000 Unemployment Rate July: 7.7% Aug: 7.6 Sep: 7.5 **Factory Orders**
5 Auto Sales July: 8.3 Mil. Aug: 7.9 Sep: 8.2 f	6 **FOMC Meeting**	7	8	9 **FOMC Minutes**
12 **COLUMBUS DAY HOLIDAY**	13	14 Producer Prices Total Core July: +0.1% +0.2% Aug: +0.1 −0.1 Sep: +0.3 f +0.3 f Retail Sales July: +1.0% Aug: −0.5 Sep: +0.6 f **10-DAY CAR SALES**	15 Consumer Prices Total Core July: +0.1% +0.2% Aug: +0.3 +0.2 Sep: +0.3 f +0.3 f Inventories June: +0.5% July: +0.1 Aug: +0.3 f	16 Merch. Trade June: −$6.7 Bil. July: − 7.8 Aug: − 8.3 f Industrial Production July: +0.6% Aug: −0.5 Sep: −0.2 f
19	20 Housing Starts & Permits July: 1.120 M 1.080 M Aug: 1.237 1.076 Sep: 1.250 f 1.070 f	21	22	23 **10-DAY CAR SALES**
26 Consumer Confidence Aug: 59.0 Sep: 56.4 Oct: 58.0 f	27 GDP & Price Index 92 Q1: +2.9% +3.6% Q2: +1.5 +3.0 Q3: +2.3 f +3.0 f Employment Cost Index Mar: +0.9% June: +0.8 Sep: +0.8 f	28 Durable Orders July: −2.7% Aug: −0.1 Sep: +1.0 f Personal Income & Outlays July: +0.2% +0.6% Aug: −0.5 −0.1 Sep: +0.4 f +0.4 f	29 Export/Import Prices	30 New Home Sales July: 607,000 Aug: 570,000 Sep: 600,000 f

ECONOMIC FORECASTING SERVICES   f = forecast; all other values are actuals   October 2, 1992
at the time of the forecast

Although the information in this report has been obtained from sources which we consider reliable, we do not guarantee its accuracy.

poor performance of the economy, so low consumer confidence was a partial result.

New home sales is one of a series of reports on the homebuilding industry. New home sales are usually reported about a month after the period covered. For instance, the data for August 1992 were released on September 30. The series is volatile because the source data—builders' reports of contracts signed on new homes built—are seldom reported in a systematic way. The decline to a level of 570,000 reported for August was especially confusing because the level for July was revised from 563,000, first reported, to 607,000. Some bond traders actually like this volatility, because it leads to more trading. Someone in Tim Roberts's position, however, would find it frustrating because the trend is unreliable. Indeed, this unreliability of month-to-month changes is exactly why managers in construction, real estate, and related industries use these data only on a 3-month-average (or longer) basis. It is ironic that managers closer to the actual activity being measured will use the information more cautiously than those who only have an interest in it as background.

Construction put in place is a more comprehensive report on all progress on construction—residential and nonresidential, public and private—done in a month. The August data were reported on October 1, which is the usual reporting lag. The reported 0.8 percent decline reflected a decline in private nonresidential construction, which overwhelmed a sizable increase in private residential construction and a much smaller increase in public construction. As with new home sales, these data are best viewed over a longer time span than one month.

The *National Association of Purchasing Management Diffusion Index (NAPM Index)* is released the first business day each month, covering the previous month. This measure summarizes survey results by 250 purchasing managers from a cross section of manufacturing companies. The five components of the index reflect purchasing managers' evaluation of whether (1) orders, (2) production, (3) employment, (4) speed of delivery, and (5) inventories, at their companies improved, worsened, or were unchanged in the past month. An overall reading above 50 signals that the manufacturing sector is expanding. A reading between 44 and 50 implies that the manufacturing sector is slipping, but the economy as a whole is still increasing. A reading below 44 signals recession. The index receives considerable financial market attention because it is usually the first broad measure of economic activity in the month just ended.

The index reading of 49 for September 1982 was ambiguous: It slipped below the level of 50 that signals an advancing manufacturing sector but was well above the threshold of 44 that signals recession. Ominously, the main source of the weakening was a falloff in new orders, suggesting weakness in the source of future manufacturing production. On balance, the index reinforced a sense that had mounted over the summer that the economy had slowed and was in danger of stalling. This sense led to a softening in interest rates in the financial markets but raised concerns among nonfinancial managers about the prospects for continued economic growth.

The *Employment Situation* report for September, as noted earlier, was released on Friday October 2. This report is almost always issued on the first Friday of the following month. This timeliness is one reason it is so closely followed. The payroll employment data were on the weak side, but not so weak as to suggest an immediate Fed easing of interest rates. Moreover, it was widely believed that since the election was only a month away this would be the last time the Fed could make a move without appearing to take sides, so the financial markets were discouraged by the report. The message was made even more ambiguous because the *unemployment rate*, which is derived from a separate survey of households, showed a third consecutive 0.1 percentage point decline to 7.5 percent. (The unemployment rate is equal to the number of unemployed—those who have lost jobs and those who have looked for jobs unsuccessfully in the past month—as a percentage of the total number of people employed and unemployed.)

The mixed nature of the report—a small net loss in the number of jobs and in total hours worked from the payroll report and a further, welcome reduction in the unemployment rate—meant that the report was subject to various interpretations. As noted, financial market participants were disappointed that the data were not clearly weaker, so that the Fed would have lowered interest rates. (In fact, the expectation of an easing had been so great that an easing had already been "priced in" to many market rates, which "backed up"—increased—over the next few trading sessions.) Nonfinancial managers would likely have paid less attention to the details of the report and might have been modestly encouraged by the fact that the unemployment rate declined again. Many businesses, correctly, view the unemployment rate as an important influence on consumer confidence and attitudes.

The Commerce Department's report, *Manufacturers' Shipments, Inventories, and Orders* ("Factory Orders"), for August was also released Friday October 2. Traders and sales representatives in financial markets show less interest in this report because it is largely anticipated by the *Advance Report on Durable Goods Manufacturers' Shipments and Orders*, roughly a week earlier. The information in the broader report is of special interest to managers within manufacturing because the detailed industry data provide a benchmark against which a company's own performance can be gauged. Shipments are actual sales by manufacturers; orders received are important indicators of both future production and shipments; and inventories measure the raw materials, work in progress, and finished goods on hand at factories.

The report for August 1992 was strange. This more detailed report confirmed the earlier advance estimate of a 0.1 percent decline in orders for durable goods. The surprise was that orders for nondurable goods declined 3.8 percent. Usually, durable good orders are far more volatile than orders for nondurable goods, which tend to be trendlike rather than cyclic. The sharp decline in nondurable orders, because it was so unexpected, seemed to many observers a fresh sign of economic weakness. It also made the ambiguity in the *Employment Situation* report that much greater. In retrospect, it appears to have been due to transportation disruptions along the Gulf coast due to Hurricane Andrew. Because orders and shipments of nondurable goods take place at nearly the same time (shipments fell 3.7%), the disruption to shipping affected the flow of orders as well.

U.S. automobile manufacturers release data on *car and light truck sales* three times a month: the first 10 days, the middle 10 days, and the final "10" days (in seven months there are 11 days in the last "10 day" period, and in February there are either 8 or 9). These data are reported in early afternoon by each manufacturer, generally three working days after the end of the period. In 1992, there were nine domestic U.S. auto manufacturers: General Motors, Ford, Chrysler, Honda, Toyota, Nissan, Mazda, Mitsubishi, and Subaru. Curiously, the last six manufacturers—often referred to as transplants—are Japanese companies that have manufacturing plants in the United States. The report for the final "10-day" period of the month also contains monthly sales data on import car sales. The Commerce Department uses these data as a source for estimating consumption spending and provides seasonal adjustment factors for the sales data.[2]

Auto sales in September 1992 rebounded from weaker sales levels in August, providing an early sign of a firming consumer sector. One appeal of these data is their timeliness. Thus, financial market traders and sales representatives scan the sales data for signs of the latest wiggles in consumer spending. Managers in businesses related to the auto industry—from dealers, to lenders, to parts suppliers—also have a keen interest in the data. A wider group of managers regard the auto sales data as a key indicator of consumer demand. Tim Roberts's reaction to the September 1992 sales would likely have been mixed. While the figures provided reassurance that the slump in August was being reversed, they also suggested there was less reason for a monetary policy easing and so less chance of a further decline in interest rates.

The *Federal Open Market Committee* or *FOMC* of the Federal Reserve Board meets roughly every six weeks, usually on a Tuesday, to discuss the recent, current, and prospective states of the economy and the appropriate response of monetary policy. On the following Friday, the minutes of the prior meeting are released (for instance, the minutes from the August 18 meeting were released on October 9, 1992, following the October 6 meeting). The financial markets pay close attention to the FOMC minutes as a way of guessing at the direction of Fed policy. Tim Roberts would also pay close attention to the report in deciding when to refinance his company's long-term bonds. (The FOMC will be examined in more detail in Chapter 6.)

The *Producer Price Index (PPI)* and the *Consumer Price Index (CPI)* are the two main monthly measures of inflation in the United States. They are usually reported around the middle of the following month, with the PPI report preceding the CPI by a day or two. The PPI measures the change in prices of all goods produced in the United States, usually as of the middle of the month. The CPI measures the change in prices of a representative "market basket" of goods and services consumed in the United States during a month. Price changes are reported in considerable detail for both indexes and are of great interest to a wide range of business managers:

- Producer prices provide a measure of input costs on raw materials, intermediate goods that have had some processing, and finished goods. Thus, production and purchasing managers will be interested in specific price trends.

- Consumer prices provide a guide to the price changes in product categories that retail and marketing companies can use to monitor the competitiveness of their own offerings.

Financial market participants view the price indexes as the primary measure of inflation, and they view inflation as the main adverse influence on interest rates. In recent years, they have viewed a "core"—which excludes the more volatile trends in food and energy prices—as an indicator of the underlying inflation rate.

The PPI for September, released on October 14, 1992, and the CPI, released the next day, each showed fairly restrained increases in the overall price level and each showed increases of only 0.2 percent in the "core," excluding food and energy prices. These reports were regarded as reassuring: They indicated little inflationary pressure. In fact, the data showed that producer prices had only risen 1.6 percent in the prior year, while consumer inflation had been only 3.0 percent.

The *retail sales* report measures the dollar value of all sales at retail establishments including a wide range of outlets: car dealers, hardware stores, furniture and appliance stores, department stores, grocery stores, clothing stores, drug stores, restaurants, and gas stations. The data are reported around the middle of the following month and usually include revised data for the two prior months. This report is an important source of data on consumer demand, in total, and by type of good.

The September 1992 report, issued on October 14, showed a modest 0.3 percent increase but was accompanied by upward revision to sales for July (+1.1% instead of +1.0%) and for August (unchanged instead of −0.5%). This suggested that consumer spending had firmed during the summer quarter and contrasted with earlier signs of weakness. (Indeed, August data was later revised to show a 0.1% increase, and September retail sales were revised to show a 0.7% gain.)

The impression of firmer consumer spending contributed to a growing sense among financial market operatives that the economy was less fragile than had been thought, and thus there would be even less of a chance of the Fed lowering interest rates. Managers in the retail trades would know their own firm's sales but would use the retail sales report to contrast their sales against total sales trends and the specific trends for their retail segment. Many managers in businesses that support retailing—advertising firms, bank lending officers, even paper bag manufacturers—are interested in the retail sales data as a primary measure of demand.

Manufacturing and Trade Inventories, a monthly report detailing the level of inventories held by manufacturers, wholesalers, and retailers at the end of the month, is issued roughly six weeks later. The August 1992 report was released on October 15 and showed a 0.3 percent increase. This report is a measure of the interface between demand and supply. A key measure of supply is the *industrial production index*, which is usually reported by the Federal Reserve at the middle of the following month. The report for September 1992 that was released on October 16 showed a 0.2 percent decline indicating the total output of the nation's factories, mines, and utilities (goods producers) had edged down in September. These data were ambiguous because (1) there had been a 0.8 percent surge in production in July, which was seen at the time as unsustainable, (2) consumer demand appeared to be picking up, and (3) inventories were only edging up slowly. Thus, the production data were taken as one more sign that the economy was beginning to firm.

Managers in goods-producing industries use the industrial production data to assess how well their own firm is doing relative to the industry average. In addition, if a particular industry is related to another segment—for instance, box producers are interested in production trends of anything that will have to be shipped in boxes—managers will monitor those trends. The overall production trend is a primary measure of economic activity that managers use when tracking aggregate trends. Financial markets pay special attention to the industrial production index because the Federal Reserve compiles it and, so, is itself especially sensitive to it. Thus, changes in the industrial production index can point to changes in monetary policy, which is a primary influence on interest rates.

A monthly report on *merchandise trade* is issued roughly six weeks after the end of the month covered. The report provides data on the level of exports, imports, and the trade balance, which nearly always shows a deficit (imports exceed imports) for the United States. The report also contains detail by industry and by country on U.S. trade flows. The report is of greatest interest to foreign exchange market participants because the trade balance is a primary influence on demand and supply of foreign exchange. The role of international trade, however, is also an important component of the overall level of economic activity and would be viewed along with other such measures by a wider range of business managers. The widening in the trade deficit for August 1992 was viewed as a sign of weakness—U.S. exports had declined by 6.1 in that month. However, by the time the decline was reported (October 16), there had been enough other signs of a firming in domestic demand to lessen its impact.

A monthly report, *Housing Starts and Permits,* is issued in the third week of the following month and shows the number of new housing units that were begun and authorized in the month. The September 1992 report was issued on October 20 and showed that construction was started on 1,256,000 new housing units, with the biggest increase taking place for single-family units (starts of apartments are also reported). In addition, permits were issued for 1,116,000 units. (Permits are usually less than starts because they are not required in all jurisdictions.)

The housing data are of primary interest to managers in firms related to construction or the real estate market. In addition, demand for many consumer products—furniture, for instance—is tied to the new housing market. These managers would likely monitor housing data closely. Like most of the statistics we have just examined, however, housing starts reflect the overall state of economic activity. Thus, many managers with little direct relationship to the housing industry would follow the housing start data as a sign of the state of macroeconomic activity. The starts data for September 1992 indicated a second straight monthly increase to above the 1.2 million annual rate level providing one more sign of a modest firming in economic activity.

The *Advance Report on Gross Domestic Product* is reported roughly four weeks after the end of the quarter. The report on real GDP growth in the third quarter of 1992 was released on October 27. The report showed a stronger-than-expected increase of 2.7%. This was the final straw to the hopes of those who had looked for a easing in interest rates, as it showed that fairly well-balanced, moderate economic growth had been underway. (Some skepticism was expressed about such unexpected strength, reported just one week before the election. In fact, real GDP growth was ultimately revised *up* to a 3.4% annual rate.)

The monthly report on *Personal Income and Outlays* is usually reported on the next business day after the GDP report. For September 1992, the report released on October 28 showed solid 0.7 percent increases in personal income and in consumption spending. These reports suggested that growth not only occurred at a solid pace in the third quarter but ended the quarter on an upbeat note.

SUMMARY

We have merely skimmed the surface of the indicators of overall economic activity in this chapter. A large amount of economic information is published each month and is regularly reported on TV news programs or in the financial pages—occasionally on the front pages—of daily newspapers. These reports can be useful to managers in at least three ways:

1. These reports reveal a good deal about the general state of the economy. Business decisions are taken within the context of the overall economic environment, and so business managers should strive to understand as much as possible about this background.

2. The specific information about particular industries in many reports can provide important insights about the manager's business conditions. For instance, a retailer will be especially interested in the reports on retail sales and personal income, while a textile mill manager will be interested in manufacturers' orders and production, and a mortgage broker will follow new home sales and housing starts.

3. Traders and brokers in financial firms will scrutinize all the indicators from at least two perspectives. First, signs of economic strength may encourage stock market participants that business conditions are improving. Alternatively, the same evidence may signal participants in the debt markets that inflationary pressures may be increasing. If so, this could put immediate upward pressure on interest rates, and it could induce the Federal Reserve to tighten monetary policy directly.

The case of Tim Roberts showed a more complex set of reactions. His problem was to refinance long-term debt with the hope of paying lower interest rates. Thus, he would show many of the same sensitivities as financial market participants and would regard signs of economic softness as downward pressures on interest rates. On the other hand, since ultimately his company will thrive along with a growing economy, he would, on balance, prefer to see signs of strength rather than weakness.

In the particular circumstances examined, Tim Roberts would have made the best decision if he had issued the new bonds in August or September 1992, when the signs of economic activity pointed to weakness. In fact, AA-rated utility bonds averaged 8.85 percent in June 1992. They reached a low of 8.52 percent in August, when the economic indicators were signaling softness. By October, the rate had risen to 8.64 percent, and it reached 8.75 percent in November. If Roberts had refinanced $15 million of 10-year bonds, which matured in June, in the following August, he would have saved $1,047,500 in interest costs over the term of the loan. If he had waited until October, however, he would have saved only $699,900 in interest costs, and had he waited until November, he would have saved only $320,400. Thus, paying attention to the economic indicators and their message about the state of economic activity was of significant value to Roberts.

LOOK AHEAD

The next chapter focuses more closely on the indicators and nature of demand in the U.S. economy. Chapter 4 looks at economic activity from the supply, or production, side. Chapter 5 examines the nature and measurement of inflation and unemployment in more detail. Chapter 6 focuses on the monetary economy and the role of monetary policy. Chapter 7 concludes the macroeconomic section with an examination of the international economy.

3 THE BUSINESS CYCLE

Aggregate Demand and Its Components

Most business decisions are short-run determinations made under conditions of uncertainty. These uncertainties typically reflect short-term fluctuations in economic demand in response to the impact of the *business cycle*. These fluctuations, in turn, represent the reaction of the most basic economic decision makers—households and businesses—to the economic conditions that prevail at a particular time.

The business cycle was referred to several times in the preceding chapter. These cycles can be defined in one of two ways. The first, and most common, refers to the period that extends from a peak in economic activity, through a recession, ensuing recovery, and expansion until the next peak is reached. Alternatively, the cycle can extend from a trough (low point) in activity through a recovery and expansion to a new peak, and through the ensuing recession until a new trough is reached. A cycle, however it is defined, contains all the phases of economic activity: recession, recovery, and expansion.

This chapter describes the changes in economic forces that result in cyclical movements. Once again, an example will be helpful: Alice Hawkins, a buyer for a chain of department stores, must order its line of winter designer (higher priced) dresses 6 to 9 months in advance. The demand for the dresses will be affected by the economic conditions prevalent at that future time, so it is necessary for Hawkins to foresee those economic conditions. One approach is to see future conditions as an extension of present economic conditions.

This case is similar to the one concerning Tim Roberts, in Chapter 2. The distinguishing feature here is that the buyer's decisions are more related to *short-run* changes in the economy. If Alice Hawkins expects a buoyant economy, but instead it weakens, the stores will be stuck with expensive dresses they cannot sell. If she looks for a lackluster economy and, in fact, it grows strongly, the stores will miss out on sales that could have been made. Thus, misjudging the economy's strength can prove to be a costly error. It could even cost the manager her job.

It is not possible to anticipate the exact behavior of the economy all the time. It is also not necessary for most managers to worry about tracking the economy; specialists can do this. But a competent manager should (1) be aware of the effects of the short-term economic fluctuations on her business and (2) be sensitive to current economic conditions.

This chapter considers short-term fluctuations in *aggregate demand,* which is the most common means by which macroeconomic forces affect specific business situations, requiring a management reaction. This can be done by a more detailed examination of the components of demand that make up the gross domestic product (GDP).

Chapter 2 contained just one equation, but it is a key one:

$$\text{GDP} = C + I + (X - M) + G$$

This relationship represents aggregate demand, the sum of the expenditures by households (personal consumption expenditures, C, and residential investment, part of I), businesses (nonresidential investment, the rest of I), foreigners (net exports, $X - M$), and government entities (government expenditures, G) on the goods and services produced in the economy.

Table 3–1 shows examples of the major components for each of the sectoral spending groups in this basic relationship. For further reference, part of Table 2–8 from Chapter 2 is repeated and expanded in Table 3–2. This table, which shows the dollar values for a much more detailed breakdown of aggregate demand, provides perspective on Table 3–1—the major types of sectoral spending. The following discussion focuses on each of the components in the preceding relationship including its composition and its behavioral characteristics.

PERSONAL CONSUMPTION EXPENDITURES

Personal consumption expenditures, or simply consumption, is the component of aggregate demand that represents spending by households on commodities and services. One of the most basic notions in all of macroeconomics views

TABLE 3–1   Aggregate demand and its components.
                 $GDP = C + I + (X - M) + G$

	Major Category	Subcategory	Example
C	= Consumption	Durable goods	Autos
			Furniture
		Nondurable goods	Food
			Clothing
			Gasoline
		Services	Household rent and operations
			Medical care
			Transportation
I	= Investment	Nonresidential fixed	Factories, office buildings, and stores
			Producers' durable equipment
		Residential fixed	New homes
			Additions and alterations
		Change in business inventories	Farm
			Nonfarm
			Manufacturing
			Wholesale
			Retail
$(X - M)$ =	Net exports	Exports	Merchandise (goods)
			Services
		Imports	Merchandise (goods)
			Services
G	= Government spending	Federal	Defense
			Employee compensation
			Material
			Other services
		State and local	Employee compensation
			Material
			Other services

consumption as the core of aggregate demand. The other components, in one sense or another, facilitate consumption. Business investment spending ultimately provides the capacity to produce consumer goods. Exports are produced to exchange for imported consumer goods (although this may not be the intention of the exporters, it is still true in the end). It can even be argued that government spending ensures an environment within which "the pursuit of happiness" can take place. Finally, personal consumption spending is the largest economic activity; it accounts for a bit more than three-fifths of GDP.

Consumption of commodities is split between those goods expected to last for 3 years or more—durable goods—and those expected to last less than 3 years—nondurable goods. Services, which account for half of all consumer spending, are intangible. A sense of the composition and relative importances of consumer spending is provided by Table 3–3, extracted from Table 3–2.

TABLE 3–2 Aggregate demand and its components.

	1990 Billions of Dollars	1991 Billions of Dollars	1992 Billions of Dollars
Gross domestic product	5546.1	5722.9	6038.5
Personal consumption	3761.2	3906.4	4139.9
Durable goods	468.2	457.8	497.3
Motor vehicles and parts	202.9	185.5	204.3
Furniture and household equipment	174.2	180.6	194.5
Other	91.0	91.6	98.5
Nondurable goods	1229.1	1257.9	1300.9
Food	604.8	621.4	633.7
Clothing and shoes	207.3	213.0	228.2
Gasoline and oil	108.4	102.9	103.4
Fuel oil and coal	13.2	13.0	13.8
Other	295.6	307.6	321.8
Services	2063.8	2190.7	2341.6
Housing	547.5	574.4	600.0
Household operation	215.6	227.1	234.4
Transportation	142.5	146.2	155.4
Medical care	526.2	577.1	628.4
Other	632.0	663.9	723.5
Residential construction	215.3	189.6	223.6
Single family structures	108.7	95.4	116.5
Multifamily structures	19.3	15.1	13.1
Other	87.3	79.1	94.0
Nonresidential fixed investment	586.7	555.9	565.5
Structures	201.6	182.6	172.6
Producer's durable equipment	385.1	373.3	392.9
Information processing and related equipment	125.6	125.0	135.5
Industrial equipment	88.7	86.0	87.2
Transportation and related equipment	85.3	84.9	90.7
Other	85.5	77.5	79.5
Change in business inventories	6.9	−8.6	7.3
Nonfarm	3.8	−8.6	2.3
Manufacturing	3.4	−7.0	−6.0
Wholesale trade	7.3	7.6	6.1
Retail trade	−1.8	1.3	6.5
Other	−5.1	−7.5	−4.3
Farm	3.1	0.0	5.0
Net exports	−71.4	−19.6	−29.6
Exports	557.1	601.5	640.5
Merchandise	398.7	426.4	448.7
Services	158.4	175.1	191.7
Imports	628.5	621.1	670.1
Merchandise	509.0	500.7	544.5
Services	119.5	120.4	125.6
Government purchases	1047.4	1099.3	1131.8
Federal	426.5	445.9	448.8
Defense	314.0	322.5	313.8
Nondefense	112.5	123.4	135.0
State and local	620.9	653.4	683.0

Source: Bureau of Economic Analysis, U.S. Department of Commerce.

TABLE 3–3 Personal consumption expenditures and their components.

	1990		1991		1992	
	Billions of Dollars	Share (%)	Billions of Dollars	Share (%)	Billions of Dollars	Share (%)
Personal consumption	3761.2	100.0	3906.4	100.0	4139.9	100.0
Durable goods	468.2	12.4	457.8	11.7	497.3	12.0
Motor vehicles and parts	202.9	5.4	185.5	4.7	204.3	4.9
Furniture and household equipment	174.2	4.6	180.6	4.6	194.5	4.7
Other	91.0	2.4	91.6	2.3	98.5	2.4
Nondurable goods	1229.2	32.7	1257.9	32.2	1300.9	31.4
Food	604.8	16.1	621.4	15.9	633.7	15.3
Clothing and shoes	207.3	5.5	213.0	5.5	228.2	5.5
Gasoline and oil	108.4	2.9	102.9	2.6	103.4	2.5
Fuel oil and coal	13.2	0.4	13.0	0.3	13.8	0.3
Other	295.6	7.9	307.6	7.9	321.8	7.8
Services	2063.8	54.9	2190.7	56.1	2341.6	56.6
Housing	547.5	14.6	574.4	14.7	600.0	14.5
Household operation	215.6	5.7	227.1	5.8	234.4	5.7
Transportation	142.5	3.8	146.2	3.7	155.4	3.8
Medical care	526.2	14.0	577.1	14.8	628.4	15.2
Other	632.0	16.8	665.9	17.0	723.5	17.5

Source: Bureau of Economic Analysis, U.S. Department of Commerce.

- *Durable goods,* in addition to being longer lasting, tend to be more expensive than other types of consumer spending. That is one reason spending for durables tends to be more volatile. In particular, as Figure 3–1(a)–(c) shows, consumption of durable goods shows a much more *cyclical* behavior pattern than spending for either nondurable goods or services. Because durable goods such as autos and furniture are expensive, their purchase can be postponed when overall economic activity is weak and then the purchases can be made when the economy revives.

- *Nondurable goods* consist of the type of goods—food, clothing, and fuel—that typically are regarded as necessities. As such, they follow a more *secular* growth trend showing less of a response to the stage of the business cycle. (Within nondurable goods purchases, say food, it is still possible to switch from high-priced purchases, such as steak, to low-priced substitutes, such as hamburger.)

- *Services* comprise more than half of all consumer spending and largely represent spending on such necessities as housing—both basic rent and operations—and medical care. In addition, consumer spending on services includes spending for various discretionary items such as recreation, education, and travel.

FIGURE 3–1   Consumption of goods and services.

(a) Consumption of durable goods.

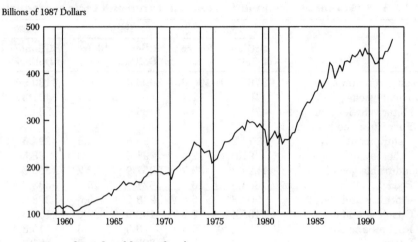

(b) Consumption of nondurable goods.

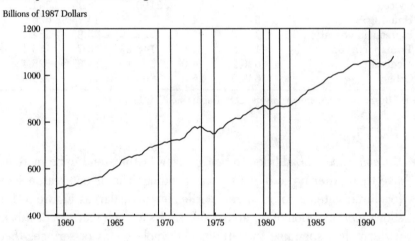

(c) Consumption of services.

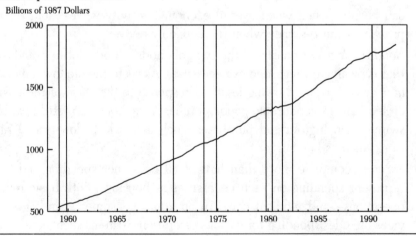

Figure 3–1 shows the trends in each of these consumer spending sectors over the past three decades. The strongly *procyclical* trend of consumption of durable goods (Figure 3–1(a)) contrasts starkly with the barely cyclical trend for consumer spending on nondurable goods (Figure 3–1(b)), and even more strongly with the nearly *secular* trend for spending on services (Figure 3–1(c)).

One of the most basic relationships in economics is that between income and consumer spending. In *The General Theory of Employment, Interest, and Money*, [1] the basis for modern macroeconomics, John Maynard Keynes noted:

1. Consumer spending tends to increase as income increases, but,
2. The increases in spending are less than the full increase in income (some of the increased income is saved).

These two aspects of the aggregate income-spending relationship are presented in Figures 3–2 and 3–3. Figure 3–2 contrasts real personal consumption expenditures (PCE) with real GDP, while Figure 3–3 contrasts real PCE with real disposable personal income (DPI). The graphs also show estimates of the average historical relationships between these variables.

The relationship between real PCE and real GDP is:

$$PCE = -272 + 0.73 \times GDP$$

FIGURE 3–2   Real personal consumption expenditures versus real gross domestic product.

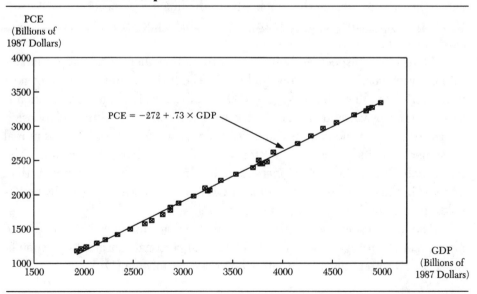

FIGURE 3-3 Personal consumption expenditures versus disposable personal income.

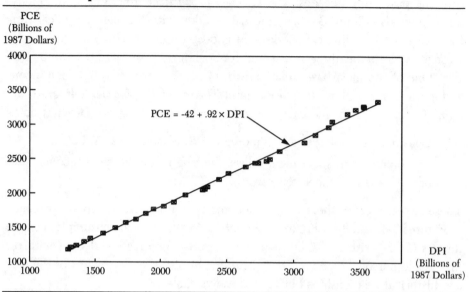

The relationship between consumer spending and total GDP is captured in the chart by a commonly used technique, known as regression analysis, which fits an estimated straight line through the actual data. The closer the actual data—the little squares in the graph—lie to the line, the stronger is the statistical relationship. (This can be quantified in a statistic known as the coefficient of determination, or R^2.)

Mere visual inspection, however, confirms that there is a strong relationship between consumer spending and GDP: The little squares all lie on or next to the estimated line (the R^2 suggests 99.8% of the variation in consumption is accounted for by variation in GDP). The basic interpretation of this relationship is that for every $1 increase in real GDP, there is an increase of 73 cents in real consumer spending. (The constant term, equal to -272, is unimportant.) The reason only 73 cents of each $1 increase in income is spent by consumers is that, as noted in the previous chapter, some of GDP is not received directly by households, namely profits.

The relationship between consumer spending and income is captured more precisely in Figure 3–3, which relates real personal consumption expenditures (PCE) to real disposable (after-tax) personal income (DPI):

$$PCE = -42 + 0.92 \times DPI$$

This result indicates that for every $1 increase in after-tax income, individuals spend 92 cents (saving the remaining 8 cents). Moreover, the graph shows that the relationship between consumer spending and after-tax income is equally strong as that to GDP (in fact, the R^2 also shows that 99.7% of the variation in PCE is explained by variation in DPI).

This is an important validation of Keynes's theory of the consumption function, using actual data for the past three decades. These estimated relationships also provide important explanations of the behavior of aggregate demand in the U.S. economy. The relationships suggest that consumption spending—accounting for roughly 60 percent of total economic activity—grows at nearly three-quarters the rate of total GDP and increases by 92 cents for every dollar that disposable income increases.

This is a useful fact for someone like Alice Hawkins to know. The precise relationship is less important than the general fact that as GDP and after-tax income increase, consumer spending will increase as well. Since knowledge that the economy is growing is a basis for expecting increases in consumer spending, Alice must have a sense of the pace and direction of overall economic activity to determine the prospects for designer dresses. Since it is now so easy to estimate these kinds of relationships with spreadsheet packages (for example, EXCEL or LOTUS 1-2-3), Alice could use that approach to estimate a direct relationship between sales of designer dresses and GDP. At any rate, two fundamental conclusions can be drawn and applied to her decision making:

1. Since dresses are nondurable goods—they have a useful life of less than 3 years—the demand for dresses is closely linked to the rate of growth in overall GDP.

2. As will be discussed in Chapter 9, because these are relatively high-priced items, they are likely to be more responsive to the rate of GDP growth than purely necessary goods.

These relationships, which underlie the demand for a particular product, will be examined in more detail in Chapters 8 and 9.

INVESTMENT

Table 3–2, shows that investment within GDP comprises three major components: residential construction, nonresidential fixed investment, and the change in business inventories. These are widely varied in terms of the decision makers, the types of spending, and the influences that affect the decision-making process. Moreover, as Figure 3–4(a)–(c) shows, these spending components are

FIGURE 3–4   Major investment components.

(a) Residential construction.

Billions of 1987 Dollars

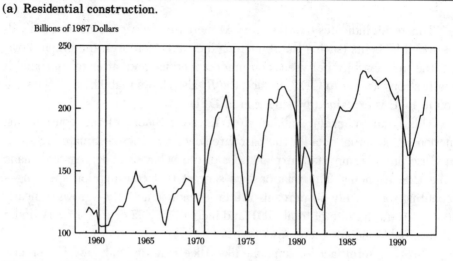

(b) Nonresidential fixed investment.

Billions of 1987 Dollars

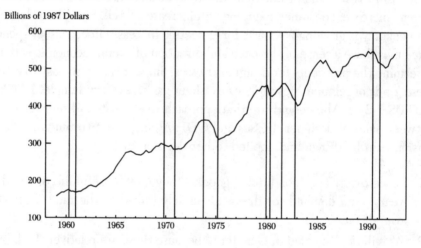

(c) Change in business inventories.

Billions of 1987 Dollars

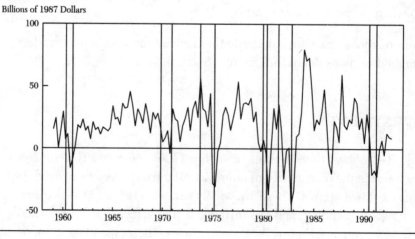

highly cyclical. In fact, they represent the most cyclically sensitive components of aggregate demand.

Residential construction resembles consumer spending in some respects: The decision to spend is most often made by individuals for their own use. A house, however, is such a major expenditure and such a long-lived asset that it is considered investment in capital rather than merely a purchase to be consumed in the near term. Nonresidential fixed investment is the most conventional form of investment spending: Business managers make the decision to spend to increase a firm's capacity for producing other goods. The change in business inventories is a necessary expenditure to carry on business. The intentional decision to spend is made by a business manager, who hopes the investment will be short-lived.

To examine these expenditures in more detail, it makes sense to juggle the order, looking at nonresidential fixed investment first, then residential construction, and finally the change in business inventories.

Nonresidential Fixed Investment

As already suggested, nonresidential fixed investment conforms to the commonly held notion of investment. It consists of spending for structures: plants, office buildings, and commercial buildings; and for equipment: industrial machinery, office machinery (from computers to desks to pencil sharpeners), transportation equipment (cars, trucks, ships, and aircraft), and tools. These items represent the capital goods used to produce goods. Capital goods are long-lasting factors of production that are purchased with a large outlay "up front" but yield a stream of income over an extended period. This rate-of-return-over-time aspect of investment leads to two key features of the "investment decision": (1) investment is related to interest rate levels and (2) the chief use of this relationship is as a benchmark for comparing the rate of return (expressed as a percentage) of the investment.

The usual textbook discussion of investment refers to an "inverse relationship between investment and interest rates." In fact, however, the relationship between investment and interest rates is far more complex. Figure 3–5 shows an estimated relationship between real nonresidential fixed investment and bond rates for the past three decades. A surprising aspect of this relationship is that it is direct; investment increases as interest rates increase. A second point that can easily be discerned is that the relationship is very loose (the R^2 shows that only about 56% of the variation in investment spending is explained by variation in bond rates). These points reflect a significant aspect of investment: Interest rates are an important consideration in the decision to invest, but investment is

FIGURE 3–5 Nonresidential investment versus bond rates.

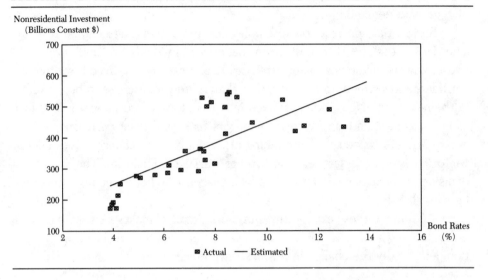

Nonresidential Investment
 (Billions Constant $)

Bond Rates (%)

■ Actual — Estimated

not undertaken merely because interest rates are low; it can still occur in the presence of relatively high interest rates.

This is true because the more important influence on investment is the prospect of earning a profit. Figure 3–6 shows a relationship between investment and the level of profits in the prior year. This is also a direct relationship, and as can be discerned from visual examination, the actual data lie much closer to the estimated line (the R^2 suggests a bit more than 86% of the variation in

FIGURE 3–6 Nonresidential investment versus lagged profits.

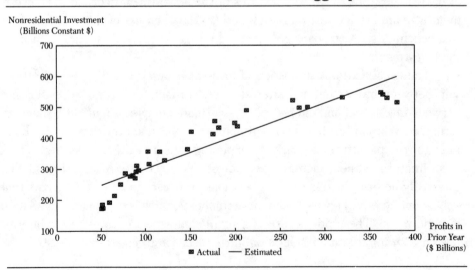

Nonresidential Investment
 (Billions Constant $)

Profits in Prior Year ($ Billions)

■ Actual — Estimated

investment is explained by the variation in lagged profits). This gives substance to an important behavioral characteristic: *Businesses invest in increased plant and equipment only if they can envision increased profits as a result. Investments are not made simply because interest rates are low.*

In fact, interest rates serve as a benchmark for comparing the *rate of return on the investment.* If the expected returns from an investment in increased capacity, as a percentage of its cost, exceeds the interest rate that could be earned on the same money if invested in interest-bearing securities, then the firm will choose investment in productive capital. This is most likely when the business cycle is in an upswing. In turn, business cycle upswings are often periods of strong credit demands and rising interest rates.

Thus, it is entirely consistent that nonresidential fixed investment shows a direct relationship to interest rates, as shown in Figure 3–5. It is not the level of interest rates alone that determines investment, but rather the *level of interest rates relative to the rate of expected return on investment.* That rate of return is most likely to be rising when profits are on an uptrend, and this is as probable in a period of rising as falling interest rates.

The state of nonresidential fixed investment is somewhat remote from Alice Hawkins's business. This investment spending concept reflects the general state of business activity, which is important in a general sense to Alice, but it has much less to suggest about the state of consumer demand in general, let alone for dresses. However, if Ms. Hawkins were in a slightly different business—say purchasing manager for an office equipment store—she would be quite sensitive to investment indicators. Also, some quite large regional centers have a dominant industrial goods manufacturer as the major employer; for instance, Boeing in Seattle, Washington, Caterpillar Tractor in Peoria, Illinois, or the combination of Kodak and Xerox in Rochester, New York. Changes in investment demand for the products of these capital goods manufacturers could exert considerable influence on consumer goods in the region. If Alice Hawkins were buying for a store in such a region, she would do well to pay attention to trends in nonresidential investment demand.

Residential Construction

Residential construction spending, as noted earlier, may be decided on and committed by households but is in the realm of an investment, because housing structures are such long-lived assets: New homes are presumed to have a useful life of at least 50 years. In addition, Figure 3–4 shows that residential construction is the most cyclically sensitive of the investment components (which, as was already noted, is itself the most cyclical of the major GDP components). Moreover, closer scrutiny of Figure 3–4 reveals that residential construction often reaches a peak before the peak for the overall economy and reaches a trough before the overall business cycle hits bottom. This reflects three important aspects of residential construction spending:

1. Many factors influence investment in residential construction. Intuitively, interest rates would seem to be high on the list. However, as Figure 3–7 shows, there is an extremely loose relationship between residential construction and mortgage interest rates (the R^2 is so low it suggests that only about 6% of the variation in residential construction is explained by the variation in mortgage rates). The explanation is understandable after a little reflection. Given the enormity of a decision to buy a home, other factors—a family's income and its prospects for future income, the employment environment, tax laws, and the rate of inflation—may be more important to the decision to commit to a 30-year payment schedule than wiggles in the mortgage interest rate.

2. The second point is related. Important influences, such as income prospects and employment conditions, are most likely to be favorable when the business cycle as a whole is in an upswing. A cyclical upturn is also a time when interest rates are likely to be rising.

3. A more important factor in new home purchases than the *level* of interest rates is the *availability* of mortgage funds. Potential long-term borrowers can be grouped into three classes: the U.S. Treasury, private businesses, and households. Among these, the household sector is the least competitive as overall credit demand intensifies. The U.S. Treasury—with the best credit rating in the world—is interest rate insensitive and can always borrow what it needs (it can simply borrow the money to pay back its past borrowing). Business borrowers are likely to demand more credit and to accept higher interest rates in business cycle upswings because the rate of return on their investments is likely to be higher. Potential new home buyers, on the other hand, have no such advantage as a business cycle matures and, historically, have been the first group to be "crowded out" of credit markets.

This last fact explains why residential construction tends to reach a peak before the overall economy reaches a peak. As such, trends in residential construction provide useful signals to business managers such as Alice Hawkins even though the activity seems remote from her own business. Signs that residential construction has reached a peak can be regarded as an indicator of an approaching peak in overall economic activity—a leading indicator. (Residential construction can also be a useful indicator of an approaching upturn in recession, because it begins to recover before the overall economy.)

FIGURE 3–7   Residential construction versus mortgage rates.

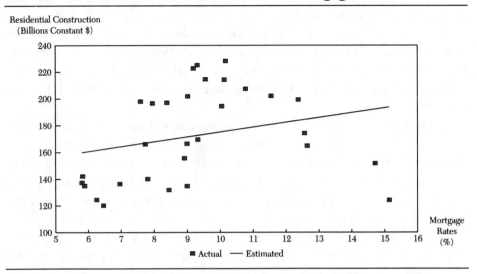

Residential Construction
(Billions Constant $)

Change in Business Inventories

Business investment is not restricted to spending on *fixed* capital—structures and equipment—but also includes stocks of raw materials, goods still in production, and finished goods ready for sale. These inventories are held by manufacturers, wholesalers, retailers, and farmers and represent the wherewithal businesses need to carry out their business every bit as much as bricks, mortar, and tools.

As can be seen from Figure 3–4, the change in business inventories is far more volatile than any other major component of GDP. This reflects a key aspect of business investment in inventories, which can be most easily seen if we think in terms of retail inventories of finished goods. Retailers desire to hold inventories for the obvious reason that it facilitates sales to have samples on hand. For Alice Hawkins, for instance, the sale of dresses is dependent on having dresses on hand for customers to try on. This means that the retailer must pay for the dresses in order to have them available for sale. Thus, the retailer must *invest* in stock, or inventory.

Investment in inventories is related to the retailers' *sales expectations*, which are, in turn, related to past sales trends. If sales have been strong, then sales in the near future probably will continue strong, so inventories will be increased. (A company would want to avoid missing sales due to insufficient stock on hand.) On the other hand, if sales have been faltering, a store will likely wish to curtail future orders, relying on existing inventories to meet future sales.

The crucial role of past sales to the decision of how much to invest in inventories is a key reason for the volatile pattern seen in Figure 3–4. Businesses can be caught off guard by sudden changes in demand. Consequently, inventories may continue to rise even after sales have turned down because of insufficient information about the state of sales on the part of business decision makers (alternatively, inventories may continue to be reduced even after sales have turned up).

These informational lags are even greater when the connection of the business to final sales is less intimate. For instance, manufacturers continue to produce goods based on past orders from retailers after the retailers begin to notice a falloff in sales. At the same time, wholesalers will continue to stock goods based on past retail sales rates. The message that sales have softened may pass through the distribution-production chain with a variety of lags.

As a result, inventories have often continued to increase well into a recession—the 1973–1975 recession was the most striking recent example—so that the eventual "inventory correction" (the need to cut production and reduce inventories to a level more in line with sales) was even deeper and more pronounced. Since the 1980 and 1981–1982 recessions, businesses, particularly manufacturers, have followed a more cautious inventory policy, called "just in time." This approach aims at minimizing the stocks of raw materials and finished goods that businesses maintain. If sales pick up, the business increases its orders, transferring the burden to suppliers, who must fill the orders. The result is that the primary business shares its sensitivity to near-term demand with its suppliers.

Inventory management is a vital concern to Alice Hawkins. As a buyer, she is one of the people who determine the inflow to inventories. Because the inventories have to be paid for and financed until they can be sold, her buying has a profound effect on the costs of her company. She must pay attention to current sales trends, in coordinating her buying of dresses for future sale. The change in business inventories is a crucial indicator for many business managers across a wide range of business types.

NET EXPORTS OF GOODS AND SERVICES

In the past two decades, the U.S. economy has become much more integrated with foreign economies. The foreign sector's impact on aggregate demand is in the form of net exports. This is a complex component of GDP for many reasons. First, it represents the interaction of two major economic activities: exports of goods and services and imports of goods and services. Other complexities stem from this interaction. Import demand originates in our economy, but production occurs abroad. Conversely, export demand arises abroad for goods and services produced domestically.

The last point explains why we look at the foreign sector on a *net* basis. One purpose of GDP is to measure production, or output. To see net output, it is necessary to measure total output—including goods and services produced for export—and to offset this production with the goods that are demanded domestically but produced abroad. An unusual aspect from the aggregate demand side is that exports have little to do with domestic demand.

Figure 3–8 presents graphs of (a) net exports, (b) exports of goods and services, and (c) imports of goods and services in constant dollar terms for the past three decades. The graphs display two features of foreign sector behavior. First, throughout most of the past three decades, U.S. net exports have been negative: the *trade deficits* reflect that import growth has outpaced export growth. The second feature of the graph of net exports is that it lacks a clear cyclical pattern. This is true although the graph for imports does have a cyclical pattern: Imports, like other types of consumer and business demand, strengthen in expansions and fall off in recessions. There is much less of a cyclical pattern for exports, however, which have only a faint connection to the domestic business cycle. (Essentially, in mature expansions, when capacity begins to constrain production—as in 1973 and 1979, but not 1989–1990—production for export may fall off so that producers can more easily supply domestic customers.) Exports are determined more by business cycle conditions in foreign economies, and fortunately, the U.S. and foreign business cycles are not always synchronized. When synchrony occurs, (as in 1973–1975), the recessions are more severe.

Two other sets of related economic influences—interest rates and foreign exchange rates—exert considerable effect on net exports (see in-depth discussion of these influences in Chapters 6 and 7, respectively). This has been especially true since the early 1970s, as can be seen by examining Figure 3–9(a)–(c), which presents net exports, exports, and imports in billions of *current* dollars. These graphs show the trade deficit as it is most often viewed.[2] It can be readily seen that there are three distinct phases to the behavior of net exports over this period:

1. During the period up through 1973, there was approximate balance in foreign trade and exports and imports represented a fairly small portion of U.S. GDP (about 5% or less).

2. From 1974 through 1982, as the first rise in oil prices pushed through by the Organization of Petroleum Exporting Countries (OPEC) became institutionalized, trade deficits became more persistent even though both exports and imports expanded to 8 to 10 percent of GDP.

FIGURE 3–8   Foreign sector behavior.

(a) Net exports.

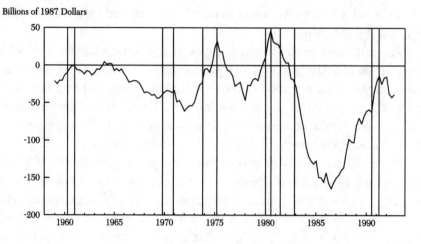

(b) Exports of goods and services.

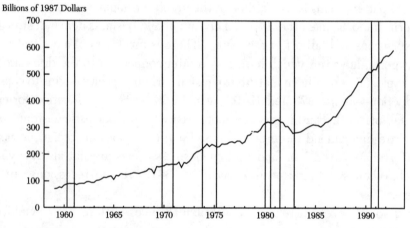

(c) Imports of goods and services.

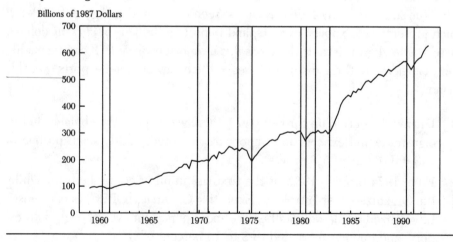

occurs abroad. Conversely, export demand arises abroad for goods and services produced domestically.

The last point explains why we look at the foreign sector on a *net* basis. One purpose of GDP is to measure production, or output. To see net output, it is necessary to measure total output—including goods and services produced for export—and to offset this production with the goods that are demanded domestically but produced abroad. An unusual aspect from the aggregate demand side is that exports have little to do with domestic demand.

Figure 3–8 presents graphs of (a) net exports, (b) exports of goods and services, and (c) imports of goods and services in constant dollar terms for the past three decades. The graphs display two features of foreign sector behavior. First, throughout most of the past three decades, U.S. net exports have been negative: the *trade deficits* reflect that import growth has outpaced export growth. The second feature of the graph of net exports is that it lacks a clear cyclical pattern. This is true although the graph for imports does have a cyclical pattern: Imports, like other types of consumer and business demand, strengthen in expansions and fall off in recessions. There is much less of a cyclical pattern for exports, however, which have only a faint connection to the domestic business cycle. (Essentially, in mature expansions, when capacity begins to constrain production—as in 1973 and 1979, but not 1989–1990—production for export may fall off so that producers can more easily supply domestic customers.) Exports are determined more by business cycle conditions in foreign economies, and fortunately, the U.S. and foreign business cycles are not always synchronized. When synchrony occurs, (as in 1973–1975), the recessions are more severe.

Two other sets of related economic influences—interest rates and foreign exchange rates—exert considerable effect on net exports (see in-depth discussion of these influences in Chapters 6 and 7, respectively). This has been especially true since the early 1970s, as can be seen by examining Figure 3–9(a)–(c), which presents net exports, exports, and imports in billions of *current* dollars. These graphs show the trade deficit as it is most often viewed.[2] It can be readily seen that there are three distinct phases to the behavior of net exports over this period:

1. During the period up through 1973, there was approximate balance in foreign trade and exports and imports represented a fairly small portion of U.S. GDP (about 5% or less).

2. From 1974 through 1982, as the first rise in oil prices pushed through by the Organization of Petroleum Exporting Countries (OPEC) became institutionalized, trade deficits became more persistent even though both exports and imports expanded to 8 to 10 percent of GDP.

FIGURE 3–8 Foreign sector behavior.

(a) Net exports.

Billions of 1987 Dollars

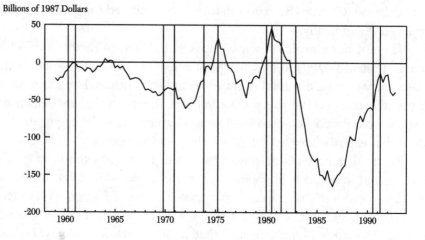

(b) Exports of goods and services.

Billions of 1987 Dollars

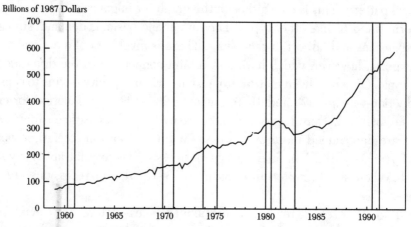

(c) Imports of goods and services.

Billions of 1987 Dollars

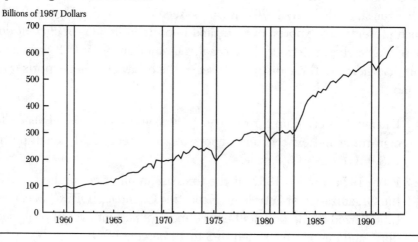

FIGURE 3–9 Exports and imports.

(a) Net exports.

Billions of Current Dollars

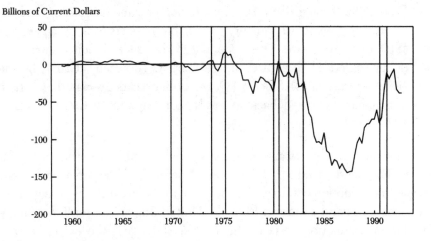

(b) Exports of goods and services.

Billions of Current Dollars

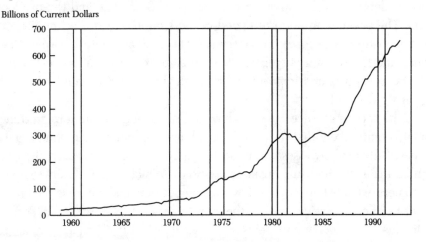

(c) Imports of goods and services.

Billions of Current Dollars

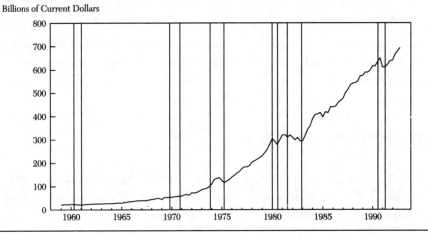

3. From 1982 through 1987, the trade deficit became far greater than earlier, as exports grew to 10 percent of GDP, but imports took up an even larger (11% or more) share. This widening in the trade deficit occurred as the dollar soared on foreign exchange markets (boosted, at first, by sharply rising interest rates). Since 1987, the dollar has depreciated and the trade deficit has narrowed back to levels more similar to those prevailing in 1974–1982.

Demand for exports and imports is complicated by the role of foreign exchange. Foreign demand for U.S. exports is determined by, among other factors, income in the foreign country, and the price of the good in the foreign country. The price of a good exported from the United States in a foreign country is a function of production costs in the United States and the exchange rate between the U.S. dollar and the foreign currency. Similarly, U.S. demand for imports is determined by, among other factors, U.S. income and the price of the good. The price of an imported good in the United States is a function of production costs in the foreign country and the exchange rate between the U.S. dollar and the foreign currency. Thus, foreign exchange rates exert important effects on exports and imports and through them exert a prominent effect on aggregate demand.

The actions of Alice Hawkins have a direct effect on the foreign trade sector. It is quite likely that in her role as a buyer she must often choose between domestically made dresses and imported ones. In most such cases, the decision will be made on the usual business concerns: Which is most likely to appeal to customers, what is being offered by the competition, and where is the best value in terms of cost relative to what the stores can sell the merchandise for? These individual *micro* economic decisions have considerable impact on aggregate *macro* economic measures. In addition, the complex feedback between the trade deficit and foreign exchange rates (to be examined in Chapter 7), and between foreign exchange rates and export demand, means that the business decisions of someone like Alice Hawkins are a factor. Finally, sensitivity on her part to foreign trade trends—and their likely effect on costs—is important to her buying decisions.

GOVERNMENT SPENDING

The government spending sector is an important large component of aggregate demand. During the 1950s and 1960s and for most of the 1970s, real government spending accounted for 20 percent to 25 percent of real GDP. Since 1976, government spending has accounted for just under 20 percent of GDP. Figure 3–10 shows the trends for government spending in total, at the federal level, and by state and local governments over the past three decades. Three points are significant:

1. First, government spending in the GDP covers only spending on goods and services. It specifically excludes spending on transfers such as Social Security payments, unemployment benefits, welfare payments, and government retirement payments. (These *transfer payments* are excluded from GDP because they are not payments for current production.) Thus, there is a considerable difference between the government spending in GDP and that which is contained in the appropriate governmental budgets.

2. The lion's share (two-thirds to three-quarters) of federal government expenditures is accounted for by defense spending on material and civilian and military salaries. Nearly two-thirds of state and local government spending is for employee compensation. Teachers make up the largest single group of state and local government employees.

3. This point follows from the previous one. As can be seen from Figure 3–10, government spending has no clear cyclical trend. This is because so much of government spending is for national defense and education, spending that must continue regardless of the state of the business cycle.

Figure 3–10(b) shows two more extended cycles. The pronounced run-up in real spending from 1965 to 1969 shows the impact from the increase in defense spending as the Vietnam War intensified. From 1969 through 1980, there was a falloff in federal government spending as the war wound down and defense spending subsided. Federal government spending began rising sharply again during the Reagan administration (1981–1988) and has since been more stable, but at the higher level. These trends—particularly the sharp run-ups and the falloff from 1969–1974—were unaffected by business cycles, although the longer government spending cycles may have affected the shorter business cycles they included.

State and local government spending show a clearer secular pattern over the past three decades, which appears to have been unaffected by business cycles.

Government spending affects Alice Hawkins in two ways. First, as noted, government spending accounts for a major share of total GDP and so affects aggregate demand. To the extent demand in her business responds to changes in aggregate demand, Alice will be interested in the changes in government spending that affect aggregate demand. An informed business manager will know about the distinctions between government spending, as it is represented in

FIGURE 3-10   Local, state, and federal government spending.

(a) Total government spending.

Billions of 1987 Dollars

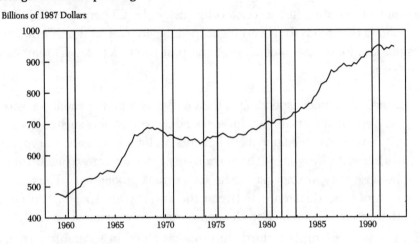

(b) Federal government spending.

Billions of 1987 Dollars

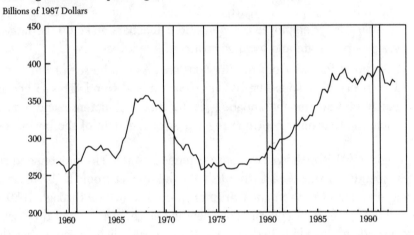

(c) State and local government spending.

Billions of 1987 Dollars

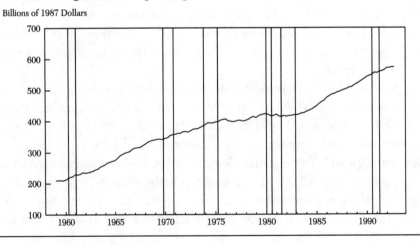

aggregate demand, and the larger concept of government spending, including transfers, that is part of fiscal budgets. Alice's second interest is as an informed citizen. In this respect, her interest will be in the fiscal as well as the aggregate demand effects.

SUMMARY

Aggregate demand, the spending component of GDP, is important to all those business managers whose businesses respond to customer demands—in other words, most businesses in the United States. Aggregate demand shows considerable short-term variability because it is affected by a number of *variables*, both integrally related (for example, disposable income) and seemingly "external" (for example, employment levels, prices, interest rates, lending conditions, and foreign exchange rates).

A famous representation of the role of aggregate demand in determining the *equilibrium* level of output is the intersection of the aggregate demand curve with the longer-run output curve, as shown in Figure 3–11. Aggregate demand, as shown, comprises PCE, which is shown as the same function of real GDP presented in Figure 3–2, and the other components (investment, net exports, and government spending), which are not functions of real GDP. Thus, aggregate demand is shown as a parallel line to the consumption

FIGURE 3–11   Aggregate demand and output.

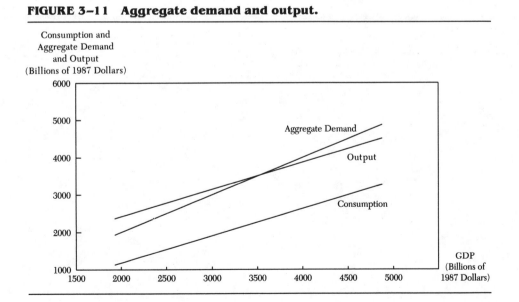

curve. The point at which aggregate demand intersects output is where equilibrium occurs in the short run.

In the next chapter, we look at the supply, or output, side of the aggregate economy: the production of goods and services. In some respects, output is less variable than demand. Nevertheless, the interaction between demand and output is a key factor in explaining the behavior of some of the external variables. In subsequent chapters, we will look at how the general price level and employment conditions are determined (Chapter 5); how interest rates, lending, and monetary policy react to these other variables (Chapter 6); and the interaction of foreign trade, capital flows, and exchange rates (Chapter 7).

4 PRODUCING GOODS AND SERVICES

Aggregate Supply—Labor, Capital, and Output

Gross domestic product measures aggregate economic activity as both expenditure and as output. The preceding chapter viewed the expenditure approach as *aggregate demand.* These expenditures were seen to be quite susceptible to *cyclical* forces, resulting in considerable short-run volatility. Output—the other side—represents the production of the goods and services that are demanded. *Aggregate supply* is a longer-term concept, which can be viewed as a response to short-term demands.

This chapter looks at the elements that make up supply: the factors of production, principally the labor force and capital stock, and how they are organized to produce the output that is demanded. At the microeconomic level, this is a vital concern of managers (explored in detail in Chapter 10), since managing is nothing less than organizing production. From a macroeconomic perspective, the availability and growth of the factors of production determine the potential for growth by the overall economy. Specifically, in examining aggregate supply, we are looking at the ability of the productive sectors to respond to aggregate demand.

In this chapter, we will view the effect on a business manager through the example of Bill Angelo, who is responsible for production planning at the plants of a large container manufacturer. Since nearly all goods are shipped or sold in containers—anything from crates to cartons to bags to shrink-wrap—this example offers a chance to view the response of the supplying sectors of the economy from the point of sale back through the production process.

PRODUCTION SECTORS

The goods and services produced in the U.S. economy represent a wide range of business types. Table 4–1 provides an extended view of the shares of total output (first seen in Table 2–5) produced by the seven major industry sectors. Although these sectors could be classified more finely, they provide a useful starting point, because the categories represent activities or entities that differ from each other and that have grown or shrunk in relative importance as the business of the nation has evolved. The seven sectors include the following industries:

1. *Agriculture, forestry, and fisheries* represent the earliest occupations and industries in the United States. They have in common that they involve cultivation and harvesting *renewable* resources.

2. *Mining*, by contrast, refers to the extraction of *nonrenewable* resources. In addition to extraction of metallic ores, mining includes drilling for and extraction of oil and natural gas.

3. *Construction* includes the building of residential and nonresidential structures, highways, infrastructure, and telecommunications facilities.

4. *Manufacturing* involves the production of durable goods lasting three years or more, such as steel, turbines, computers, and automobiles; and shorter-lived nondurable goods such as food, textiles, paper, and chemicals. This kind of production traditionally takes place in factories, although some "high-tech" manufacturing is done under conditions closer to laboratories than factories.

5. *Private services* include (1) transportation and public utilities (communications, electric, gas, and sanitary services); (2) distributive services (wholesale and retail trade); (3) finance, insurance, and real estate; and (4) other services, including business and health services. The principal feature these industries have in common is that their output is *intangible* in contrast to the *goods-producing* sectors.

6. *Government* refers to the services produced by governments at all levels: federal, state, and local. These services fall into three major types: defense, social welfare, and education.

7. *Rest of the world* captures the contribution to total output from foreign trade and is included on a net basis (exports less imports).

LONG- AND SHORT-TERM TRENDS

As shown in Table 4–1, there has been a considerable shift in the relative importance of these sectors in the past 60 years. In fact, this period can be divided

TABLE 4-1 National income shares.

	Agriculture, Forestry, and Fisheries	Mining	Construction	Manufacturing	Private Services	Government	Rest of World
1930	8.7%	2.3%	4.2%	24.1%	52.7%	7.0%	0.9%
1935	11.5	2.1	2.3	23.3	48.2	11.8	0.5
1940	7.6	2.3	3.2	27.5	48.2	10.8	0.5
1945	8.6	1.5	2.4	28.5	38.7	20.2	0.2
1950	7.5	2.2	5.1	31.1	43.9	9.7	0.6
1955	4.8	1.7	5.2	31.8	44.3	8.4	0.8
1960	4.2	1.3	5.3	29.2	46.7	12.5	0.8
1965	3.6	1.0	5.5	29.4	46.2	13.2	0.5
1970	3.1	1.0	5.7	25.8	47.7	15.9	0.9
1975	3.7	1.6	5.3	24.2	48.3	15.9	1.0
1980	2.7	1.9	5.6	23.5	49.9	14.2	2.1
1985	2.0	0.8	5.2	20.3	57.0	14.4	0.2
1990	2.2	0.8	5.0	19.0	57.9	14.7	0.5

Source: Bureau of Economic Analysis, U.S. Department of Commerce.

into three major swings lasting longer than typical business cycles. These three periods are (1) 1930–1940, reflecting the overwhelming influence of the depression, (2) 1940–1955, reflecting the effects of World War II, the Korean conflict, and the associated postwar influences, and (3) the past three decades, which, lacking the major traumas of the other two eras, have exhibited more continuity in their trends. This period since 1960 is our main focus in this book for examining the U.S. economy. However, a familiarity with the trends of the longer period is helpful to put the more recent years in perspective.

Some industry shifts have reflected forces particular to one or another of these individual eras, while other shifts have gone on across all periods. An instance of the former can be seen in the manufacturing boom relative to service production from 1940 through 1955. This reflected the emphasis on (1) production of war-related material during World War II, (2) the efforts to fulfill pent-up civilian demand after the war, and (3) compounded in the early 1950s by renewed military production related to the Korean conflict. While these demands were being met by the manufacturing sector, the expansion of the service sector lagged.

Another long-term cycle can be seen for the construction industry, reflecting the effects of demographic and other economic influences on residential construction activity. In the 1930s and during World War II, construction declined not only absolutely, but also relatively, as a share of total output. (Between 1930 and 1935, there was an absolute decline in total output, but the decline in construction's share is a sign that construction fell off at nearly twice the rate of total output.) This partly reflected the delayed effects of declining birth rates from 1910 to 1940, which led to slower subsequent growth for housing. In addition, it reflected a heightened caution, induced by the depression, that deterred households and businesses from making the long-term commitment implicit in a construction project.

The baby boom following World War II unleashed a housing boom in the 1950s, 1960, and 1970s. This boom was facilitated by the highway construction programs of the 1950s and early 1960s, which made more outlying areas accessible to urban commuters. In turn, this outmigration resulted in the suburban sprawl that characterizes the peripheries—East, West, and Gulf coasts and the areas bordering the Great Lakes.

Other long-term trends are also evident from the table. The most striking is the decline in importance of extractive industries. The decline in agriculture, forestry, and fisheries reflects the ongoing development of the U.S. economy. These occupations were among the earliest in the settlement of North America, let alone the evolving U.S. economy. The output from these sectors represented only about 3 percent of national income in 1990 compared with 11 percent to 14 percent in the 1930s—a testament to the increased importance of more advanced (higher value-added) industries.

A special aspect of the decline in the importance of mining is that increased petroleum exploration and production only interrupted the long-term decline in the 1970s and, ultimately, failed to reverse it.

The shift from manufacturing to service industries has received a great deal of media attention in recent years, but as Table 4–1 shows, it has been a fairly recent development. For most of the period since 1960, the service sector constituted a fairly stable share of output, while manufacturing declined from its level in the 1950s and 1960s, but then held fairly stable until the mid-1980s. Since then, the service share has gained, partly at the expense of manufacturing. Since the role of the rest of the world sector has also declined, the shift from manufacturing to service production may be regarded as a reflection of a change in underlying demand. The increased share of services in national income is evidence of the increased value ultimate consumers (demanders) place on this production.

Bill Angelo would be aware of the differing relative importance of industry sectors, although he might not think about the distinctions in those terms. His container plant could conceivably supply containers in all the major sectors:

- Much agricultural produce is shipped in cardboard boxes.
- Construction materials are shipped in cardboard and other fiber containers and wrappings.
- The container plant itself is a part of the manufacturing sector, and practically all manufactured goods are packaged in some form.

- The retail sector is a major segment of services and uses containers of various forms—boxes, cartons, and bags—extensively. The growth of retailing has been a part of the growth in relative importance of the service sector, and it has been accompanied by a dramatic increase in packaging. (Indeed, other representatives of the service sector—environmental consultants—are concerned with the effects of the growth in packaging.)

- Even governments use containers of one form or another to hold all their paperwork, if nothing else.

Thus, without paying much attention, Bill has a good insight to the intensity of activity in the various industrial sectors of the U.S. economy and the way these sectors work together to produce the national output.

Production, whether viewed in total, or by major sector, involves the combination of factors of production. The most elemental factors are labor and capital, while the manner in which they are combined is the technology. Labor is the more variable of the two factors in the short term and will be examined first. We will then look at the way in which capital is formed. Finally, we will examine how the two factors of production combine to produce the total output of the United States and will compare actual output with potential output.

LABOR INPUT

There are a number of different ways to view the use of labor in production. Figure 4–1 (a)–(c) presents trends for three measures that track various aggregates from which labor inputs are derived:

1. The *noninstitutional civilian population over age 16* (Figure 4–1 (a)) is the pool of (potentially) economically active people. It excludes children under the age of 16, people in the armed forces, and institutionalized adults, who are not active participants in the economy. The category includes students, retirees, and other adults—including parents at home—who are not actively involved in the labor force. Nevertheless, this category represents the potential number of human factors of production because those members of the group outside the paid labor force may still be active consumers and affect aggregate demand.

2. The *labor force* (Figure 4–1 (b)) is a narrower concept, consisting of the employed and those who are not currently employed but are seeking employment. Thus, this group provides a more precise notion of *potential* labor input to production.

FIGURE 4–1   Measures of labor input.

(a) Noninstitutional population over 16.

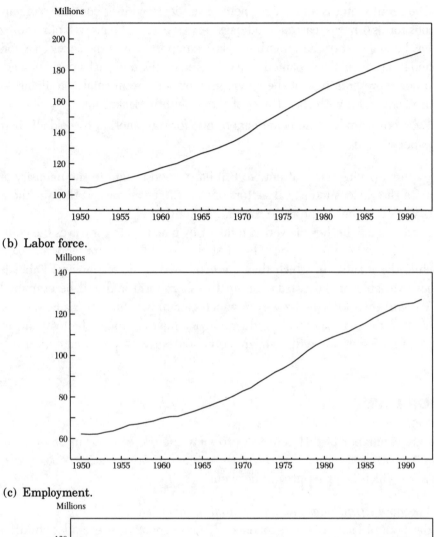

(b) Labor force.

(c) Employment.

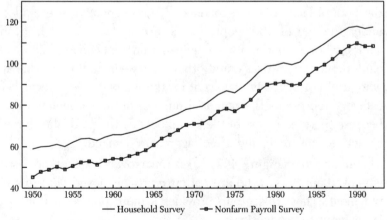

— Household Survey   —■— Nonfarm Payroll Survey

3. *Employment* (Figure 4–1 (c)) measures the labor input to production that is actually utilized. There are, however, two differing measures of employment. The one based on the *household survey* counts the number of workers and is drawn from the labor force data. The purpose of this measure is to count the number of workers among all those seeking to be employed (the labor force). Thus, if one worker has two jobs, that worker is counted only once. Moreover, workers are counted as employed even if they are not at work due to a work stoppage, vacation, or illness.

The so-called *nonfarm payroll survey* counts the number of jobs rather than workers. If one worker has two jobs, each of those jobs would be counted. On the other hand, groups that are included in the household survey—farm workers, self-employed workers, and doctors and lawyers in partnerships—are excluded from the payroll survey. In addition, workers must be receiving pay to be counted. Strikers are not counted.

The household and payroll employment concepts track each other quite closely, as can be seen in Figure 4–1 (c). The two series trace the same cyclical patterns and grow nearly in tandem. The payroll employment concept, however, is closer to the notion of labor input in production. The payroll survey also measures the weekly hours and hourly earnings of production workers (those who earn hourly wages rather than salaries).

When the number of payroll jobs is multiplied by the number of hours in the workweek, the resultant measure, *employee-hours worked,* provides an even more precise measure of labor input. The number of jobs, employment, provides a broad, *extensive* measure of labor utilization. Hours worked gives insight to the *intensity* of labor utilization. Figure 4–2 contrasts the trend for real GDP with that for employee-hours worked in the private nonfarm sector. As can be seen, the trends track quite closely. The trends would be even closer if just private nonfarm output were used instead of GDP, but the point is that the growth in hours worked closely tracks real GDP because the growth of labor input is a key determinant of real output.

The intensity of labor utilization represents the "fine tuning" of production at the margin. If Bill Angelo decides to order an increase in container output, he is likely to follow a series of options:

1. The easiest, short-term expedient is to lengthen the workweek by adding overtime.

2. A longer term response is to hire new workers thus adding to payrolls.

3. Increasing the workforce may ultimately be limited by the plant and other available capital the workers can utilize. Thus, increased investment—additions to the capital stock—represent a more permanent response to increased demand.

FIGURE 4–2   Real gross domestic product versus hours worked.

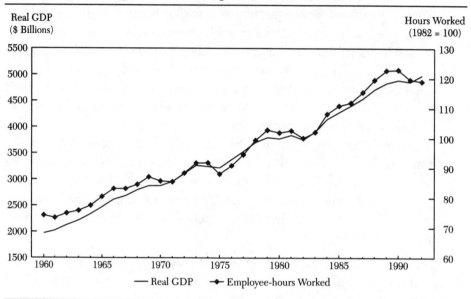

The difference between the trend for real GDP growth and for hours worked is productivity, which itself is partly determined by the growth of capital.

CAPITAL INPUT

The more capital labor has to work with, the more productive (the greater the output per hour) the labor can be. Thus, growth in capital—the tangible non-human input to production—is an essential ingredient to the growth of total output. In theory, investment is equal to the change in the capital stock. Non-residential fixed investment, the concept contained in GDP, however, measures not only the net new capital created but also the replacement of worn out, obsolete, or otherwise depreciated capital. Figure 4–3 (a) contrasts the change in net capital stock with nonresidential fixed investment, Figure 4–3 (b) contrasts net capital stock with nonresidential fixed investment.

The stock of capital (or any stock) is a "balance sheet" concept: It is a count as of a particular date of all the capital available. Investment, representing the change in the stock of capital, is equal to the *flow* of new capital over some period. Thus, investment is more of an "income statement" concept. As Figure 4–3 (a) shows, real nonresidential fixed investment has exceeded the real change in the net capital stock over the past four decades, and the difference has widened because the nonresidential fixed investment concept in GDP

FIGURE 4-3   Comparison of net capital stock with investment.

(a) Capital and nonresidential investment.

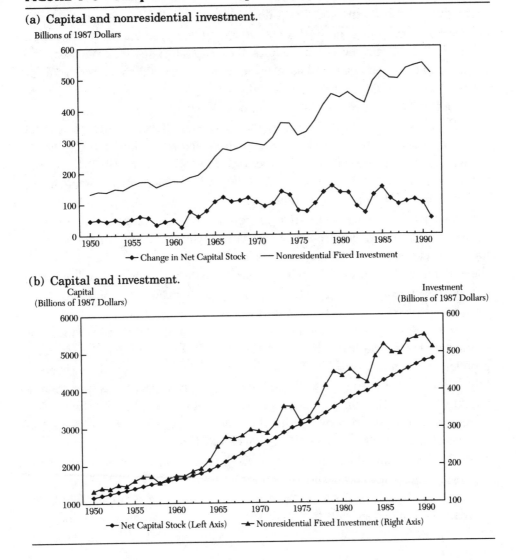

(b) Capital and investment.

is a *gross* concept. Both net new investment (the net addition to the capital stock) and replacement investment (the amount intended to replace worn-out and obsolete capital, which is financed by depreciation charges) are included. Indeed, this is the reason for the *gross* in gross domestic product.

The widening gap between nonresidential fixed investment and the change in the net capital stock over time (Figure 4–3 (a)), represents the increased importance of replacement investment as a share of total investment spending as the capital stock has grown. The relatively steady growth of the capital stock (Figure 4–3 (b)) requires that replacement needs will grow apace.

The large share of replacement investment in total investment spending highlights a difficulty in a manager's decision to add to the capital stock. Unlike the case of lengthening the workweek, or adding new workers to the payroll, it is more difficult to reverse an addition to capital. The workweek can be trimmed and workers can be laid off, but once the capital stock has been increased, the only way to "lay off" capital is to decide not to replace obsolete or worn-out units on schedule. Capital equipment cannot be fired.

Figure 4–3 (a) shows, however, that both the change in the net capital stock and nonresidential fixed investment have followed similar cyclical patterns. Note the decline during the recessions of 1973–1975, 1981–1982, and 1990–1991 and the oil-price shock in 1986–1987 (when oil prices declined, making much of the previous drilling capacity unprofitable). In periods of weak economic activity—recessions—firms defer new investment and allow existing capital to wear out without replacement. This is why the change in the net capital stock and nonresidential investment follow similar cyclical patterns, even if the long-term trends diverge. The downturns in capital formation result in periods of slower real output growth because as labor utilization increases, with longer workweeks and new hires, capital imposes a constraint.

Bill Angelo would be familiar with the constraint imposed by capital on production even if he had little say in the capital investment decision. In fact, production managers typically feel such constraints first. Capacity utilization rates—the ratio of output to available fixed capital, or capacity—is for capital a measure of utilization similar to the unemployment rate for the labor force. The difference is that the capacity utilization rate (see Figure 4–4) measures the portion of fixed capital that is utilized, whereas the unemployment rate measures the portion of labor that is *not* utilized. In periods of strong activity (for instance, 1966), the capacity utilization rate is high (91.1%), and the unemployment rate is low (3.8%). Conversely, in recession years (for example, 1982), the capacity utilization rate falls (to 72.8%), while the unemployment rate soars (to 9.7%). As Figure 4–4 shows, the two measures provide virtual mirror images of each other.

Capacity utilization is a key measure for a production manager to monitor. Planning production involves estimating future demand, given available resources (labor and capital). The availability of capital is more likely to impose a constraint because it is more difficult to increase the capital stock suddenly. Thus, Bill Angelo needs to pay close attention to the pace of demand relative to the available factors of production—labor and capital—in order to plan production for his container plants. At the macroeconomic level, the growth of the labor force (available for employment) and of nonresidential capital set the *potential* pace at which output can grow.

FIGURE 4-4   Unemployment versus capacity utilization rate.

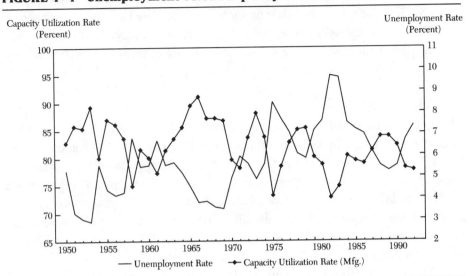

OUTPUT

A key distinction is between *actual* GDP, or output, and *potential* GDP, where potential GDP represents the output of goods and services that would be produced if there was full employment of all resources, both labor and capital. Thus, the unemployment rate would be at a "full employment" level and the capacity utilization rate would indicate that fixed capital is being fully utilized, when the economy is growing at potential.

The notion of "full employment" needs some clarification. Indeed, the concept of the "full-employment unemployment rate" may sound odd to non-economists. While this measure may sound like a contradiction in terms, it stems from the fact that there are three different types of unemployment:

1. The key portion represents those unemployed workers who are *cyclically* unemployed due to weak cyclical demand—a temporary inadequacy of aggregate demand. This unemployment reflects a degree of failure in macroeconomic management and so requires a policy response (analyzed in detail in Chapter 5).

2. Another segment is the *frictionally* unemployed: workers who are between jobs, but expect to be employed again soon. The crucial aspect of frictional unemployment is that it does *not* represent a market failure but rather is a concept akin to "voluntary" unemployment.

3. A final group consists of the *structurally* unemployed. These are workers who lost their jobs or cannot find jobs because they lack the experience or job skills employers are seeking. Structural unemployment is unlikely to respond to countercyclical macroeconomic policy measures. Structural unemployment is rooted in a mix of demographic, social, and microeconomic forces.

Changes in structural unemployment are important because they are the source of change in the "full-employment unemployment rate." As the foregoing suggests, "full employment" is not the same as an unemployment rate of zero. A working definition of "full employment" is the condition where experienced workers, and those seeking jobs with basic skills that are of a contemporary standard, can find employment. This definition implies a positive "full-employment unemployment rate," which is essentially equal to the frictionally and structurally unemployed.

There is a further complication. The amount of structural unemployment, in particular, has changed over the years. These changes reflect shifts in the composition of the labor force, three of which became particularly important in the 1970s and early 1980s: (1) employment of women, (2) the baby boom, and (3) reduction of the armed forces.

Unemployment, particularly among workers entering the job market for the first time or after a long absence is related to the length of job search, which in turn involves matching workers' job skills with employment openings. The longer it takes for workers to find jobs, the higher will be the unemployment rate. In a growing economy, the length of the job search varies in inverse proportion to the skill and experience of the job seeker: the more skilled and experienced the worker, the shorter the search. In the 1950s and 1960s, the labor force was composed predominantly of men. Beginning in the late 1960s, however, much of the labor force growth stemmed from two new groups.

The first was adult women, who either entered the labor force for the first time or reentered after a prolonged absence. In either case, the adult female participation rate (the portion of females 20 years and over in the labor force; see Table 4–2) rose from an average of 34.7 percent in the 1950s, to 38.2 percent in the 1960s, to 45.2 percent in the 1970s, to 53.8 percent in the 1980s, and to 58.1 percent in 1992. In other words, female participation in the labor market went from roughly one-third in the 1950s to nearly three-fifths in just four decades. This led to longer job searches for those women entering the labor market for the first time or after a long absence (typically, after raising a family). As a result, the overall unemployment rate felt upward pressure as the economy had to absorb an increased share of less experienced workers.

TABLE 4–2 Participation rates* (percent).

| | 20 Years Old and Over | | 16–19 Years Old |
	Male	Female	Both Sexes
1954–1959	87.1	34.7	48.6
1960–1969	84.2	38.2	47.0
1970–1979	81.2	45.2	54.0
1980–1989	78.8	53.8	54.9
1992	77.8	58.1	51.3

Source: Bureau of Labor Statistics, U.S. Department of Labor.

*Civilian Labor Force as a percentage of noninstitutional population group shown.

A second major change that operated in a similar manner was the entrance of baby boomers into the labor force beginning in the late 1960s. (The "baby boom" refers to the increase in the birth rate that began in 1946 and peaked in 1960.) Table 4–3 shows the distribution of the U.S. population for selected years from 1950 through 1991. The children of the baby boom can be seen in the share of the population under 16 years of age, which reached its peak of nearly one-third in the years between 1960 and 1965. The earliest wave of the baby boom, those born in 1946, began entering the labor force as low-skilled,

TABLE 4–3 Population distribution by age and unemployment rates* (percent).

| | | | | | Unemployment Rates | |
	Under 16	16–19	20–64	65 & Over	Actual	NAIRU**
1950	28.3	5.6	57.9	8.1	5.3	
1955	30.9	5.3	55.1	8.8	4.4	5.1
1960	32.6	5.9	52.3	9.2	5.5	5.2
1965	32.3	7.0	51.2	9.5	4.5	5.6
1970	30.2	7.5	52.5	9.8	4.9	5.6
1975	27.1	7.9	54.5	10.5	8.3	6.0
1980	24.3	7.5	56.9	11.3	7.0	5.9
1985	23.2	6.3	58.6	11.9	7.1	5.8
1990	23.0	5.8	58.7	12.5	5.5	5.6
1991	23.1	5.5	58.8	12.6	6.7	5.6
1992					7.4	5.5

Sources: Bureau of the Census, U.S. Department of Commerce; Bureau of Labor Statistics, U.S. Department of Labor.

*Population distribution shows each age group as a percentage of total population. Actual unemployment rate is shown as a percentage of civilian labor force.

**NAIRU is the nonaccelerating inflation rate of unemployment used by the Congressional Budget Office for computing potential GDP.

inexperienced teenagers in 1962, while those born in 1960 would have entered the labor force in the late 1970s. The likelihood that this group would have a longer job search is another reason the unemployment rate was under upward pressure in the 1970s.

The end of the Vietnam War, the end of the draft, and the consequent reduction in the size of the armed forces made up the third factor that led to a higher full employment unemployment rate. From its peak in 1968 to 1979, the resident armed forces decreased from 2,253,000 to 1,597,000. This meant that, just when the numbers of inexperienced youth were bulging, there was one less alternative to their entering the labor force.

The last two columns of Table 4–3 compare the actual civilian unemployment rate with one version of a full employment unemployment rate, the nonaccelerating inflation rate of unemployment (NAIRU). This concept attempts, first, to weight the labor force for changes in age and sex, so as to maintain comparability with the mix in the mid-1950s. Second, the intent is to maintain a constant rate of inflation, rather than a zero rate. This foreshadows the notion of a tradeoff between inflation and unemployment, which will be a focus of Chapter 5.

Thus, the actual unemployment rate in 1955 was below the NAIRU, suggesting the economy was straining its capacity limits and growing at a pace that would worsen inflationary pressures. By 1975, the demographic and social changes discussed earlier had raised the NAIRU to 6.0 percent. The 1973–1975 recession had resulted in an even higher actual inflation rate, but the point is this represented less slack in 1975 than the same rate would have suggested in 1955. More recently, the NAIRU has edged back to its mid-1960s level, as the social and demographic pressures on labor force absorption have eased. The 1990–1991 recession, however, represents a fresh cyclical falloff in labor market tightness that is reflected in the rise in the actual unemployment rate.

The key point is that the U.S. economy's *potential*, or *full employment*, real output growth rate has changed over the post-World War II era, in line with changes in the definition of the full employment unemployment rate. Figure 4–5 presents a comparison between *actual* real GDP growth from 1955 through 1992 and a *potential* real GDP growth concept, which the Commerce Department refers to as the "middle-expansion trend rate"[1].

As Figure 4–5 shows, the economy's actual growth has been fairly close to its potential for most of the past four decades. In fact, for 111 of the 152 quarters plotted, or 73 percent of the time, actual GDP has equaled or exceeded potential. When actual GDP growth is above potential, the difference is called an *inflationary gap,* implying that output is exerting a strain on capacity that, in turn, exerts upward pressure on the price level. During the rest of the time, when actual GDP is below the economy's potential growth rate, a *recessionary*

FIGURE 4–5   Potential versus actual gross domestic product.

Billions of 1987 Dollars (Ratio Scale)

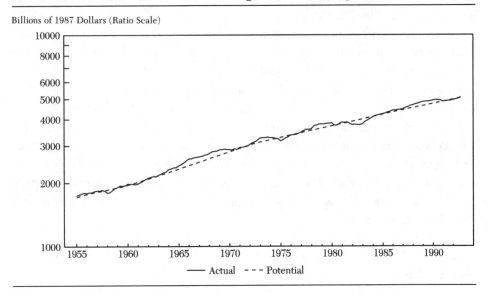

—— Actual   - - - Potential

gap is said to exist. Under these conditions, the unemployment rate is likely to be increasing and inflationary pressure lessening.

Table 4–4 compares actual real GDP growth rates with potential GDP growth rates for the six complete business cycles between 1958 and 1990 (where a business cycle extends from the trough in one recession through the ensuing recovery, expansion, and recession to the subsequent trough). The early 1970s and the early 1980s stand out as periods when actual real growth fell seriously short of potential growth for the full cycle. In the late 1950s and late 1970s, real growth exceeded potential by 0.5 percent per year, while in the two long cycles, the 1960s and most of the 1980s, actual growth and potential growth were quite close.

The relationship between aggregate demand, which underlies actual GDP growth, and aggregate supply is crucial to the determination of the two main

TABLE 4–4   Business cycle real GDP growth rates (expressed as percent at average annual rates).

Cycle	Potential	Actual
QII 1958–QI 1961	2.9%	3.4%
QI 1961–QIV 1970	3.7	3.9
QIV 1970–QI 1975	3.0	2.2
QI 1975–QIII 1980	2.5	3.1
QIII 1980–QIV 1982	2.5	0.3
QIV 1982–QIII 1990	2.4	2.9

macroeconomic disequilibrium conditions—inflation and unemployment (examined in detail in Chapter 5).

The relationship between aggregate demand and aggregate supply is one that a production manager like Bill Angelo can relate to quite easily. The fixed factors of production he must adjust to, impose limitations on his ability to increase production. Most likely, he would have experience of running operations at above their theoretical capacity limitations for short times. It is true that the overall economy can do this at times, too. In effect, the periods when the overall economy has run an inflationary gap are periods when not only Bill Angelo, but *most* production managers have operated at above their capacity. It is usually more apparent when the macroeconomy is running a recessionary gap. In those periods, the depressed state of general economic conditions likely affects individual firms as well.

SUMMARY

The ability to relate a firm's operations to that of the overall economy is a valuable asset for a manager. The macroeconomy comprises the individual economic operators. Thus, the firm's own activity must relate to the economy as a whole. If operations are strong, it may be a sign that the overall level of economic activity is straining its noninflationary limits. Alternatively, if the firm's business conditions are weakening, then this may be a signal of harder times in general.

5 INFLATION AND UNEMPLOYMENT

Much of economic theory focuses on equilibrium conditions, giving the impression that equilibrium is the usual economic state. In fact, this has been more the exception than the rule for the U.S. economy in the past four decades. Instead, either inflation or high unemployment has often existed—occasionally both at the same time.[1]

The macroeconomic ideal is to have (1) economic growth, (2) full employment, and (3) stable prices. This may be referred to as a *dynamic* equilibrium. The term dynamic is used here to differentiate equilibrium in a growing economy from a stagnant state. More often, however, one of three *dis*equilibrium states exist: (1) inflation with growth, (2) high unemployment with recession, or (3) inflation and high unemployment at the same time. In 1973, Paul Samuelson coined the term *stagflation* for this latter condition.

It is useful at the outset to define some reference points for inflation and high unemployment:

- *Inflation* refers to a *general* rise in the price level (as opposed to occasional rises in specific prices). In general, inflation rates of 3 percent or less have been tolerated in much the same way that unemployment rates close to the full employment unemployment rate have been accepted.
- *Unemployment rates* have been regarded as high when the rate has been more than a percentage point above the full employment unemployment rate.

Table 5–1 presents annual inflation and unemployment rates since 1950, while Figure 5–1 depicts these rates since the early 1960s.

TABLE 5–1   Unemployment and inflation trends 1950–1992.

	Civilian Unemployment Rate (%)	CPI Year–Year Changes (%)
1950	5.3	1.3
1951	3.3	7.9
1952	3.0	1.9
1953	2.9	0.8
1954	5.5	0.7
1955	4.4	−0.4
1956	4.1	1.5
1957	4.3	3.3
1958	6.8	2.8
1959	5.5	0.7
1960	5.5	1.7
1961	6.7	1.0
1962	5.5	1.0
1963	5.7	1.3
1964	5.2	1.3
1965	4.5	1.6
1966	3.8	2.9
1967	3.8	3.1
1968	3.6	4.2
1969	3.5	5.5
1970	4.9	5.7
1971	5.9	4.4
1972	5.6	3.2
1973	4.9	6.2
1974	5.6	11.0
1975	8.5	9.1
1976	7.7	5.8
1977	7.1	6.5
1978	6.1	7.6
1979	5.8	11.3
1980	7.1	13.5
1981	7.5	10.3
1982	9.7	6.2
1983	9.6	3.2
1984	7.5	4.3
1985	7.2	3.6
1986	7.0	1.9
1987	6.2	3.6
1988	5.5	4.1
1989	5.3	4.8
1990	5.5	5.4
1991	6.7	4.2
1992	7.4	2.9

Source: U.S. Department of Labor.

Shaded years represent years in which there was a recession in all or part of the year.

FIGURE 5–1   Inflation versus unemployment rate.

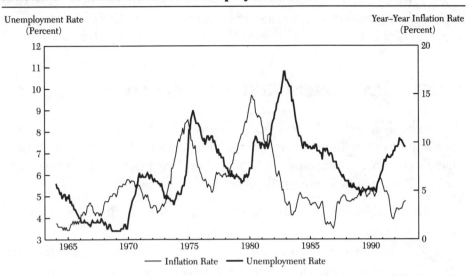

In this chapter, we will view the effects of inflation and unemployment through the eyes of Michael Sullivan, a personnel manager in the Northeast regional office of a large insurance company. Short-term changes in these macroeconomic conditions can have the following direct effects on how Sullivan performs his job:

- In periods of weak economic activity, unemployment is likely to be high and inflationary forces weak. This may affect the insurance company's personnel policies in three ways: (1) The large pool of unemployed workers will make it easier to fill job openings, while (2) the weak inflationary forces act to hold down the costs of hiring workers, but (3) the weak economy is likely to lessen the need for additional workers.

- When economic activity is strong, unemployment is likely to be shrinking and inflationary pressures may be building. These conditions will have opposite effects on the company's personnel policies. A growing economy may spur demand for workers, but the declining unemployment rate and the likelihood of an intensifying inflation rate will put upward pressures on the cost of new hires from a shrinking pool of available workers.

Thus, the short-term *cyclical* pressures on prices and labor markets are important considerations for Michael Sullivan in managing his company's personnel operations.

The preceding discussion hints at the existence of a tradeoff between unemployment and inflation. While this is a topic of some controversy among academic economists, business managers commonly observe such a tradeoff. Before refining the notion of a unemployment-inflation tradeoff, we will examine three topics: (1) the ways in which prices are measured in the United States, (2) the measurement of unemployment, and (3) seasonal effects on these measures.

PRICE MEASUREMENT IN THE U.S. ECONOMY

As previously noted, inflation refers to a *general* rise in the price level, rather than a spurt in the price for a specific good or service. This statement presumes that general price movements can be measured. The price measures used in the United States can be conveniently classed into four categories:

1. The Producer Price Index measures the prices of all domestically produced goods.
2. The Consumer Price Index measures the prices for a representative "basket of goods and services" consumed by a cross section of ordinary people.
3. These two approaches are combined in the various price indexes associated with GDP.
4. There are also a number of labor cost measures, which when combined with productivity, translate labor input cost directly to output prices.

We will examine each of these concepts briefly.

The Producer Price Index, or PPI, is intended to measure the selling prices of all domestically produced commodities (goods). Prior to 1978, this concept was known as the Wholesale Price Index (WPI), but this was a misnomer. The index measures the selling price of goods produced and ready for sale to the ultimate user, but there is really no connotation of "wholesale" as opposed to retail.

Well over 3,000 commodities are covered in the PPI, which manages to include just about all the output of the nation's goods-producing sectors—manufacturing, mining, agriculture, forestry, and fishing—as well as natural gas and electricity. The PPI actually consists of three indexes compiled separately for three stages of processing: crude, intermediate, and finished goods. These classifications depend on (1) the class of buyer and (2) the amount of physical processing or assembling the products have undergone:

- *Crude* materials for further processing are unprocessed commodities that are not sold to final consumers, but rather are the raw material inputs to further production. Wheat is an example of a crude food good; iron and steel scrap are examples of crude nonfood goods.
- *Intermediate* materials are goods that have had some processing, but are not yet ready for final sale. Flour is an example of a intermediate food; sheet steel is an intermediate nonfood commodity.

- *Finished* goods are commodities ready for sale to the final user—whether a consumer or business user—exclusive of any taxes. Bakery products are consumer finished food goods, passenger cars are consumer finished non-food goods, and heavy trucks are capital finished goods.

In general, the main focus is on the finished goods index (this is typically the focus of newspaper reports on the PPI), although the other stage of processing indexes is useful analytical measures. (For instance, a manufacturing manager, such as Bill Angelo in Chapter 4, might well find useful inputs to production planning in the earlier stage of processing measures.)

Table 5–2 shows annual percent changes for the crude, intermediate, and finished goods indexes. In addition, four components of the finished goods index are shown: food, energy, other consumer goods, and capital goods.[2] It is useful to separate the food and energy components because they are often subject to considerable volatility. This volatility stems from food and energy prices being subject to much greater changes in supply—crop failures or cartel (OPEC) price increases—while other consumer finished goods and capital goods prices are much more subject to short-term demand forces.

The weights of the components in the index represent the relative value of shipments of each component in the gross value of shipments of goods in the domestic economy.

The Consumer Price Index, or CPI, is a less inclusive measure of the prices urban consumers[3] pay for a representative "basket" of goods and services. There are several differences from the PPI:

- The CPI includes both commodities and services. Indeed, more than half the index consists of services.

- The CPI includes imported goods as well as domestically produced goods. This means that foreign exchange rate movements may also have an impact on the prices U.S. consumers pay.

- Since the CPI looks at the prices consumers pay, it includes all components of that final price: excise and other taxes as well as the costs of producing and distributing the good or service.

The weights of the goods and services in the CPI are derived from regularly conducted surveys of consumer expenditures. Table 5–3 presents annual changes for the CPI and for three key components: foods, energy, and all other commodities and services (electricity and natural gas are considered energy services). This so-called "core" measure of inflation is often regarded as a less volatile, basic measure of price pressure.

Both the PPI and CPI are fixed-quantity indexes, meaning that the index is calculated by dividing the sum of the products of current prices (P_t) times

TABLE 5–2 Producer price indexes by stage of processing (year–year percent changes).

	Crude All Items	Intermediate All Items	Finished All Items	Consumer Foods	Energy*	Other Consumer	Capital Equipment
1960	−2.3	0.0	0.9	2.0		0.6	0.3
1961	−0.7	−0.6	0.0	−0.3		−0.3	0.3
1962	1.0	0.0	0.3	0.8		0.0	0.3
1963	−2.0	0.3	−0.3	−1.1		0.0	0.3
1964	−1.0	0.3	0.3	0.3		−0.3	0.9
1965	5.1	1.3	1.8	4.0		0.9	1.2
1966	6.4	2.6	3.2	6.5		1.5	2.4
1967	−5.4	0.6	1.1	−1.8		1.8	3.5
1968	1.6	2.5	2.8	3.9		2.3	3.4
1969	6.6	3.3	3.8	6.0		2.3	3.5
1970	3.8	3.8	3.4	3.3		3.0	4.7
1971	2.3	4.0	3.1	1.6		3.5	4.0
1972	2.5	3.8	3.2	5.4		1.8	2.6
1973	47.7	11.0	9.1	20.5		4.6	3.3
1974	12.7	23.8	15.4	14.0		17.0	14.3
1975	0.3	10.5	10.6	8.4	17.2	9.2	15.2
1976	2.9	5.0	4.5	−0.3	11.7	5.1	6.7
1977	3.3	6.6	6.4	5.3	15.7	5.7	6.4
1978	12.1	7.1	7.9	9.0	6.5	7.3	7.9
1979	17.0	12.8	11.2	9.3	35.0	9.1	8.7
1980	10.9	15.2	13.4	5.8	49.2	11.4	10.7
1981	8.1	9.2	9.2	5.8	19.1	7.7	10.3
1982	−2.9	1.4	4.1	2.2	−1.5	5.7	5.7
1983	1.3	0.6	1.6	1.0	−4.8	3.1	2.8
1984	2.2	2.5	2.1	4.4	−4.2	2.5	2.3
1985	−7.4	−0.4	1.0	−0.8	−3.9	2.6	2.2
1986	−8.5	−3.5	−1.4	2.6	−28.1	2.5	2.0
1987	6.8	2.4	2.1	2.1	−1.9	2.8	1.8
1988	2.5	5.5	2.5	2.8	−3.2	3.8	2.3
1989	7.4	4.6	5.2	5.4	9.9	4.6	3.9
1990	5.6	2.2	4.9	4.8	14.2	3.9	3.5
1991	−7.1	−0.1	2.1	−0.2	4.1	3.8	3.1
1992	0.9	0.3	1.2	−0.8	−0.4	2.7	1.9

Source: U.S. Department of Labor.

*Prior to 1974, finished energy prices are included in other finished consumer goods prices reflecting the fact that energy prices showed virtually no change.

base-period quantities (Q_0) by the sum of the products of base-period prices (P_0) times base-period quantities (Q_0):

$$I = \frac{\Sigma P_t \times Q_0}{\Sigma P_0 \times Q_0}$$

GDP-related price measures are hybrid measures in two senses: (1) they use a combination of PPI and CPI components, and (2) the weighting of the

TABLE 5–3 Consumer price index and components (year–year percent changes).

	All Items	Foods	Energy	All Other
1960	1.7	1.7	2.3	1.3
1961	1.0	1.0	0.4	1.3
1962	1.0	1.0	0.4	1.3
1963	1.3	1.3	0.0	1.3
1964	1.3	1.3	−0.4	1.6
1965	1.6	1.6	1.8	1.2
1966	2.9	2.2	1.7	2.4
1967	3.1	3.4	2.1	3.6
1968	4.2	4.5	1.7	4.6
1969	5.5	5.4	2.5	5.8
1970	5.7	6.0	2.8	6.3
1971	4.4	4.6	3.9	4.7
1972	3.2	2.9	2.6	3.0
1973	6.2	4.0	8.1	3.6
1974	11.0	9.8	29.6	8.3
1975	9.1	9.4	10.5	9.1
1976	5.8	6.7	7.1	6.5
1977	6.5	6.4	9.5	6.3
1978	7.6	7.2	6.3	7.4
1979	11.3	11.4	25.1	9.8
1980	13.5	14.5	30.9	12.4
1981	10.3	10.9	13.6	10.4
1982	6.2	6.5	1.5	7.4
1983	3.2	3.5	0.7	4.0
1984	4.3	4.3	1.0	5.0
1985	3.6	3.8	0.7	4.3
1986	1.9	1.7	−13.2	4.0
1987	3.6	3.5	0.5	4.1
1988	4.1	4.1	0.8	4.4
1989	4.8	4.6	5.6	4.5
1990	5.4	5.3	8.3	5.0
1991	4.2	4.5	0.4	4.9
1992	3.0	1.2	0.5	3.6

Source: U.S. Department of Labor.

measures vary. The first aspect refers to the *deflation* of the various components of the GDP. This is done at a fairly disaggregate level. For instance, the current dollar amount of new car purchases of personal consumption expenditures for durable goods is deflated using the CPI component for new passenger cars, whereas the current dollar spending on heavy trucks in the producers' durable equipment component of nonresidential fixed investment is deflated using the PPI component for heavy trucks included in finished capital equipment. There are also components in the government sector, for instance, where the Commerce Department must develop its own price indexes for deflation, while a separate set of export and import price indexes are used to deflate the spending in the foreign trade sector.

The more unique aspect is in the way the prices are weighted to arrive at an overall price index and a measure of the change in overall prices. There are at least three major approaches. The most familiar is the *fixed-weight* price index, which uses constant weights, determined by the relative share of an expenditure category in some base year (currently 1987 = 100). This is computed just like the equation shown for the PPI and CPI, where the quantities are kept constant and only the prices are allowed to change.

The problem with the fixed-weight approach is it ignores that purchasers will substitute goods whose prices are rising less rapidly for goods with more rapid price rises. To approximate a price index in which both prices and the quantity weights change simultaneously, the Commerce Department uses an *implicit price deflator*, where the weighting of the various GDP components essentially reflects the relative share of the current-dollar spending components in current-dollar GDP. This measure is somewhat less popular with financial market participants because it is less comparable to the CPI and PPI measures than the fixed-weight price index. Its virtue, however, is that it provides a better "standard of living" measure because it recognizes the economizing nature of households, firms, and other economic entities: They will substitute goods whose prices are rising less rapidly for goods that are rising rapidly—for instance, consumers may substitute chicken for beef because beef prices are surging.

A third alternative is the *chain price index*, where the weights are the expenditures in the just-previous period. This permits a constant updating of expenditure weights, but always with a one-quarter lag. The chain price index has some features of both the preceding approaches, but like most compromise measures, it is less popular than either of the other two. Figure 5–2 compares trends for the three measures over the past three decades and shows that the differences have been slight.

LABOR COST AND PRODUCTIVITY MEASURES

The primary importance of labor as an input to production places a great stress on the importance of labor costs to inflation. This fact establishes a key linkage between the two main subjects of this chapter. The Labor Department publishes quarterly data on the effects of labor costs and productivity on business sector output in the U.S. economy.[4] Labor productivity data are estimated for four subsectors of the business sector: (1) the total business sector, (2) nonfarm business, (3) nonfinancial corporations, and (4) manufacturers. There are three measures of particular importance: (1) compensation per hour, (2) productivity or output per hour, and (3) unit labor costs.

FIGURE 5–2 Gross domestic product price measures.

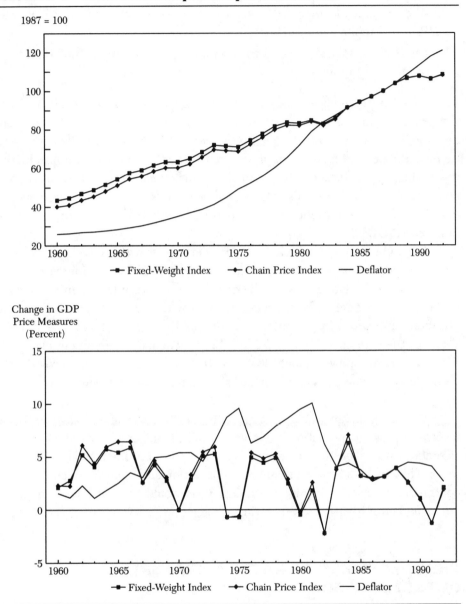

1. *Compensation per hour* measures the hourly costs to employers of basic wages and salaries, as well as supplemental payments. These latter include employers' contributions to Social Security, unemployment insurance taxes, and payments for private health insurance and pension plans. These are the costs to an employer of obtaining an hour's labor.

2. *Productivity* measures the real (physical) output per hour of labor input. For the business sector, this is the portion of constant dollar GDP

originating in the particular sector divided by the total hours worked
(the number of employed times the hours worked per week) from the
Payroll Employment Survey.

3. *Unit labor costs* are equal to compensation per hour minus the offset from
   productivity growth.

Generally, the percentage changes in these concepts, as shown in Table 5–4, are
the primary focus of those who observe productivity data. Thus, the percent
increase in unit labor costs is equal to the percent increase in hourly compensation less the percent increase in productivity growth. The growth in productivity is important because it permits noninflationary increases in hourly
compensation. In other words, productivity increases allow for a rising standard
of living. (The rate of productivity increase is closely tied to the rate of growth
in potential GDP.)

As can be seen from Table 5–4, productivity growth slowed in the 1970s
while compensation per hour surged ahead, resulting in a sharp increase in output prices. In the late 1970s, strong output growth resulted mainly from the
gains in hours worked. Thus, productivity growth was mediocre at best, and
inflation—measured by output prices—remained high. After the long, deep
slump of the combined 1980 and 1981–1982 recessions, the percent change in
hourly compensation was much slower, so the modest productivity growth that
accompanied it was enough to maintain a restraint on the percent change in
output prices.

Michael Sullivan would be especially sensitive to these changes. His job
involves setting compensation levels, and one of the major inputs to his own considerations would be the behavior of national productivity and labor cost patterns. These would, at a minimum, serve as a standard against which he would
contrast compensation in his own industry, as would be true for any manager
concerned with hiring or even setting a budget.

THE UNEMPLOYMENT RATE—A MEASURE
OF EXCESS LABOR

Until now, we have mainly considered employment as the labor input to production. This has led us to focus on the *Establishment* (or *Payroll*) *Employment
Survey*. This survey measures the number of *jobs,* hours per job, and earnings
per hour, but only counts the number of *people* employed indirectly. (There may
be multiple counting of people because the same person may work two jobs.)
Nor does it look at the split between those actually employed and those who
desire employment.

TABLE 5–4 Productivity, labor costs, and output prices (percent changes).

	Output	Hours Worked	Output per Hour	Compensation per Hour	Unit Labor Costs	Output Prices*
1960	1.7	0.1	1.6	4.3	2.7	1.5
1961	2.1	−1.6	3.7	3.9	0.1	0.5
1962	5.1	1.6	3.5	4.7	1.2	2.0
1963	4.6	0.5	4.1	3.8	−0.3	0.8
1964	6.0	1.6	4.3	5.2	0.9	1.1
1965	6.0	3.2	2.7	3.8	1.1	2.5
1966	5.2	2.3	2.8	7.0	4.1	3.3
1967	2.2	−0.3	2.5	5.7	3.1	2.9
1968	4.5	1.4	3.0	8.2	5.0	4.4
1969	2.9	2.4	0.5	7.3	6.7	4.7
1970	−0.5	−1.9	1.4	7.6	6.1	4.3
1971	2.9	−0.4	3.3	6.4	3.0	4.9
1972	6.4	3.2	3.1	6.3	3.1	3.8
1973	6.2	3.6	2.6	8.7	5.9	6.1
1974	−1.8	0.1	−1.8	9.9	11.9	9.5
1975	−1.9	−4.1	2.3	10.0	7.5	10.0
1976	5.8	2.8	2.9	9.1	6.0	5.8
1977	5.6	3.8	1.7	8.0	6.3	6.5
1978	5.5	4.9	0.6	8.8	8.2	8.0
1979	2.0	3.1	−1.1	9.8	11.0	9.1
1980	−1.6	−0.9	−0.7	10.7	11.5	9.7
1981	1.9	0.6	1.3	9.4	8.0	10.1
1982	−2.3	−2.5	0.1	7.6	7.4	5.8
1983	4.1	1.8	2.2	3.7	1.5	3.4
1984	8.2	5.7	2.3	4.2	1.9	4.1
1985	3.6	2.1	1.4	4.5	3.0	3.3
1986	2.8	0.7	2.0	4.9	2.8	2.2
1987	4.1	3.1	1.0	3.5	2.5	2.6
1988	4.3	3.3	0.9	4.3	3.3	3.6
1989	1.7	2.6	−0.8	3.4	4.2	4.4
1990	0.2	0.0	0.3	5.6	5.3	4.1
1991	−2.2	−2.5	0.3	4.9	4.6	3.8
1992	2.3	−0.6	2.9	3.7	0.9	2.1

Source: Bureau of Labor Statistics, U.S. Department of Labor.

*Output prices refer to the implicit price deflator for gross domestic product originating in the business sector.

These considerations are the subject of the *Household Employment Survey,* which focuses on the size of the labor force—both the number of employed workers and those actively seeking employment—and its composition according to various demographic and racial characteristics. The best way to understand how the unemployment rate is estimated is to explain some of the questions in the Household Employment Survey.

The survey is conducted among a sample of households (a subsample of the Census Bureau's Current Population Survey). The population group that the Labor Department is concerned with is the *noninstitutional civilian population over 16 years of age*. As noted in Chapter 4, this is the economically active segment of the population. The Survey divides this segment into two further subgroups: (1) those who are in the *labor force* and (2) among the members of the labor force, the split between those who are *employed* and those who are *unemployed*. These classifications are as follows:

Noninstitutional civilian population (over 16 years of age)
    Labor force
        Employed
        Unemployed
    Not in labor force

The survey participants are asked if they were employed during the calendar week (from Sunday through Saturday) containing the twelfth day of the month. The *employed* consist of those respondents who either (1) did any work at all during the survey week or (2) had jobs but were temporarily away from work (because of vacation, illness, bad weather, strikes, or personal reasons). In addition to being counted as employed, these individuals are included in the *labor force*.

Unemployed persons include those who did not work at all during the survey week, were looking for work, and were available for work during the week. This group also includes (1) anyone who made a specific effort to find work during the preceding four-week period, (2) those waiting to be recalled to a job from which they have been laid off, and (3) anyone waiting to report to a new job within 30 days. The unemployed constitute the rest of the *labor force*.

The *unemployment rate* is equal to the number of unemployed divided by the total number in the labor force, expressed as a percentage. Figure 5–3 compares the noninstitutional civilian population with the labor force and the household employment measure; Figure 5–4 presents the employment and unemployment trends; and Figure 5–5 shows the pattern for the unemployment rate. The unemployment rate and the number of unemployed show the strongest cyclical patterns. (The number of employed complements the cyclical pattern for unemployment, but the dips are smaller relative to the total size of the employed.)

The labor force shows a less pronounced cyclical pattern (the log scales used in Figure 5–3 and Figure 5–4 dampen the long-term increases by showing growth rates proportionately). To the extent there is cyclical pattern at all, it

FIGURE 5–3 Civilian population labor force and employment.

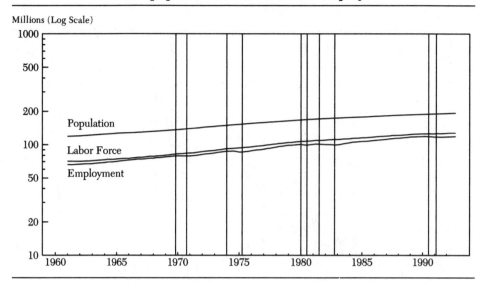

reflects that in periods of weak economic activity, there will be a slower total growth in the labor force because some potential workers will be so discouraged at the prospect of finding a job that they will not actively seek work. In recent years, the Labor Department has attempted to count these so-called "discouraged workers" on a quarterly basis. The opposite is true in economic booms; labor force growth strengthens.

FIGURE 5–4 Civilian employment and unemployment.

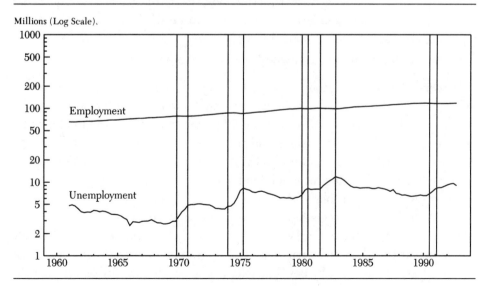

FIGURE 5–5   Civilian unemployment rate.

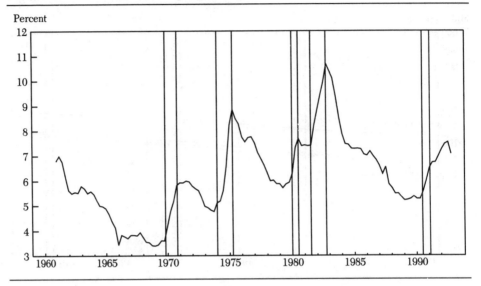

The preceding discussion suggests that there can be a number of reasons for unemployment, among which four represent the main categories:

1. *Job losers* are those who have lost jobs either permanently or due to temporary layoff.
2. *Job leavers* are people who quit or otherwise ended their employment voluntarily and immediately began looking for work.
3. *Reentrants* are people who worked previously but were out of the labor force prior to looking for work. (In recent years, this group has largely consisted of women who left the labor force to raise a family and are returning after several years unpaid work.)
4. *New entrants* are persons who have never worked before.

Job losers represent the group that most closely conforms to the common notion of unemployment as a failure of the economy to supply jobs for all those who want them. Job losers typically make up 50 percent or more of the total number of unemployed during recessions and in the months immediately following a business cycle trough. Job leavers, on the other hand, represent a smaller portion of the unemployed during recessions and in the early stages of an upturn: People are less willing to quit jobs when the prospects of finding a new one are poor.

The other two groups have reflected some longer-term changes. For instance, reentrants became a larger segment of the unemployed from the late 1960s onward, as the female participation rate rose. Similarly, the portion of the unemployed represented by new entrants rose from the late 1960s through the early 1980s as the baby boomers reached an age to enter the labor force and were looking for jobs. Reentrants and new entrants to the labor force are more likely to be unemployed than other segments of the labor force because their lack of work experience is likely to result in a longer job search.

A separate factor affecting new entrants is that they are likely to have a strong seasonal pattern to their unemployment.

SEASONAL FORCES

Seasonal forces affect many economic and business data series. Seasonal forces are *regular, periodic* factors that can affect a time series. For example, Figure 5–6 contrasts trends for the household employment data since January 1980 on a *seasonally adjusted (SA)* and a *not seasonally adjusted (NSA)* basis. As can be seen, the NSA data display a much more volatile pattern around the seasonally adjusted trend. The similarity of the patterns for the NSA data (regardless of the cyclical forces at work, note the cyclical downturns in 1981–1982 and 1990–1991) indicate that both are *regular* forces and that they are periodic. The major seasonal factor affecting employment is the increase in summer hiring that is accompanied by students seeking part-time employment for the summer vacation (or first-time, full-time jobs after graduation). Thus, as Figure 5–6 shows,

FIGURE 5–6   Employment—Seasonally adjusted and unadjusted.

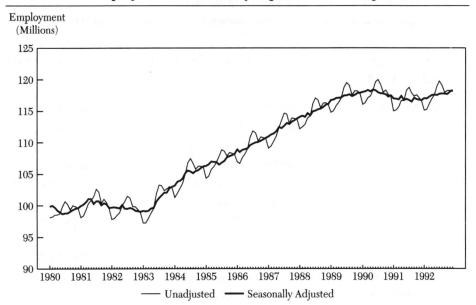

employment begins to rise in the spring months, hits a peak in August, and declines through the early autumn, before another more modest upswing as temporary holiday workers are hired at the end of the year. Employment typically hits its low point in January or February.

These purely seasonal movements introduce a lot of "noise" to the information that analysis of the employment trend is intended to provide. Seasonal adjustment is the term used for the procedure[5] followed to remove this noise. The intent is to recognize that since seasonal forces are regular, their noise should be squelched in order to extract the underlying cyclical and trend patterns.

Seasonal forces are important in a wide range of economic measures:

- *Housing starts* are typically lower in the winter months and higher in the summer due to the unfavorable/favorable mix of weather.

- *Retail sales* are much stronger in November and December than in the remaining winter or summer months. This is especially so for the department store component, which accounts for half of annual sales between Thanksgiving and Christmas.

There are strong seasonal patterns for certain components of the price indexes, reflecting weather and social customs:

- *Turkey* prices rise more in November than any other month.

- *Education costs* tend to rise in September and January.

- *Property taxes* (included in housing expense) tend to rise in January, July, and September, depending on local fiscal years.

- *Apparel* prices tend to rise in November–December, March–April, and August–September and to be under downward pressures in other months.

- *New car* prices are most likely to be under upward pressure at new model introduction time in October.

There are many more examples, but there are two reasons knowledge of and recognition of seasonal patterns are of importance to all managers. First, knowledge of a seasonal pattern can allow a manager to anticipate the effect and either take advantage of it, or defend against its impact. For instance, Michael Sullivan would certainly be aware of the seasonal increase in availability of unskilled (but likely low-wage) labor each summer. He would probably plan to hire some of these seasonal workers each year, even to the extent of planning the workload around the availability of seasonal workers.

A second reason managers need to know and recognize seasonal patterns is that, while nearly all official (government-compiled) economic data is available in a seasonally adjusted form, most company data are only available in unadjusted form. For instance, most records—on sales, payrolls, hours worked, even nonwage bills—are compiled in raw form. These data, however, may have a distinct seasonal pattern. Firms that are able to recognize such patterns have greater insight about their own business and can anticipate problems, rather than simply react to them.

A TRADEOFF BETWEEN INFLATION AND UNEMPLOYMENT

There has long been a notion that there is a tradeoff between inflation and unemployment. Most managers in a position such as Michael Sullivan's would *know* that such a tradeoff existed, based on their own experience. The topic, however, has created considerable debate among economists.

The controversy stems from a famous article by an English economist, A. W. Phillips, entitled "The Relation between Unemployment and the Rate of Change of Money Wage Rates in the United Kingdom, 1861–1957."[6] Phillips found empirical evidence that there was an inverse relationship between the rate of change in money wages (uncorrected for price changes) and unemployment: When unemployment rose, the rate of change in money wages slowed; whereas when unemployment declined, the rate of change in money wages sped up—for the 1861–1913 period (the golden age of the gold standard in the United Kingdom). Moreover, Phillips found that the tradeoff conformed to the 1861–1913 relationship in subsequent years, so long as allowances were made for the impact of wars and import prices on wage rates.

There was a sound theoretical basis for the existence of a tradeoff. When unemployment is high, it is a sign of an excess supply of labor, relative to demand, and so the price of labor—the wage rate—is bound to come under downward pressure. Since labor costs are a major input to output prices, it is perfectly sound to expect that the tradeoff is ultimately between the unemployment rate and the rate of output inflation. The dangerous aspect of Phillips's findings was the specificity of his results: They suggested an exact unchanging tradeoff. It is but a short extension to conclude that the economy could be brought closer to "full employment" by accepting a modest increase in the inflation rate. This was dangerous.

Milton Friedman[7] and Edmund Phelps[8] pointed out this danger;[9] in separate papers published in 1968, they stressed that this tradeoff could only be so for a brief time. Otherwise, the theory assumed that workers were *consistently* fooled by unanticipated inflation. Instead, Friedman and Phelps agreed that workers would recognize the way in which inflation eroded the purchasing power of their income and would adjust their wage rates upward. This meant that any tradeoff was temporary and could not be relied on as the basis for policy. The remarkable aspect of these views is that they were put forth when the empirical evidence still supported the Phillips Curve tradeoff.

It was only in the mid-1970s—specifically during the 1973–1975 recession and the ensuing recovery—that the unemployment and inflation data started to indicate stagflation, rather than a tradeoff. Much intellectual effort was invested in arriving at an answer to the dilemma of simultaneous high unemployment and rapid inflation. Among the more satisfying answers was one propounded by George Perry of the Brookings Institution. In a 1978 article entitled "Slowing the Wage-Price Spiral: The Macroeconomic View,"[9] Perry developed an ingenious answer. He said "something like a Phillips Curve existed," but in addition it could be shown that there was a great deal of "inertia" in wage setting. In other words, there was a long, lagged response on the part of wages to past increases in inflation. Thus, even as the unemployment rate mounted during the 1973–1975 recession (and remained high in the first year or so of recovery) wage rates continued to increase in response to the rapid inflation of previous years.

Perry's answer is a wonderful compromise. It retains the notion that there is some tradeoff between unemployment and wage rate increases. Most practical business managers would agree that such a tradeoff exists in the "real world" that they operate in. Perry's answer also resolves the tendency for the relationship between unemployment and inflation to shift, as Friedman and Phelps accurately suggested it would. He also focused attention on the fact that the longer inflation persisted, the more difficult it was to rein it in.

Perry suggested that, to bring the wage-price spiral of the 1970s to an end, it might be necessary to resort to a very severe dose of monetary restraint. The mechanics of this approach will be examined in the next chapter.

SUMMARY

Despite the fact that macroeconomics focuses on equilibrium, two of the main features of the U.S. economy since World War II have been alternating bouts of unemployment or inflation. These disequilibrium conditions, in turn, have often shaped the economic environment in which managers make business decisions. A familiarity with and understanding of the principal employment and price measures are essential if managers are going to be able to react to these two alternatives to economic stability. Most business managers see these two conditions as alternatives, although the notion of a "tradeoff" between inflation and unemployment has been an area of controversy among economists. Tightness in labor markets—and the resulting upward pressures on wages—has been shown to have been an important factor in explaining inflation in output prices.

6 ECONOMIC LUBRICANTS
Money, Credit, and Interest Rates

Money and credit are the lubricant and fuel that drive the macroeconomy. In Chapters 2, 3, and 4, we focused on measures of real (constant-dollar) economic activity such as employment, consumer and business investment spending, output, and income. The discussion of inflation in Chapter 5 implicitly dealt with money, since inflation is a monetary phenomenon, but the context was still a view of inflation as a disequilibrium state of the *real* economy.

This chapter focuses more directly on money, specifically the demand for money, its supply, and the role of interest rates in bringing about a balance between the two.

An understanding of how money interacts with economic activity and the role of credit is fundamental to the role of the manager. All managers—from the sole proprietor of a small business, to an assistant treasurer of a corporation, or to the CEO of a large multinational—deal with financial issues such as managing a firm's cash balances, extending and receiving short-term credit, and planning the long-term capital needs of the firm. These concerns, in turn, require a working knowledge of the functions of the overall monetary economy, the functions and instruments of the credit markets, and the operations and tools of monetary policy.

In this chapter, we will view the monetary economy through the eyes of Marie Lee, a lending officer at a large commercial bank. As noted earlier, almost any type of manager could serve as a model since financial management is such a universal function. A bank lending officer, however, has a particularly broad view of such operations.

The chapter begins with an overview of the monetary economy, provided by the *flow of funds*, or *uses and sources* of funds raised in credit markets for the economy. The *uses*, or demand, for credit will be examined first, followed by an examination of the *sources*, or supply, of credit. We will then look at the principal instruments of the credit markets and their associated interest rates and yields. Finally, we will examine the overall demand and supply of money in the economy and the role of monetary policy in determining money supply.

THE FLOW OF FUNDS: AN OVERVIEW OF THE MONETARY ECONOMY

In Chapter 3, we viewed the gross domestic product accounts in detail to obtain an overview of the behavior of aggregate demand in the goods and services sectors of the economy. The *flow of funds* accounts presented in Tables 6–1 and 6–2 provide an analogous overview for the financial side of the U.S. economy.

Table 6–1 shows the uses, or demands, for credit in nonfinancial[1] sectors; while Table 6–2 presents the sources, or supply of credit to the nonfinancial sectors, for 1987–1991. Two things are immediately evident:

1. The uses and sources for each year are equal. These are the two sides of the credit ledger, and so they *must* be balanced.

2. There is a considerable amount of variation from year to year. Not only do these years represent the crest of the great debt creation in the 1980s, but they encompass October 19, 1987, which will be remembered as the greatest stock market crash since 1929. Yet, the effect on the annual credit flows (note the figures in 1988 and 1989) was less disruptive than had been widely feared at the time. The more pronounced slowdown in credit growth in 1990–1991 reflects the impact of the recession in those years on credit demands.

The tables can be used as a road map to follow the flows of credit in the U.S. economy.

Demand: Uses of Credit

Table 6–1 presents the uses, or demand, for credit in the United States. The table is split into three sections. Part A distinguishes between official borrowing by the U.S. government through the Treasury and government agencies, and "private" domestic borrowing by state and local governments, households, and nonfinancial businesses. This private borrowing is classified by type of

**TABLE 6-1   Uses of total funds raised in credit markets in nonfinancial
sectors, 1987-1991 (billions of dollars).**

Uses	1987	1988	1989	1990	1991
Total net borrowing by domestic nonfinancial sectors	721.2	775.8	740.8	665.0	452.7
A. U.S. Government	143.9	155.1	146.4	246.9	278.2
Treasury issues	142.4	137.7	144.7	238.7	292.0
Agency issues and mortgages	1.5	17.4	1.6	8.2	-13.8
Private domestic nonfinancial sectors	577.3	620.7	594.4	418.2	174.4
Debt capital instruments	487.2	474.1	441.8	342.3	254.6
Tax-exempt obligations	83.5	53.7	65.0	51.2	45.8
Corporate bonds	78.8	103.1	73.8	47.1	78.8
Mortgages	325.0	317.3	303.0	244.0	130.0
Home mortgages	235.3	241.8	245.3	219.4	142.2
Multifamily residential	24.4	16.7	16.4	3.7	-2.0
Commercial	71.6	60.8	42.7	21.0	-9.4
Farm	-6.4	-2.1	-1.5	-0.1	-0.8
Open-market paper	1.6	11.9	21.4	9.7	-18.4
Other	45.7	43.6	49.3	44.2	-15.8
B. By borrowing sector	577.3	620.7	594.4	418.2	174.4
State and local governments	83.0	48.9	63.2	48.3	38.5
Households	296.4	318.6	305.6	254.2	158.0
Nonfinancial business	197.8	253.1	225.6	115.6	-22.1
Farm	-10.6	-7.5	1.6	2.5	0.9
Nonfarm noncorporate	65.3	61.8	50.4	26.7	-23.6
Corporate	143.1	198.8	173.6	86.4	0.6
C. Foreign net borrowing in the United States	6.2	6.4	10.2	23.9	14.1
Bonds	7.4	6.9	4.9	21.4	14.9
Bank loans (n.e.c.)	-3.6	-1.8	-0.1	-2.9	3.1
Open-market paper	3.8	8.7	13.1	12.3	6.4
U.S. government and other loans	-1.4	-7.5	-7.6	-6.9	-10.2
Total domestic plus foreign	727.4	782.2	750.9	688.9	466.8

Source: Board of Governors of the Federal Reserve System.
n.e.c. = not elsewhere classified.

instrument, long-term versus short-term. Part B includes the main borrowing sectors—state and local governments, households, and nonfinancial businesses. Finally, Part C details the types of foreign *net* borrowing in the United States. It is important to keep in mind that the table measures *flows* of credit, the net increase in borrowing of each type each year.

The U.S. government borrows directly through the issuance of Treasury bills (with maturities of less than 1 year), notes (with maturities of 1 to 10 years), and bonds (maturities of over 10 years). These are direct borrowings backed by the "full faith and credit" of the U.S. government. As such, they have

**TABLE 6–2   Sources of total funds raised in credit markets in
nonfinancial sectors, 1987–1991 (billions of dollars).**

Sources	1987	1988	1989	1990	1991
Total funds supplied to domestic nonfinancial sectors	721.2	775.8	740.8	665.0	452.7
Private domestic nonfinancial sectors	423.1	460.7	424.6	290.4	50.1
Deposits and currency	185.7	234.5	215.1	86.6	28.5
Checkable deposits and currency	17.5	27.3	11.7	21.9	69.4
Time and savings deposits	120.2	165.3	105.6	16.5	−66.0
Money market fund shares	28.9	20.2	86.4	54.5	33.8
Security repurchase agreements	21.6	32.9	6.9	−18.2	−18.7
Foreign deposits	−2.5	−11.2	4.4	12.0	10.0
Credit market instruments	237.4	226.2	209.6	203.8	21.6
Foreign funds	105.5	105.6	64.1	82.3	20.6
At banks	43.7	9.3	−9.9	23.8	−24.1
Credit market instruments	61.8	96.3	74.1	58.4	44.7
U.S. Government and related loans, net	8.1	−14.3	−46.3	17.3	32.0
U.S. Government cash balances	−5.8	7.3	−3.4	5.3	5.5
Private insurance and pension reserves	107.8	182.8	210.2	175.9	204.3
Other sources	82.5	33.7	91.5	93.9	140.1

Source: Board of Governors of the Federal Reserve System.

been the most creditworthy debt instruments in the world, although there has
been an enormous increase in U.S. government borrowing and debt[2] since 1980
(see Figures 6–1 and 6–2). There are also a number of independent federal
agencies; for instance, the Government National Mortgage Association (Ginnie
Mae), the Federal National Mortgage Association (Fannie Mae) the Federal

FIGURE 6–1   U.S. budget deficits.

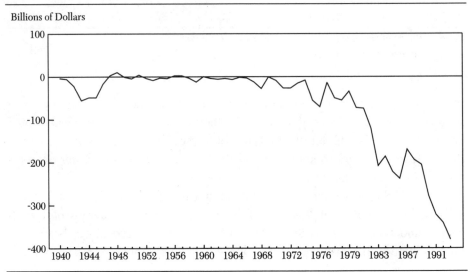

FIGURE 6–2 Gross federal government debt.

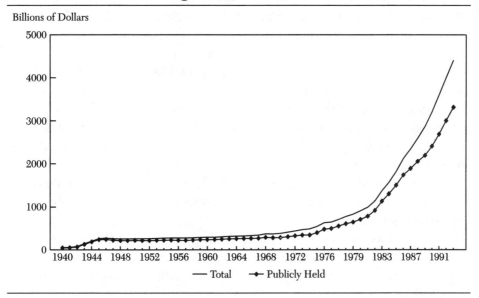

Billions of Dollars

Home Loan Mortgage Corporation (Freddie Mac), and the Student Loan Marketing Association (Sallie Mae), which have independent borrowing authority. As such, their borrowing does not affect the deficit, and they are not backed by the "full faith and credit" of the U.S. government.

The private domestic nonfinancial sectors use credit for a variety of reasons. Long-term borrowing—in the form of debt capital instruments—can generally be regarded as having a maturity of beyond 1 year. *Tax-exempt obligations* are most often issued by *state and local governments*—referred to as municipal or "munis"—and as the term implies are exempt from taxation at all levels.[3] As a rule, state and local governments have less freedom to resort to deficit financing than the federal government, and so more of their debt is to finance specific projects, such as bridges, turnpikes, or college dormitories. State and local governments do little short-term borrowing, but when they do, it is usually in the form of short-term notes (with maturities from 1 month to 1 year) in anticipation of funds from either general tax revenues or bond proceeds.

Households' long-term borrowing mainly consists of home mortgage loans, where the debt is secured by the home itself. Because home mortgage credit is linked to real estate sales, it is quite cyclical, as shown in the sharp decline in home mortgage credit in 1991. Consumer credit refers to four types of short-term consumer borrowing: (1) automobile loans (the average auto loan has a maturity of 4 to 5 years), (2) revolving credit (for instance, credit card loans), (3) mobile home loans, and (4) other credit extended by banks, finance companies, retailers, and so forth. Consumer credit is also quite cyclical, closely following consumer spending trends for durable goods. In 1991, following the recession that ended in March, households actually paid down consumer debt, more than reversing the small increase recorded in 1990.

Nonfinancial businesses consist of corporations, farms, and unincorporated, nonfarm businesses. Corporations tend to have the most credit options. For long-term credit, they can issue their own bonds, assuming their credit rating is high enough. A corporation can also take out a mortgage to acquire or maintain real property. For short-term credit needs, large corporations often issue commercial paper, which are short-term negotiable securities (usually with a maturity of 30 days, but no more than 270 days) that can be sold in secondary markets. In addition, corporations may borrow from banks and are likely to avail themselves of trade credit.

As a lending officer, Marie Lee is likely to deal primarily with corporate or small business, noncorporate borrowing. Unincorporated businesses cannot issue bonds or open-market paper, so they are mainly dependent on banks for loans and mortgages.

The credit demands of these business borrowers—whether incorporated or unincorporated—are closely linked to the business cycle. Short-term borrowing is mainly to finance production and inventories, while long-term business borrowing is typically for capital spending. These purposes depend on economic growth. Note the shift from nonfinancial business borrowing in 1990 to net repayment in 1991 following the recession. The net repayment was in the non-farm, noncorporate sector, but corporate borrowing showed an even more dramatic slowdown.

The farm sector is much smaller than the other two components of the business sector but is shown separately because of the particular nature of farm credit demand. Aside from mortgages (which showed net repayment for the years presented in Table 6–1), farm credit demands are closely tied to crop cycles and the results of harvests. It is, therefore, helpful to segregate these demands from other business credit demands.

Foreign net borrowing in the United States is appreciable because of the important role the U.S. capital markets, concentrated in New York, play in world capital markets. The depth of the U.S. financial markets makes them an attractive source of borrowing by both foreign governments and private borrowers. A notable feature in recent years has been the increased importance of foreign buyers of U.S. Treasury securities. As can be seen from Table 6–1, foreigners were net lenders to the U.S. government in each of the 5 years.

Credit demand is an important dimension to understanding the working of the U.S. economy. These credit demands stem from a variety of economic forces, and in turn, the availability of credit affects real economic activity.

Supply: Sources of Credit

The sources of credit, presented in Table 6–2, are more concentrated than the uses. One point to note at the outset is that an important source of funds is *private insurance and pension reserves*. These funds remained committed and continued to grow throughout the 5-year period shown. Because of the greater variation in other sources of capital, however, the importance of private insurance and pension reserves rose from just under 15 percent of the total funds raised in 1987 to just under 45 percent in 1991, although the rate at which these funds increased did not quite double over the period.

Private domestic nonfinancial sectors normally account for the bulk of funds raised through their holdings of various types of deposits and currency and through their purchases of credit market instruments. These flows contracted sharply in 1990 and in 1991, however, partly as a result of the recession and partly due to the decline in interest rates, which led to either outright contraction (time and savings deposits) or slower growth (Money Market Mutual Fund shares) in interest-sensitive types of deposits and credit market instruments. In fact, the faster growth for checkable deposits and currency—which yield no interest—in 1991 is a sign of the indifference of those depositors to the low yields of other interest-bearing deposits.

INTEREST RATES AND YIELDS

There is a vast array of interest rates, just as there is a wide range of credit instruments. Tables 6–3 and 6–4 present annual average rates for a number of key interest rates over the past three decades. The rates in Table 6–3 show interest on short-term credit instruments (maturities of less than 1 year); while those in Table 6–4 show rates for longer-term instruments (maturities greater than 1 year).

A better grasp of the different interest rates can be gained by examining some of the features that different rates have in common and those features that distinguish them from each other.

A starting point is to recognize that interest rates are expressed in percentage and basis points, where the percentage point is the digit(s) to the left of the decimal point. In addition, there are 100 basis points in each percentage point of interest, shown to the right of the decimal point.

For example, the federal funds rate for 1992 presented in Table 6–3 was 3.52 percent, 217 basis points below the level of 5.69 percent for 1991:

$$5.69\% - 3.52\% = 2.17\%, \text{ or } 217 \text{ basis points}$$

TABLE 6–3 Short-term interest rates, 1960–1992.

	Federal Funds (%)	FRB of NY Discount Rate (%)	Commercial Bank Prime (%)	3-Month Treasury Bills (%)	6-Month Commercial Paper (%)
1960	3.22	3.53	4.82	2.93	3.85
1961	1.96	3.00	4.50	2.38	2.97
1962	2.68	3.00	4.50	2.78	3.26
1963	3.18	3.23	4.50	3.16	3.55
1964	3.50	3.55	4.50	3.55	3.97
1965	4.07	4.04	4.54	3.95	4.38
1966	5.11	4.50	5.63	4.88	5.55
1967	4.22	4.19	5.61	4.32	5.10
1968	5.66	5.16	6.30	5.34	5.90
1969	8.20	5.87	7.96	6.68	7.83
1970	7.18	5.95	7.91	6.46	7.71
1971	4.66	4.88	5.72	4.35	5.11
1972	4.43	4.50	5.25	4.07	4.73
1973	8.73	6.44	8.03	7.04	8.15
1974	10.50	7.83	10.81	7.89	9.84
1975	5.82	6.25	7.86	5.84	6.32
1976	5.04	5.50	6.84	4.99	5.34
1977	5.54	5.46	6.83	5.27	5.61
1978	7.93	7.46	9.06	7.22	7.99
1979	11.19	10.28	12.67	10.04	10.91
1980	13.36	11.77	15.27	11.51	12.29
1981	16.38	13.42	18.87	14.03	14.76
1982	12.26	11.02	14.86	10.69	11.89
1983	9.09	8.50	10.79	8.63	8.89
1984	10.23	8.80	12.04	9.58	10.16
1985	8.10	7.69	9.93	7.48	8.01
1986	6.81	6.33	8.33	5.98	6.39
1987	6.66	5.66	8.21	5.82	6.85
1988	7.57	6.20	9.32	6.69	7.68
1989	9.21	6.93	10.87	8.12	8.80
1990	8.10	6.98	10.01	7.51	7.95
1991	5.69	5.45	8.46	5.42	5.85
1992	3.52	3.25	6.25	3.45	3.80

Source: Economic Report of the President (Washington, D.C.), January 1993.

TABLE 6–4 Long-term interest rates and yields, 1960–1992.

	3-Year* Treasury Note (%)	10-Year* Treasury Bonds (%)	High-Grade Municipal Bonds (%)	Aaa Corporate Bonds (%)	Baa Corporate Bonds (%)	New-Home Mortgage Yields** (%)
1960	3.98	4.12	3.73	4.41	5.19	
1961	3.54	3.88	3.46	4.35	5.08	
1962	3.47	3.95	3.18	4.33	5.02	
1963	3.67	4.00	3.23	4.26	4.86	5.89
1964	4.03	4.19	3.22	4.40	4.83	5.83
1965	4.22	4.28	3.27	4.49	4.87	5.81
1966	5.23	4.92	3.82	5.13	5.67	6.25
1967	5.03	5.07	3.98	5.51	6.23	6.46
1968	5.68	5.65	4.51	6.18	6.94	6.97
1969	7.02	6.67	5.81	7.03	7.81	7.81
1970	7.29	7.35	6.51	8.04	9.11	8.45
1971	5.65	6.16	5.70	7.39	8.56	7.74
1972	5.72	6.21	5.27	7.21	8.16	7.60
1973	6.95	6.84	5.18	7.44	8.24	7.96
1974	7.82	7.56	6.09	8.57	9.50	8.92
1975	7.49	7.99	6.89	8.83	10.61	9.00
1976	6.77	7.61	6.49	8.43	9.75	9.00
1977	6.69	7.42	5.56	8.02	8.97	9.02
1978	8.29	8.41	5.90	8.73	9.49	9.56
1979	9.71	9.44	6.39	9.63	10.69	10.78
1980	11.55	11.46	8.51	11.94	13.67	12.66
1981	14.44	13.91	11.23	14.17	16.04	14.70
1982	12.92	13.00	11.57	13.79	16.11	15.14
1983	10.45	11.10	9.47	12.04	13.55	12.57
1984	11.89	12.44	10.15	12.71	14.19	12.38
1985	9.64	10.62	9.18	11.37	12.72	11.55
1986	7.06	7.68	7.38	9.02	10.39	10.17
1987	7.68	8.39	7.73	9.38	10.58	9.31
1988	8.26	8.85	7.76	9.71	10.83	9.19
1989	8.55	8.49	7.24	9.26	10.18	10.13
1990	8.26	8.55	7.25	9.32	10.36	10.05
1991	6.82	7.86	6.89	8.77	9.80	9.32
1992	5.30	;7.01	6.41	8.14	8.98	8.28

Source: Economic Report of the President (Washington, D.C.), January 1993.

*Yields on the more actively traded issues adjusted to constant maturities by the Treasury Department.

**Effective rate on conventional mortgages, reflecting fees, and charges as well as contract rate and assuming, on the average, repayment at the end of 10 years.

Interest Rate Composition

There are four basic components of interest rates: (1) maturity, (2) default risk, (3) tax treatment, and (4) inflation expectations:

1. *Maturity,* or liquidity preference refers to the fact that the longer repayment is deferred, the higher the interest rate payment must be to reward the lender for forgoing the use of the money. The liquidity premium is an opportunity cost concept and, in many ways, the most fundamental interest rate payment.

2. The *default risk premium* is the payment the lender receives against the possibility that the loan will not be paid back at all (or on time). The greater is this risk, the higher is the risk premium included in the interest rate. Loans of similar maturity can be classified according to their risk, with the riskier ones earning higher interest rates.

3. *Tax treatment* is especially important for state and local government obligations, "munis." The federal government assists the state and local governments by exempting their interest payments from taxation. It essentially reduces the cost of financing for the state and local governments. For instance, if a 30-year Treasury bond (the interest on which is subject to federal tax) is yielding 10 percent, and the top federal tax rate is 37 percent, then a 30-year "muni" (assuming no difference in risk) would have a 6.63 percent interest rate. Or, expressed another way, the *taxable-equivalent* rate for a municipal bond yielding 6.63 percent—given a 37 percent federal tax rate—would be 10 percent.

4. The final, but in many ways most important, component of interest rates is an *inflation expectations premium.* Inflation, the loss of purchasing power, is the greatest enemy of interest-bearing wealth. If the liquidity premium is a payment for the basic loss of liquidity—the lender's loss of the use of the money—then inflation exacerbates this loss. The existence of inflation averaging 5 percent over a 5-year period means that the purchasing power of the principal paid back after the 5 years is only 78.4 percent[4] of what it was at the beginning of the loan. Since the future inflation rate is not known with certainty at the time the loan is made, the premium reflects the inflation *expectations* of the lender. These expectations may be higher or lower than recent inflation experience but are likely to be based, in part, on such experiences.

Tables 6–3 and 6–4 show these relationships. The *maturity* premium can be seen by comparing three Treasury securities: Table 6–3 lists the yield on the 3-month Treasury bill, while the 3-year note and 10-year bond yields are presented in Table 6–4. Since these are all Treasury issues, the only difference is the maturity premium attached to each issue. Selected years are extracted in Table 6–5 for clearer reference.

In 1960, 1970, and 1990, the relationships are normal, in that the interest rate increases as the maturity lengthens. The relationship for 1980 is unusual because the interest rate on the 3-month bill rate was nearly as high as for the note and both the bill and note yields were higher than for the bond. This *"inverted"* yield curve relationship occurs when (1) inflation is very high, as it was in 1980 and (2) there is an expectation that either economic weakness, tighter monetary policy, or a combination of the two will shortly bring about a reduction in inflationary pressures.

Under those conditions, investors (the people who buy the securities and are thus the lenders) require a greater *inflation premium* for the near term, when they expect inflationary pressures to be greatest, and are willing to accept a somewhat lesser premium for the more distant period, when they expect inflationary forces to have eased.

The full maturity range of yields for Treasury issues can be depicted in a *yield curve,* as shown in Figures 6–3 and 6–4. These two figures depict the interest rate levels on the Treasury's issues as of June 21, 1985 and June 18, 1993, almost exactly eight years apart. Both curves have a "normal" shape; interest rates generally rise as the maturities lengthen. However, the curve for June 18, 1993 is roughly 400 basis points lower than the earlier curve for all maturities, because of the general lowering of the inflation premium. This reflects (1) the contrast between the still-recent experience of rapid inflation in the early 1980s for the earlier curve compared with the extended period of subdued inflation for the 1993 curve and (2) the belief by financial market participants that the monetary authorities would oppose an increase in inflationary pressures.

The *default risk premium* can be seen in an analogous examination of the data in Table 6–4. Table 6–6 compares yields on Treasury bonds with two grades of corporate bonds, Aaa and Baa.

TABLE 6–5 Treasury yields and spreads (yields in percentage, spreads in basis points).

	3-Month Bill (%)	3-Year Note (%)	10-Year Bond (%)	3-Month vs. 3-Year (bp)	3-Year vs. 10-Year (bp)
1960	2.93	3.98	4.12	105	14
1970	6.46	7.29	7.35	83	6
1980	11.51	11.55	11.46	4	−9
1990	7.51	8.26	8.55	75	29

FIGURE 6–3   Treasury yield curve, June 21, 1985.

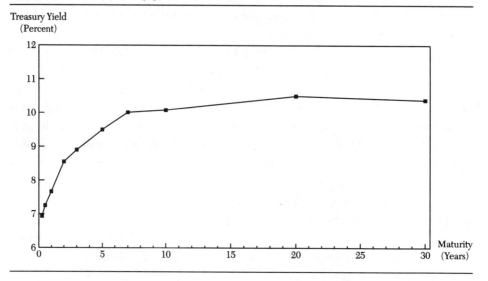

Corporate bonds are evaluated for risk by rating services such as Standard & Poor's, Moody's, or Fitch's, which assign ratings to the bonds issued (the ratings shown in the tables are by Moody's). Thus, the Aaa rating represents Moody's highest rating for corporate bonds, with the least risk of default. (The main difference with Treasury bonds is that the corporate bonds are subject to

FIGURE 6–4   Treasury yield curve, June 18, 1993.

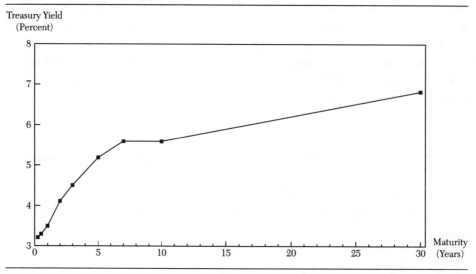

TABLE 6-6 Bond yields and quality spreads (yields in percentage, spreads in basis points).

	Treasury Bond (%)	Aaa Bond (%)	Baa Bond (%)	Aaa vs. T-Bond (bp)	Baa vs. T-Bond (bp)
1960	4.12	4.41	5.19	29	107
1970	7.35	8.04	9.11	69	176
1980	11.46	11.94	13.67	48	223
1990	8.55	9.32	10.36	77	181

state and local taxes, the Treasury's are not.) The Baa rating represents a lower rating, a greater degree of default risk, which is apparent in the widened spread. The yield spread to Treasury bonds is called a "quality spread" because the difference marks degree of risk.

The yields on non-Treasury debt securities are often cited in terms of "[basis] points off the Treasury curve." In other words, the Treasury yield curve is used as the benchmark for liquidity relationships, and the quality spread superimposes the dimension of default risk on the liquidity premium. Tax treatment and inflation expectations would be a function of the time and type (in the case of tax treatment) of issue and so are similar for corporate securities.

At least three of these considerations—liquidity, default risk, and inflation expectations—are included in the interest rates on administered loans, such as the bank loans that Marie Lee would be concerned with. Rather than using a credit rating agency, such as Moody's or Standard & Poor's, however, she would evaluate the quality of the loan with a similar approach, using the bank's own *credit policy guidelines*. In addition, there would be an extra *administrative premium*, reflecting the bank's costs of administering the loan. This premium is subject to economies of scale: The larger the loan, the smaller the administrative costs as a percentage. This is one reason consumer installment loan interest rates are so much higher than market interest rates.

Interest Rate Concepts

There are at least three key interest rate concepts to become familiar with before looking at the instruments themselves: investment, or bank, yields; compound rates; and discount rates.

Investment yields are the usual form of interest rate and are the rates associated with most bank loans and money market instruments with maturities of a year or longer. These rates can best be understood by looking at the notion of *simple* annual interest. In the case of a 1-year bank loan with an interest rate of

10 percent, the principal and interest would be payable in 1 year. Thus, the simple interest rate would be calculated according to the following formula:

$$\frac{\text{Principal plus interest paid} - \text{Principal lent}}{\text{Principal amount lent}} = \text{Annual simple interest rate}$$

For example:

$$\frac{\$1,100 - \$1,000}{\$1,000} = 10\%$$

Compound annualized interest rates are the usual form of expressing interest rates because the interest on most loans and deposits is computed more often than once a year. Essentially, the compound interest rate (r_c) depends on the number of times per year (n) that the nominal rate of interest is compounded. This is shown in the following formula:

$$r_c = (1 + r/n)^n$$

Thus, for a 10 percent rate compounded quarterly (four times a year), the compound annualized rate would be 10.38 percent.

$$10.38\% = (1 + (.10/4))^4$$

A *discount basis* is used for interest rates on money market instruments with maturities of less than 1 year[5]—federal funds, bills, commercial paper, and bankers acceptances. There are two special characteristics of discount securities:

1. Generally, because the term of the loan is short, the lender provides less than the face amount of the loan. The difference is the "*discount.*" At maturity, the borrower pays the full face amount. Thus, the lender receives back the original principal and the discount, which represents the interest payment.
2. For purposes of calculating discount rates, the convention is actual days to maturity over 360 days.

For example, if the interest rate on a 6-month Treasury bill (actually having a maturity of 182 days) is 5 percent, then the discount on a $10,000 face amount would be $252.78.

$$\$10,000 \times .05 \times (182/360) = \$252.78$$

The investor (lender) would pay $9,747.22 at the outset of the loan and receive $10,000 at maturity.

Credit Instruments

As we saw with the sources of funds, there are many ways in which credit can be extended to borrowers in the U.S. economy. There are two major avenues along which credit flows: (1) bank lending and (2) the money market.

Bank Lending

The term "bank" is used quite specifically in economics, usually applying to a commercial bank, which takes in demand deposits (checking accounts), and whose primary business is making loans to businesses. Marie Lee is associated with this type of institution. The category includes such large financial institutions as Bank of America, Citicorp, Chase Manhattan Bank, Chemical Bank, First Chicago, and Pittsburgh National Bank. It also includes some 14,000 smaller commercial banks that serve local areas.

Commercial banks extend credit through a variety of loan types, but as can be seen in Table 6–7, nearly 90 percent of bank loans in 1991 fell into just three categories: (1) commercial and industrial (C&I) loans, (2) real estate loans, and (3) individual loans.

Commercial and industrial loans (C&I) used to be the core business of commercial banks. These loans are made to business firms to meet the costs of production and inventory carrying costs before the firm can sell the goods produced. The loans are short term in the sense that they are typically repayable within a year, but the credit can usually be extended. The interest rate is determined on the basis of the borrower's creditworthiness, which is assessed by someone like Marie Lee using the bank's credit guidelines. However, the interest rate is usually expressed relative to the *prime rate,* a reference rate representing what the theoretical "best" customer would pay.

Real estate loans include both residential and commercial mortgages. Mortgages (the word is derived from two old French words that translate literally as "dead grip") are loans secured by the asset the borrower is attempting to purchase. The successful mortgage borrower has the use of the asset but cannot dispose of it since it is pledged as collateral for the loan. Hence, the "dead grip."

TABLE 6–7   Commercial bank loans and leases (billions of dollars).

	Total	C&I	Real Estate	Individual
1975	517.2	189.3	134.4	104.9
1980	913.5	325.7	262.6	179.2
1985	1,459.8	500.2	425.8	294.7
1990	2,098.8	643.2	843.3	379.6
1991	2,096.6	618.0	873.1	363.5

Mortgage loans are long-term loans: Residential mortgages are generally made for either 20 or 30 years, while commercial mortgages are more usually made for 10 to 20 years. Mortgages are made at either fixed rates for the length of the mortgage or according to some sort of annual adjustable formula. For instance, the mortgage interest rate may be adjusted once a year (either with or without a maximum "cap" placed on the adjustment), based on movements in some reference rate such as the 6-month Treasury bill rate.

Individual loans refer to the various consumer credit loans that banks make for purchases of automobiles, boats, mobile homes, or other durable goods and for such purposes as education. Also, small business loans may fall into this category. The maturity of the loan is generally geared to the asset or purpose, and the interest rate is generally fixed for the term of the loan and is higher than for other types of loans.

Money Market Credit

There are an extensive array of money market instruments. Indeed, the multiplicity of money market instruments is evidence of the creativity—especially in the past 20 years—of money market participants, who have tailored instruments for particular credit needs. The following are among the most important:

1. Federal funds.
2. Negotiable certificates of deposit.
3. Commercial paper.
4. Eurodollars.
5. Treasury securities.
6. Municipal securities.
7. Corporate bonds.

Federal funds refer to loans of immediately available reserve balances at the Federal Reserve bank, to be discussed later in this chapter. These loans are typically made between banks, where one bank with "excess" reserves lends to a second bank with a reserve "shortage," although the loans can also be made through a broker. Federal funds loans are usually "overnight" (or "over the weekend"), but longer, "term Fed funds" (Federal funds loans made for a longer term, such as 30 days) lending takes place. Because of the shortness of the loan, it is done on a discount basis, with the rate determined by the nationally traded Fed funds rate. (The Fed funds rate, a very important focus of monetary policy, is also discussed later in this chapter.)

Negotiable certificates of deposit (CDs) are an important source of bank funding. These are short-term securities (maturities of 2 weeks to 1 year) issued in amounts of at least $100,000 and eligible for trading in the secondary market. The interest rate is expressed on an investment yield basis.

Commercial paper is essentially a short-term (most commonly, 15- to 60-day) promissory note issued directly to money market investors by corporate borrowers with good credit ratings. Commercial paper is issued in minimum amounts of $100,000, but blocks of $5 million or $10 million are more common. The issues can be traded on secondary markets, like certificates of deposit, but are sold on a discount basis.

Eurodollar deposits are deposits of U.S. dollars in U.S. bank branches abroad. Since the deposits are outside the United States, they are not subject to reserve requirements or Federal Deposit Insurance Corporation (FDIC) premiums. Eurodollar certificates of deposit (known as Euro CDs) are similar to domestic negotiable certificates of deposit, usually issued in maturities of a year or less in minimum amounts of $1 million. The rise of the Eurodollar market in general, and the Euro CD market in particular, is a sign of the globalization of capital markets, which was reflected in the *flow of funds* by the role of foreigners as both borrowers and lenders.

Treasury securities consist of bills, notes, and bonds with maturities as previously described. These securities are issued at auction but are traded extensively in secondary markets. Treasury bills—usually 3-month (91-day), 6-month (182-day), and 1-year (52-week) maturities—are issued in minimum amounts of $10,000 with additional amounts available in $5,000 increments. They are discount instruments.

The Treasury currently issues 2-, 3-, 5-, and 10-year notes and a 30-year bond. These securities are also offered at auctions: the 2- and 5-year notes in monthly auctions, the 3- and 10-year notes at quarterly auctions, and the 30-year bond twice a year. They also are traded in secondary markets. The minimum for auction purchase is $5,000 for the 2- and 3-year notes and $1,000 for the longer-dated securities; interest is calculated on an investment basis.

Municipal securities are debt instruments issued by state and local governments and by some special authorities (bridge, turnpike, port authorities, etc). They are distinctive for having their interest exempt from federal tax. Another oddity is that securities with a maturity of a year or less are referred to as "notes"; all other maturities are called "bonds." These securities are typically issued through banks and brokerages that underwrite the issues, and many "munis" trade actively in secondary markets. Interest is computed on an investment yield basis.

Corporate bonds are direct long-term debt instruments issued by corporations, based on their own credit ratings. A majority of corporate bonds in recent years have been issued with maturities under 10 years, but the term may be much longer. In late 1993, there were a number of 50-year corporate bond issues and even one issue with a 100-year maturity. Corporate bonds are usually sold through underwriting syndicates of brokerages and/or investment bankers and can be resold on secondary markets. Interest is computed on an investment yield basis.

Corporate bonds also often have a "call" feature that allows them to be repurchased by the issuer at an agreed-on price after some years (usually 5–10 years) from the initial issue date. This feature is especially important for bonds issued in periods of high interest rates if market interest rates subsequently decline. It is then attractive to the issuer to call the old bonds and reissue new bonds at the lower rate. The danger, from the investor's standpoint, that this might happen typically means that there is an added call premium for corporate bonds.

MONEY DEMAND, SUPPLY, AND MONETARY POLICY

It would seem that money hardly needs an introduction: Any adult—manager or not—is familiar with money. Nevertheless, it is helpful to have a formal definition of money. Money is the means we use for carrying out economic transactions, for comparing the value of different goods, and for gauging our wealth (composed of monetary and nonmonetary assets). In addition to these conceptual definitions, the Federal Reserve uses three main measures of what it refers to as the *money stock* or *monetary aggregates*. These concepts—M1, the narrowest monetary concept; M2, a broader concept; and M3, the broadest concept—and their main components are presented in Table 6–8.

The Monetary Aggregates

The narrowest monetary aggregate, *M1*, is closest to the strict interpretation of the conceptual definitions given earlier. M1 consists of currency in the hands of the nonbank public (in other words, all currency except that held by banks in their vaults and tills, and excluding any currency held by the federal government) as well as bank deposits that can immediately be drawn on through checking accounts. These balances are drawn on to carry out normal economic transactions. M1 balances are extremely liquid; checks can be drawn "on demand" without prior notification of the bank and without restrictions as long as the funds are on deposit.

The concept of *M2* is much broader, containing a range of interest-bearing accounts in addition to the M1 components. M2 is a less "pure" concept of money than M1 because the interest-bearing accounts can, themselves, be regarded as forms of wealth. These accounts can also be used for transactions

TABLE 6–8 Money stock measures (billions of dollars).

	M1				M2						M3		
	Currency	Checkable Deposits	Total	M1	MMM Balances	Savings Deposits	Small Time Deposits	Other	Total	M2	Large Time Deposits	Other	Total
1960	28.7	112.0	140.7	140.7	0.0	159.1	12.5	0.1	312.4	312.4	2.0	0.9	315.3
1961	29.3	115.9	145.2	145.2	0.0	175.5	14.8	0.0	335.5	335.5	3.9	1.7	341.1
1962	30.3	117.6	147.9	147.9	0.0	194.7	20.1	0.0	362.7	362.7	7.0	1.8	371.5
1963	32.2	121.2	153.4	153.4	0.0	214.4	25.6	-0.1	393.3	393.3	10.8	2.0	406.1
1964	33.9	126.5	160.4	160.4	0.0	235.3	29.2	-0.1	424.8	424.8	15.2	2.5	442.5
1965	36.0	131.9	167.9	167.9	0.0	256.9	34.5	0.1	459.4	459.4	21.2	1.7	482.3
1966	38.0	134.1	172.1	172.1	0.0	253.2	55.0	-0.3	480.0	480.0	23.1	2.0	505.1
1967	40.0	143.3	183.3	183.3	0.0	263.7	77.8	-0.4	524.4	524.4	30.9	1.8	557.1
1968	43.0	154.5	197.5	197.5	0.0	268.9	100.6	-0.6	566.4	566.4	37.4	2.5	606.3
1969	45.7	158.3	204.0	204.0	0.0	263.6	120.4	1.6	589.6	589.6	20.4	5.1	615.1
1970	48.6	165.9	214.5	214.5	0.0	260.9	151.1	1.6	628.1	628.1	45.2	4.1	677.4
1971	52.0	176.4	228.4	228.4	0.0	292.2	189.7	2.4	712.7	712.7	57.7	5.8	776.2
1972	56.2	193.1	249.3	249.3	0.0	321.4	231.6	2.9	805.2	805.2	73.4	7.5	886.1
1973	60.8	202.1	262.9	262.9	0.0	326.7	265.8	5.6	861.0	861.0	111.1	12.9	985.0
1974	67.0	207.4	274.4	274.4	1.7	338.5	287.9	6.1	908.6	908.6	144.8	17.0	1070.4
1975	72.8	214.8	287.6	287.6	2.7	388.6	338.0	6.4	1023.3	1023.3	129.8	19.1	1172.2
1976	79.5	226.9	306.4	306.4	2.4	452.6	390.9	11.4	1163.7	1163.7	118.1	30.0	1311.8
1977	87.4	243.9	331.3	331.3	2.4	491.1	445.7	16.1	1286.6	1286.6	145.0	40.9	1472.5
1978	96.0	262.4	358.4	358.4	6.4	480.3	521.2	22.4	1388.7	1388.7	194.9	62.8	1646.4
1979	104.8	277.9	382.7	382.7	33.4	422.0	633.8	24.6	1496.7	1496.7	221.4	84.7	1802.8
1980	115.3	293.5	408.8	408.8	61.6	398.2	727.0	33.9	1629.5	1629.5	257.6	99.9	1987.0
1981	122.6	313.9	436.5	436.5	150.6	342.2	820.2	43.4	1792.9	1792.9	299.1	141.6	2233.6
1982	132.5	342.1	474.6	474.6	184.5	398.5	847.2	47.1	1951.9	1951.9	323.3	165.4	2440.6
1983	146.2	375.2	521.4	521.4	138.3	684.0	780.8	61.6	2186.1	2186.1	324.8	182.1	2693.0
1984	156.1	396.4	552.5	552.5	167.1	704.2	884.9	65.6	2374.3	2374.3	415.6	197.5	2987.4
1985	167.9	452.3	620.2	620.2	176.1	814.4	881.7	77.0	2569.4	2569.4	436.1	197.7	3203.2
1986	180.8	543.8	724.6	724.6	208.0	940.1	854.8	83.6	2811.1	2811.1	439.5	243.7	3494.3
1987	197.0	553.0	750.0	750.0	221.7	937.0	917.5	84.6	2910.8	2910.8	489.1	281.2	3681.1
1988	212.3	574.6	786.9	786.9	241.9	926.2	1032.9	83.3	3071.2	3071.2	541.2	310.7	3923.1
1989	222.6	571.5	794.1	794.1	316.3	891.2	1148.5	77.2	3227.3	3227.3	559.3	273.2	4059.8
1990	246.8	579.3	826.1	826.1	348.9	920.7	1168.7	74.6	3339.0	3339.0	495.2	280.7	4114.9
1991	267.3	630.8	898.1	898.1	360.5	1042.6	1063.0	75.6	3439.8	3439.8	437.1	294.1	4171.0
1992	279.6	687.0	966.6	966.6	351.6	1130.4	950.8	74.2	3473.6	3473.6	387.3	316.5	4177.4

Source: Board of Governors, Federal Reserve System.

purposes but with less ease than the checkable deposits in M1. Thus, M2 is less liquid than the narrower M1 measure.

Three of the interest-bearing components are shown separately in Table 6–8:

1. *Money market mutual fund (MMMF) balances* are general purpose and broker/dealer accounts owned by individuals.[6] These funds are invested in money market instruments, but investors can write a limited number of checks (usually for a minimum amount, such as $500) against them. Thus, they have some of the characteristics of money but less liquidity than the checkable deposits included in M1.

2. *Savings deposits* include passbook accounts at both commercial banks and thrift institutions (mutual savings banks, savings and loan institutions, and credit unions) and money market deposit accounts (MMDAs) at commercial banks. Again, these accounts are less liquid than the checkable deposits in M1 (MMDAs are usually restricted to three checks per month, checks cannot be written against passbook accounts).

3. *Small-denomination time deposits* refer to certificates of deposit (CDs) of less than $100,000. Unlike the negotiable CDs previously examined, these do not trade in secondary markets, so investors must hold them to maturity or incur high penalties. Again, they are much less liquid than the components of M1.

There are also a number of more exotic balances—overnight repurchase agreements (known as RPs, these are agreements to sell a security for one day, with a simultaneous agreement by the seller to buy it back at an agreed price) and overnight Eurodollar balances.

The concept of *M3* implies even less liquidity than M2 and mainly differs by the inclusion of *large-denomination time deposits,* those negotiable CDs over $100,000. There are also a number of more exotic, nontransaction components—money market funds owned by institutions, term RPs (the agreement is for longer than one day), and term Eurodollar balances.

The M1 concept is intuitively closer to the ordinary concept of money than the broader aggregates. M2 and M3, however, have maintained a more stable relationship with overall economic activity. This relationship, known as velocity, derives from the relationship between money and total economic activity, summarized in the *equation of exchange:*

$$\text{Money} \times \text{Velocity} = \text{GDP}$$

or

$$\text{Velocity} = \text{GDP/Money}$$

Figure 6–5(a)–(c) shows the velocity trends for 1960–1992. As can be seen, there has been a fairly strong trend (1.92 percent per year) for M1 velocity. This means that the public has become increasingly efficient in their use of M1 money: Less money supports more GDP in the 1990s than in the 1960s. By contrast, there is hardly any trend (0.13% per year) to M2, and a slightly negative trend (−0.64% per year) to M3. The near absence of any trend for M2 velocity, in particular, has made M2 a favored aggregate for monetary policy to focus on, as discussed in the following section. The unstable relationship between M1 and economic activity, on the other hand, has led to a deemphasis on M1 as a policy focus.

The Demand for Money

There are two major aspects to the demand for money. The first, and more straightforward, is the *transactions demand*. This simply recognizes that the primary demand for money is to carry out transactions, whether in cash or by check. Thus, as economic activity increases, the demand for money also grows. The heightened nominal economic activity implies a larger number of transactions thus increasing the demand for money to carry out these transactions. Notice, as well, that the relationship is to *nominal* GDP. Inflation can actually exert a positive effect on the demand for money.

The second aspect of the demand for money is less obvious and used to be controversial. The *portfolio* demand for money recognizes that money is an alternative to interest-bearing assets. When interest rates are high, people will prefer to hold their wealth in some interest-bearing form. On the other hand, when interest rates are low, people will wish to avoid getting locked into low-yielding assets. They will be more likely to hold some of their wealth in money balances, waiting for better opportunities to invest in an interest-bearing asset once interest rates have started to rise again. It is essential to note that the demand for these "idle cash balances" represents an alternative to more conventional forms of wealth. This demand is unrelated to short-term liquidity but reflects the public's expectation of future interest rates, relative to the present.

The portfolio demand is most relevant to M1, because M2 and M3 have components that are, themselves, interest sensitive. The behavior pattern suggested by the portfolio demand was strongly in evidence during the low-interest-rate periods of 1991–1993. As can be seen from Table 6–9, the transaction-oriented M1 aggregate grew much faster than the hybrid M2 and M3 measures. This was particularly evident in 1992, when falling interest rates led to liquidation of the interest-sensitive components (labeled "nontransactions components" by the Fed), fueling a sharp run-up in stock market values.

FIGURE 6–5 Velocity trends.

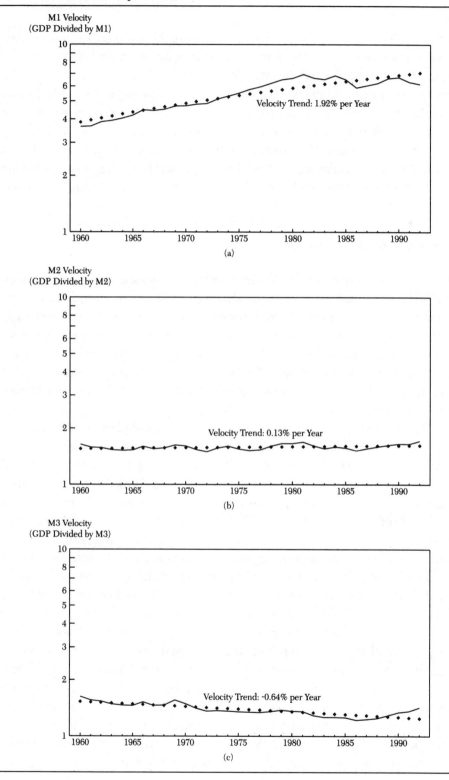

(a)

(b)

(c)

TABLE 6–9 Annual growth rates.

Years	M1 (%)	M2 (%)	M3 (%)
1990–1991	8.7	3.0	1.4
1991–1992	7.6	0.1	0.2
1992–first 6 months of 1993*	9.3	1.1	1.8

*Compound annualized rate.

Thus, the demand for money is positively related to the level of GDP and inversely related to interest rates. The second aspect, the portfolio demand, is complicated by the fact that some components of M2 and M3 yield interest themselves sometimes raising problems for monetary policy.

The Supply of Money

Money is supplied through the joint actions of the commercial banking system and the Federal Reserve. The commercial banks fulfill the more active role. They create money through their extension of credit. When a bank makes a loan (C&I loans are the best example), it credits (or establishes) the borrower's checking account for the amount of the loan, thus adding to the money supply. The Federal Reserve plays a regulatory role, setting reserve requirements—the amount of reserves the banks must put aside relative to the amount of deposits outstanding—and regulating the supply of reserves to the market.

The commercial bank's role in money creation is rooted in credit creation, the processes underlying the flow of funds, which we examined at the start of the chapter. We can get a fuller sense of this by looking at simplified bank balance sheets.

Table 6–10 presents a set of balance sheets for Bank A and Bank B. The first sheet shows the balance sheet for Bank A just after $100,000 has been deposited. Keep in mind this key rule: *Anything that the bank owes to someone else is a liability, while anything owed to the bank is an asset.*

Thus, the demand deposit, which is owed to the depositor, is a liability of the bank; the capital stock represents net worth, which is owed to the stockholders. The $100,000, along with an initial $10,000 in cash represent the reserves of the bank. Since there is a 20 percent reserve requirement against deposits, $20,000 of these reserves are *required reserves*. The remaining $90,000 are *excess reserves*, representing resources that are earning no return, merely sitting idle.

This is where a loan officer, like Marie Lee, earns her salary. She will work to find a borrower who meets all the credit requirements of the bank and who desires to borrow money, in this case, we assume, for business reasons. If

TABLE 6–10 Simplified balance sheets.

Bank A: Balance Sheet 1

Assets		Liabilities and Net Worth	
Reserves	110,000	Capital stock	250,000
(required)*	20,000		
(excess)	90,000		
Property	240,000	Demand deposits	100,000
Total	350,000		350,000

*20% reserve requirement.

Bank A: Balance Sheet 2

Assets		Liabilities and Net Worth	
Reserves	110,000	Capital stock	250,000
(required)*	30,000		
(excess)	80,000		
Loans	50,000		
Property	240,000	Demand deposits	150,000
Total	400,000		400,000

*20% reserve requirement.

Bank B: Balance Sheet 1

Assets		Liabilities and Net Worth	
Reserves	60,000	Capital stock	250,000
(required)*	10,000		
(excess)	50,000		
Property	240,000	Demand deposits	50,000
Total	300,000		300,000

*20% reserve requirement.

Bank B: Balance Sheet 2

Assets		Liabilities and Net Worth	
Reserves	60,000	Capital stock	250,000
(required)*	20,000		
(excess)	40,000		
Loans	50,000		
Property	240,000	Demand deposits	100,000
Total	350,000		350,000

*20% reserve requirement.

Bank A decides to loan Marie's customer $50,000, it will simply create a demand deposit credit to the borrower's checking account. This creates a new liability of $50,000 and an asset, the loan (which is *owed to the bank*) of $50,000. Total reserves are unchanged, but their composition has changed: Required reserves have risen to $30,000 (an extra $10,000 representing 20% of the new demand deposit created for the borrower) and $80,000 of excess reserves. While $80,000 of the reserves are not *required to meet reserve requirements,* these reserves cannot be fully regarded as "excess." There is a likelihood that the borrower will draw down the entire new checking account balance for the purposes of the loan. (After all, borrowers do not borrow money just to have the satisfaction of looking at a large balance on their checking account statement once a month.) Conservative bank management, therefore, requires setting aside reserves equal to the full amount of the loan.

If the borrower does, in fact, withdraw all the loan proceeds to buy inventories, the proceeds may well end up as a deposit in another bank, Bank B. In this case, Bank B already had $10,000 of reserves, which are sufficient to meet the reserve requirement on the new deposit. If Bank B creates a loan of $50,000, a new asset will result (the loan of $50,000), a liability will be added (the newly created demand deposit of $50,000), and the composition of reserves will change ($20,000 of reserves will be required; there will be $40,000 of excess reserves although these reserves are likely to be drawn down quickly).

In this way, commercial banks "create" money through loaning excess reserves and recycling the proceeds from bank to bank until the reserves are "all loaned out." There are three key aspects of this process:

1. There is a theoretical maximum amount of money that can be created. This maximum is determined by a *money multiplier* times the excess reserves:

$$\text{excess reserves} \times \frac{1}{\text{reserve requirement}}$$

    in this case with an initial $90,000 of excess reserves,

$$\$90,000 \times \frac{1}{0.20} = \$450,000$$

    This example implies that the initial $90,000 of excess reserves, given a 20 percent reserve requirement, could lead to a maximum expansion in the money supply of $450,000.
2. The theoretical maximum expansion of the money supply depends on two behavioral responses: (a) the banks have to lend all their excess reserves, and (b) the borrowers have to spend all the loan proceeds.
3. The reserve requirement is set by the Federal Reserve System, which substantially controls the supply of reserves to the banking system.

The two behavioral characteristics—the efficiency with which banks use their reserves and the extent to which borrowers draw on their loan proceeds—are each largely dependent on the level of interest rates. If interest rates are high, banks will incur a high "opportunity cost" in maintaining idle reserve balances. Moreover, periods of high interest rates are also periods of strong business activity and credit demand. Thus, it is likely that the banks will fully use their excess reserves. The high interest rates are also an inducement for the borrowers to use all their loan proceeds; the cost of financing idle bank balances is too high.

These behavioral responses are reversed during low interest rate periods. The borrowers with good credit ratings are fewer (remember the falloff in business borrowing during the 1990–1991 recession, shown in Table 6–1), and the cost of idle reserves for banks or idle cash balances for businesses is less. Thus, the theoretical maximum on money creation is less likely to be met.

These relationships are the basis for an upward sloping (direct) relationship between the money supply and interest rates. The role of the Federal Reserve in the creation of money is crucial, however. This is where monetary *policy* enters the analysis.

The Federal Reserve and Monetary Policy

The Federal Reserve System—usually referred to simply as the "Fed"—is the monetary authority for the United States. It has a unique organization, reflecting the national and regional character of the nation.

The Federal Reserve Board consists of seven governors appointed for 14-year terms;[7] the terms have a staggered (beginning every 2 years) sequence. One governor serves as chairman for a 5-year term. Federal Reserve Board governors are appointed by the President of the United States, but must be confirmed by the Senate. The Federal Reserve Board is headquartered in Washington, D.C.

The regional differences in the U.S. economy are addressed by the 12 Federal Reserve banks arranged in Federal Reserve Districts throughout the country. Table 6–11 lists the Federal Reserve districts, banks, and branches. Each Federal Reserve bank is owned by the member banks in that district, who elect a board of directors. The chief officer of each bank is the president, who is appointed by the Federal Reserve Board in Washington, D.C.

The board of governors and the presidents of the Federal Reserve banks combine their efforts to direct and regulate monetary policy in the *Federal Open Market Committee* or *FOMC*, which is the main monetary policy-making body in the system. The FOMC meets eight times a year, roughly every six weeks. While all 19 members (7 governors and 12 bank presidents) take part in the meetings and discussions, only 12 vote on the policy actions to be taken: all 7 governors, the president of the Federal Reserve Bank of New York (in recognition of the central role of the New York Fed in carrying out open market operations in the money markets, centered in New York), and 4 of the remaining 11 presidents on a 1-year rotation.

TABLE 6–11 Federal reserve districts, banks, and branches.

District	Bank	Branch
1	Boston	
2	New York	Buffalo
3	Philadelphia	
4	Cleveland	Cincinnati Pittsburgh
5	Richmond	Baltimore Charlotte
6	Atlanta	Birmingham Jacksonville Miami Nashville New Orleans
7	Chicago	Detroit
8	St. Louis	Little Rock Louisville Memphis
9	Minneapolis	Helena
10	Kansas City	Denver Oklahoma City Omaha
11	Dallas	El Paso Houston San Antonio
12	San Francisco	Los Angeles Portland Salt Lake City Seattle

Theoretically, there are three main *tools of monetary policy*: (1) establishing of reserve requirements, (2) control of the discount rate, and (3) open market purchases and sales of Treasury securities. In practice, however, reserve requirements have only been reduced since 1979 to simplify the regulatory structure. Thus, the effect of reserve requirements on money creation has been mainly constant in recent years. The Fed has moved toward a more direct reserve adjustment policy, by relying on the other two tools.

The discount rate is an interest rate that the Fed charges member banks when they borrow reserves directly from the Fed. Banks that are members of the Federal Reserve System must maintain their reserves at the required level *on average* over a two-week reserve maintenance period (from Thursday to the Wednesday two weeks later). Banks with a reserve shortage can make up the shortage by either borrowing reserves in the Fed funds market—paying the existing Fed funds rate for the borrowed funds—or by borrowing directly from the Fed through its discount window facility.

When a bank borrows through the discount window, it pledges Treasury bills as collateral. The bills are literally "discounted"; the Fed pays less than their face amount and the borrowing bank pays back the full face amount of the loan to retrieve the bills. The need to repay the loan means that the bank will ultimately have to find the reserve shortage from some other source, so discount window lending may actually increase the demand for reserves in the Fed funds market. Access to the facility is restricted, however, and the restrictions are set, along with the discount rate itself, by the board of governors at the request of one or more district bank boards of directors.

The discount rate is changed infrequently. One consequence is that, when it does change, it is a notable event. From the end of 1990 through September 1992, monetary policy eased numerous times, as signaled by declines in the Fed funds rate, but the discount rate was only lowered seven times. Each discount rate cut, however, made a strong impression because it was such a rare event.

Open market operations represent the most commonly used monetary policy tool. In addition to its role as the nation's monetary authority, the Fed works as agent for the U.S. Treasury in selling U.S. Treasury securities. It does this through an auction process, in which the active bidders are 38 "primary dealers," either banks or brokerages registered with the Federal Reserve Bank of New York that make markets in Treasury securities. (See Table 6–12 for a listing of the primary dealers.)

The primary dealer connection of the Federal Reserve Bank of New York greatly facilitates monetary policy, in particular efforts to add or drain the amount of bank reserves in the monetary system. When the Fed decides to add reserves to the banking system, the traders at the domestic trading desk of the Federal Reserve Bank of New York call the traders at the primary dealers (generally between 11:30 A.M. and 11:40 A.M. New York time) and offer to buy specific Treasury issues. After contacting all primary dealers, the traders at the Fed choose the best offerings—in order from the lowest to highest price (highest to lowest interest rate)—up to the predetermined amount they wish to purchase and confirm those purchases with the dealers. The dealers are then paid in reserves credited to their own account in the case of a bank dealer (such as Bank of America or Chemical Securities) or to its clearing bank in the case of a nonbank dealer (such as Merrill Lynch Government Securities or Salomon Brothers). In either case, the banking system as a whole receives an injection of reserves that can support an increase in the money supply. The Fed can drain reserves, thus bringing about a shrinking of the money supply, by offering to buy securities in the open market.

TABLE 6–12   Primary dealers in the U.S. Treasury securities market.

Bank of America	Harris-Nesbitt Thomson Securities, Inc.
Barclays de Zoete Wedd Securities Inc.	Kidder, Peabody & Co., Incorporated
Bear, Stearns & Co.	Aubrey G. Lanston & Co., Inc.
BT Securities Corporation	Lehman Government Securities, Incorporated
Carroll McEntee & McGinley Incorporated	Merrill Lynch Government Securities, Inc.
Chase Securities, Inc.	J.P. Morgan Securities, Inc.
Chemical Securities, Inc.	Morgan Stanley & Co. Incorporated
Citicorp Securities Markets, Inc.	NationsBank of North Carolina, N.A.
Daiwa Securities America Inc.	The Nikko Securities Co. International, Inc.
Dean Witter Reynolds Inc.	Nomura Securities International, Inc.
Deutsche Bank Government Securities, Inc.	Paine Webber Incorporated
Dillon Read & Co. Inc.	Prudential Securities Incorporated
Discount Corporation of New York	Saiomon Brothers Inc.
Donaldson, Lufkin & Jenrette Securities Corporation	Sanwa-BGK Securities Co., L.P.
Eastbridge Capital Inc.	Smith Barney, Harris Upham & Co. Incorporated
The First Boston Corporation	SBC Government Securities Inc.
First Chicago Capital Markets, Inc.	UBS Securities Inc.
Fuji Securities, Inc.	S.G. Warburg & Co., Incorporated
Goldman, Sachs & Co.	Yamaichi International (America), Inc.
Greenwich Capital Markets, Inc.	

Since 1979, the Fed has used the level of reserves in the banking system as its policy objective, and since 1983, the target has been the amount of borrowed reserves (through the discount facility). The effect of reserve targeting, however, is most evident in the Fed funds rate, the rate at which banks must borrow from each other to satisfy a reserve shortage. Thus, the Fed funds rate is the "fulcrum" rate on which other interest rates and, indeed, the money supply and demand depend. When the rate is increased as a result of open-market draining of reserves, the cost of lending by banks is raised; other interest rates will then increase, ultimately acting as a retardant, if not a deterrent, to economic growth.

Most open market operations, however, are conducted for ordinary seasonal smoothing reasons, rather than to change monetary policy. For instance, the Fed will routinely supply reserves on the day before Thanksgiving because the coming Friday is the biggest shopping day of the year causing a large, purely seasonal transactions demand for money. Conversely, the Fed will drain reserves following a large snowstorm that closes airports and so disrupts check clearing, leading to exaggerated demand deposit balances.

Open market operations can be used either to smooth regular seasonal demand and supply of money, or to effect a direct policy change ordered by the FOMC.

SUMMARY

The demand and supply of money is the result of a complex set of forces. A crucial aspect of both, however, is the demand for credit by the various sectors in the economy. Satisfying this demand is the business of the entire financial sector, but at its center is the commercial banking system. By making loans, banks create money. Interest rates, however, act on both the demand and supply of money as an allocator. The Federal Reserve System exerts limited control over the banking system's ability to lend at all (through its effects on reserves) and on the rate at which loans can be made (through its effects on the Fed funds rate). Ultimately, interest rates and the stance of monetary policy affect the level of economic activity.

7 A BORDERLESS WORLD

The International Economy

So far, our discussion of the U.S. macroeconomy has been almost entirely geared to the domestic economy. The United States, however, is a major force within an integrated, international economy and is affected by strong feedbacks from that economy. This chapter looks at the international effect on domestic macroeconomic activity. There are two major focal points for international macroeconomics: international trade flows and foreign exchange and international finance. The chapter concludes with a brief inspection of the *micro* economic bases for and gains from trade.

The integration of the U.S. economy within the international economy is so complete that a thorough understanding of international economic relationships is important for a wide range of managers. In fact, the lack of such understanding may prove to be a serious deficiency in any manager. In this chapter, we will examine the impact of the international economy on business through the eyes of Alan Block, the assistant treasurer for international operations at a manufacturer of computer software. Such a function exists today in most large corporations. In many smaller companies, this role is an added responsibility for managers primarily involved with the company's domestic operations. This is all the more reason familiarity with the working of the international economy should be part of any manager's tool kit.

THE BALANCE OF PAYMENTS

The *balance of payments accounts* are the official statements of international transactions between U.S. residents and residents of foreign nations. They fulfill a similar role for the nation's international economic activity as that played by the *national income and product accounts* in summarizing the nation's domestic production and income flows, or the *flow of funds accounts* in depicting the nation's financial flows. In effect, the balance of payments accounts depict the U.S. international trade and capital positions. The concept of the balance of payments has changed since the early 1970s, when the foreign exchange value of the U.S. dollar ceased to have a fixed relationship with other currencies and began floating.

From 1946 through the 1960s, the balance of payments accounts underwent several changes in definition. These involved several different accounting methods for striking a balance between (1) a nation's *receipts* from other nations for goods and services sold and (2) *payments* to other nations for goods and services received. The balance of payments always had to balance, but the manner of achieving this balance reflected the problems or fundamental health of the domestic economy being measured. Quite often, a nation would show either a surplus or deficit on its "regular," or autonomous, accounts—those determined in the ordinary course of economic activity. In cases of deficit, the official sector (the monetary authority and the treasury or finance ministry) would have to make up the balance from "compensatory" accounts (official reserves and monetary gold). The emergence of persistent deficits on regular accounts in many nations—the United Kingdom, United States, France, and Italy—and persistent surpluses on "regular" accounts in others—especially the former West Germany—led to the breakdown of the balance of payments-foreign exchange rate system referred to as the *Bretton Woods* system.[1]

With the advent of flexible exchange rates in the early 1970s, the balance of payments concepts changed again and two major accounts emerged that represent the major categories of international transactions. The first account is the *current account,* which contrasts exports of goods, income, and services with imports of goods, income, and services. These short-term payments represent the flow of goods, factor incomes, and services on an ongoing (hence, current) basis. The second account is the *capital account,* which contrasts the inflow of capital (direct investment and long-term lending by foreigners) with the outflow of capital (direct investment by U.S. residents abroad and long-term lending to foreigners).

In essence, a current account deficit induces a capital account surplus, and a current account surplus induces a capital account deficit. For this reason, the current account dominates, at least in terms of cause and response. The current account position is, thus, most commonly used to depict the nation's balance of payments position. A current account deficit is a sign of fundamental adverse imbalance in the nation's international payments, whereas a current account surplus reflects a healthy international payments position. A capital account outflow (deficit) is a response to a current account surplus (and vice versa). Otherwise, the exchange rate must change to offset any imbalance.

Tables 7–1 and 7–2 present, respectively, summary data for the current account and the capital account for the 1946–1992 period. Each of these accounts and the main categories within each account will be described in the following sections.

The Current Account

Two aspects of the definition of the current account are especially important. First, the transactions covered are *current,* which means that their impact will generally be confined to the current year. This contrasts with the capital account, where investments made currently will lead to a flow of income over future years. Second, the flows refer to goods *and* services. Table 7–1 shows that the six columns consist of four basic components and two summary balances. The four basic components are:

1. The merchandise trade balance.
2. The services balance.
3. The balance on investment income.
4. The balance on unilateral transfers.

Summary balances are struck both excluding and including the balance on unilateral transfers. The first represents a concept closer to that used for gross domestic product (GDP), where only payments for goods or services rendered are measured. The more comprehensive current account measure includes net unilateral transfers[2] because, although these are not payments for value received, they are charges against U.S. international reserves that must be offset against inflows.

The following is a simple, but crucial accounting rule:

> If money flows into the United States, the current account is credited and it contributes to a surplus; conversely, if money flows out of the United States, the current account is debited and it contributes to a deficit.

For instance, when IBM sells a computer to a firm in Australia, or a Japanese tourist flies to Hawaii on United Airlines, or Coca Cola (United Kingdom) sends back profits to its parent corporation in the United States, money flows into this country; these are all current account credits. Alternatively, when Sony televisions are imported into the United States, or when an American family flies to Paris on Air France, or when a German insurance company receives interest on U.S. Treasury bonds that it owns, or when aid payments are made to

TABLE 7–1 U.S. international transactions on current account (billions of dollars).

	Merchandise Trade	Services	Investment Income	Balance on Goods, Services, & Income	Unilateral Transfers	Balance on Current Account
1946	6.697	0.619	0.560	7.876	-2.991	4.885
1947	10.124	0.733	0.857	11.714	-2.722	8.992
1948	5.708	0.198	1.484	7.390	-4.973	2.417
1949	5.339	0.028	1.355	6.722	-5.849	0.873
1950	1.122	0.066	1.509	2.697	-4.537	-1.840
1951	3.067	0.721	2.050	5.838	-4.954	0.884
1952	2.611	0.920	2.196	5.727	-5.113	0.614
1953	1.437	1.822	2.112	5.371	-6.657	-1.286
1954	2.576	0.938	2.347	5.861	-5.642	0.219
1955	2.897	-0.111	2.730	5.516	-5.086	0.430
1956	4.753	-0.135	3.102	7.720	-4.990	2.730
1957	6.271	-0.130	3.384	9.525	-4.763	4.762
1958	3.462	-0.996	2.965	5.431	-4.647	0.784
1959	1.148	-1.079	3.071	3.140	-4.422	-1.282
1960	4.892	-1.385	3.379	6.886	-4.062	2.824
1961	5.571	-1.377	3.755	7.949	-4.127	3.822
1962	4.521	-1.151	4.294	7.664	-4.277	3.387
1963	5.224	-1.014	4.596	8.806	-4.392	4.414
1964	6.801	-0.779	5.041	11.063	-4.240	6.823
1965	4.951	-0.287	5.350	10.014	-4.583	5.431
1966	3.817	-0.877	5.047	7.987	-4.956	3.031
1967	3.800	-1.196	5.274	7.878	-5.295	2.583
1968	0.635	-0.385	5.990	6.240	-5.629	0.611
1969	0.607	-0.516	6.044	6.135	-5.736	0.399
1970	2.603	-0.350	6.233	8.486	-6.155	2.331
1971	-2.260	0.957	7.272	5.969	-7.402	-1.433
1972	-6.416	0.973	8.192	2.749	-8.544	-5.795
1973	0.911	0.989	12.153	14.053	-6.913	7.140
1974*	-5.505	1.212	15.503	11.210	-9.248	1.962
1975	8.903	3.501	12.787	25.191	-7.075	18.116
1976	-9.483	3.402	16.063	9.982	-5.687	4.295
1977	-31.091	3.845	18.137	-9.109	-5.226	-14.335
1978	-33.927	4.164	20.408	-9.355	-5.788	-15.143
1979	-27.568	3.003	30.873	6.308	-6.593	-0.285
1980	-25.500	6.093	30.073	10.666	-8.349	2.317
1981	-28.023	11.852	32.903	16.732	-11.702	5.030
1982	-36.485	12.329	29.788	5.632	-17.075	-11.443
1983	-67.102	9.305	31.915	-25.882	-17.741	-43.623
1984	-112.482	3.427	30.843	-78.212	-20.612	-98.824
1985	-122.173	0.167	23.235	-98.771	-22.950	-121.721
1986	-145.081	6.349	15.378	-123.354	-24.175	-147.529
1987	-159.557	8.191	10.945	-140.421	-23.053	-163.474
1988	-126.959	12.706	12.466	-101.787	-24.869	-126.656
1989	-115.668	25.765	14.366	-75.537	-25.606	-101.143
1990	-108.853	32.055	19.287	-57.511	-32.917	-90.428
1991	-73.436	45.297	16.429	-11.710	8.028	-3.682
1992	-96.275	55.125	10.062	-31.088	-31.360	-62.448

Source: Bureau of Economic Analysis, U.S. Department of Commerce.

*Includes extraordinary U.S. government transaction with India.

TABLE 7-2 U.S. international transactions on capital account (billions of dollars).

	U.S. Assets Abroad				Foreign Assets in the U.S.			
	U.S. Official Reserves	Other U.S. Government Assets	U.S. Private Assets	Total	Foreign Official Assets	Other Foreign Assets	Total	Statistical Discrepancy
1946	−0.623							
1947	−3.315							
1948	−1.736							
1949	−0.266							
1950	1.758							
1951	−0.033							
1952	−0.415							
1953	1.256							
1954	0.480							
1955	0.182							
1956	−0.869							
1957	−1.165							
1958	2.292							
1959	1.035							
1960	2.145	−1.100	−5.144	−4.099	1.473	0.821	2.294	−1.019
1961	0.607	−0.910	−5.235	−5.538	0.765	1.939	2.704	−0.989
1962	1.535	−1.085	−4.623	−4.173	1.270	0.641	1.911	−1.124
1963	0.378	−1.662	−5.986	−7.270	1.986	1.231	3.217	−0.360
1964	0.171	−1.680	−8.050	−9.559	1.660	1.983	3.643	−0.907
1965	1.225	−1.605	−5.336	−5.716	0.134	0.607	0.741	−0.457
1966	0.570	−1.543	−6.347	−7.320	−0.672	4.333	3.661	0.629
1967	0.053	−2.423	−7.386	−9.756	3.451	3.928	7.379	−0.205
1968	−0.870	−2.274	−7.833	−10.977	−0.774	10.703	9.929	0.438
1969	−1.179	−2.200	−8.206	−11.585	−1.301	14.002	12.701	−1.516
1970	2.481	−1.589	−10.229	−9.337	6.908	−0.550	6.358	−0.219
1971	2.349	−1.884	−12.940	−12.475	26.879	−3.909	22.970	−9.779
1972	−0.004	−1.568	−12.925	−14.497	10.475	10.986	21.461	−1.879
1973	0.158	−2.644	−20.388	−22.874	6.026	12.362	18.388	−2.654
1974*	−1.467	0.366	−33.643	−34.744	10.546	23.696	34.242	−1.458
1975	−0.849	−3.474	−35.380	−39.703	7.027	8.643	15.670	5.917
1976	−2.558	−4.214	−44.498	−51.270	17.693	18.826	36.519	10.445
1977	−0.375	−3.693	−30.717	−34.785	36.816	14.503	51.319	−2.199
1978	0.732	−4.660	−57.202	−61.130	33.678	30.358	64.036	12.236
1979	−1.133	−3.746	−61.176	−66.055	−13.665	52.416	38.751	26.449
1980	−8.155	−5.162	−73.651	−86.968	15.497	42.615	58.112	25.386
1981	−5.175	−5.097	−103.875	−114.147	4.960	78.072	83.032	24.992
1982	−4.965	−6.131	−111.229	−122.325	3.593	88.826	92.419	41.359
1983	−1.196	−5.006	−52.654	−58.856	5.845	77.534	83.379	19.099
1984	−3.131	−5.489	−20.605	−29.225	3.140	98.870	102.010	26.038
1985	−3.858	−2.821	−27.391	−34.070	−1.119	132.084	130.965	24.825
1986	0.312	−2.022	−89.360	−91.070	35.648	187.543	223.191	15.407
1987	9.149	1.006	−72.556	−62.401	45.387	184.585	229.972	−4.096
1988	−3.912	2.967	−91.762	−92.707	39.758	179.731	219.489	−0.126
1989	−25.293	1.271	−90.922	−114.944	8.489	205.204	213.693	2.394
1990	−2.158	2.304	−56.467	−56.321	33.908	65.471	99.379	47.370
1991	5.763	3.397	−71.379	−62.219	18.407	48.573	66.980	−1.078
1992	3.901	−0.959	−47.843	−44.901	40.307	80.093	120.400	−13.052

Source: Bureau of Economic Analysis, U.S. Department of Commerce.

*Includes extraordinary U.S. government transaction with India.

127

Israel, money flows out of the United States; these are all current account debits. The following sections examine each of these accounts in more detail.

The Merchandise Trade Balance

The *merchandise trade balance* focuses on the international flows of goods. Since exports of goods induce an inflow of money, they are a credit (positive) to the merchandise trade account. The sale of the IBM computer cited earlier is such an export, and shipments by Alan Block's company of software to overseas customers are also exports. The opposite transaction, an import, occurs when goods are brought into the United States for which money must flow out. The Sony televisions cited earlier represent imports. Foreign-produced components used in the packaging of the software sold by Block's company would also be imports.

The merchandise trade balance plays a dominant role within the current account. As can be seen from Table 7–1, the merchandise trade balance, whether a surplus or a deficit, has typically been far larger than the rest of the current account taken together. Moreover, the sign of the merchandise trade balance—plus for a surplus, minus for a deficit—is usually (although not always; note 1950, 1953, 1959, 1974, 1976, 1980, and 1981) the same as for the current account.

Table 7–1 shows four distinct subperiods in the 1946–1992 period, representing changes in the United States' merchandise trade performance. These can be better understood by reference to Figures 7–1(a) through 7–1(c). These show the trade balance,[3] exports, and imports, each expressed as a share of total GDP in constant dollars. The fact that both exports (Figure 7-1(b)) and imports (Figure 7–1(c)) have risen as a share of GDP over the extended period attests to the increased importance of international flows in the U.S. economy. The four subperiods are as follows:

1. The years *1946–1960* represented the immediate postwar period. During this time, the United States reaped the benefits of emerging from World War II relatively unscathed, as the dominant economy in the developed world. While there were occasional deficits in real terms,[4] the U.S. trade surplus averaged a modest 0.4 percent of GDP. This period, however, had two important features: (1) the rest of the world experienced a "dollar shortage" where there was great demand for the dollar to import U.S.-made goods and (2) neither the export nor import sectors accounted for more than 5 percent of U.S. economic activity.

2. The years *1961–1972* were a transition period. In current dollar terms (see Table 7–1), the United States managed small merchandise trade surpluses

FIGURE 7–1   Changes in U.S. merchandise trade performance.

(a) Trade balance share of gross domestic product.

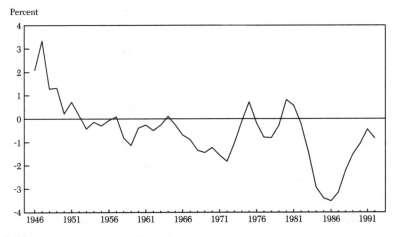

(b) Export share of gross domestic product.

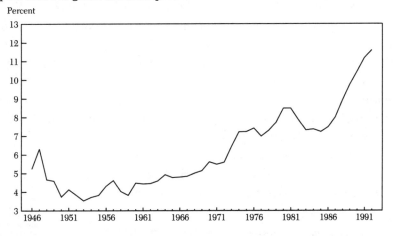

(c) Import share of gross domestic product.

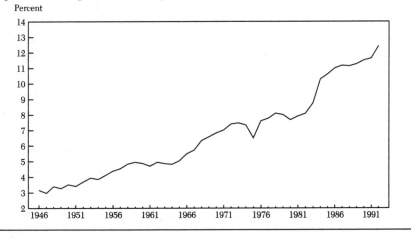

until the end of the period. In constant dollar terms (see Figures 7–1(a) through 7–1(c)), however, the United States began recording persistent small trade deficits, averaging 0.8 percent of GDP. At this time, the U.S. dominance of the international economy began to lessen; there were persistent "crises" involving the United States, the United Kingdom, France, and other nations whose trade deficits jeopardized the international payments system.

3. During the years *1973–1982*, the United States and the rest of the world had to adjust to the increase in oil prices that followed the oil embargo and price hikes initiated by the Organization of Petroleum Exporting Countries (OPEC) in 1973 and again in 1979. The steep increase in oil prices, combined with the increasing percentage of imported oil consumed in the United States, sharply raised the share of imports in GDP from an average of 5.8 percent in 1961–1972, to 7.7 percent in 1973–1982.

   The more remarkable fact is that the export share increased from an average of 5 percent of GDP in 1961–1972, to 7.5 percent in 1973–1982. Companies in the United States became much more active participants in world markets. Previously, many U.S. companies treated exports ambivalently: They were glad to export when domestic markets were weak but were willing to sacrifice foreign orders to fill booming domestic demand. In the 1970s, however, U.S. firms developed their international operations as a more important, integral part of their overall business. Thus, while the United States endured frequent deficits, they were small and there were intermittent surpluses. On average, the deficits amounted for just over 0.1 percent of GDP.

4. The *1982–1992* period reflected an even greater internationalization of the U.S. economy, but it was also a period of large, persistent deficits, averaging 2.1 percent of GDP. The reasons are complex and partly related to capital account-current account interactions. Briefly, the widening budget deficit after the tax reductions of the early 1980s (see Figure 6–1) led to an increased reliance on foreign purchases of Treasury bonds (a capital inflow). This increased the demand for dollars, leading to an increase in the foreign exchange value of the dollar. The rising value of the dollar, in turn, made U.S. goods more expensive in foreign currency terms abroad and foreign goods cheaper in dollar terms, eroding foreign demand for U.S. exports and increasing U.S. demand for imports. This became known as the "twin deficits problem."

The foregoing discussion highlights two important factors that affect trade flows and are the basic determinants of the demand for internationally traded goods:

1. There is a direct relationship between the *demand for imports* and *income*. This *income* effect means that domestic economic strength may be adverse for the trade balance because it can stimulate demand for imports. At the same time, strong economic growth abroad is favorable for a nation's exports. Indeed, the erosion of the trade surplus during the 1946–1960 period, shown in Figure 7–1(a), is largely a reflection of the stronger U.S. economic performance compared with other countries still recovering from World War II.

2. There is an inverse relationship between *the demand for foreign-traded goods* and *relative prices*. This *price* effect means that, other conditions remaining equal, consumers will purchase the cheaper of two goods of the same quality, regardless of where they were made. If Japanese radios are cheaper than U.S.-made radios, then imports will rise. Alternatively, if U.S.-made newsprint is cheaper than Swedish-made newsprint, U.S. exports of newsprint will rise. The *price* effect is complicated because at least two elements go into the price: (1) the relative costs of production (for example, in the United States and Sweden) and (2) the foreign exchange rate (for example, between the U.S. dollar and the Swedish krona).

Services Balance

The *balance on services* covers the international flow of services, consisting of four broad categories:

1. *Travel* refers to the expenditures of tourists and other travelers when abroad. For instance, the spending of the American family in Paris for meals, lodging, and gifts would all be treated as a negative flow in the services account. The similar spending by a Japanese banker visiting the United States would be treated as a positive flow.

2. *Passenger fares* represent the net spending on passenger transportation. If the hypothetical American family flies on Air France, it represents an outflow of money. Conversely, if the Japanese banker flies on United Airlines, it is an inflow of money to the United States.

3. *Other transportation payments* refer to freight payments. Thus, if imported goods arrive in this country on U.S. ships, the shipping charges represent a positive flow. The foreign exporter would have paid the U.S. shipping company for the freight charges. If U.S. goods are exported on foreign ships, however, the shipping charges would be treated as a negative charge to the services account. Insurance charges related to the flow of goods are treated similarly.

4. *Royalties and license fees* have also become an important component of the services account in recent years. For instance, if Alan Block's company licenses software production and sales abroad, the license fees would be treated as a positive item in the service and current accounts.

Investment Income Balance

The investment income account is directly related to the capital accounts. Essentially, it reflects income earned from foreign investments, *net* of income paid to foreigners with investments in the United States. Three major forms of investment income are included in the current account:

1. *Direct investment* receipts and payments represent the repatriated profits and dividends from direct investment by U.S. residents abroad (receipts) and by foreign residents in the United States (payments). The responsive nature of these flows to capital flows means that an initial capital inflow— say the investment by Honda in its U.S. manufacturing plant in Ohio—sets up a future outflow of investment income.

2. *Other private* receipts and income reflect, primarily, interest from fixed-income securities and bank lending. Here again, an initial capital flow is the basis for a stream of investment income.

3. *U.S. government* receipts and payments are treated separately (hence the "private" in the other private category). The U.S. Treasury receives interest income from holding foreign government securities. Most of these securities were acquired in past efforts by the U.S. Treasury to aid other nations' efforts at foreign exchange rate stabilization. Interest payments by the Treasury grew sharply during the 1980s, as the U.S. budget deficit grew and foreign holdings of U.S. Treasury securities increased markedly.

The United States has consistently enjoyed a surplus on investment income, much of which reflects the enormous stock of capital invested abroad. Indeed, many observers are skeptical about the degree of apparent erosion in the investment income and capital positions of the United States on the basis that the foreign assets are undervalued. In the 1980s, however, the falloff in investment income mainly reflected two factors: (1) the suspension of interest payments by Latin American borrowers to U.S. banks in the early 1980s and (2) the increased payments to foreign owners of U.S. Treasury securities.

The interaction between the investment income portion of the current account and the capital account highlights an area where the private actions of a manager, such as Alan Block, directly affect the national macroeconomy. If Block were involved in setting up an overseas facility, this would require a capital outflow from the United States in hopes of a future inflow of profits. These decisions would be made on the basis of normal business considerations, but their effects would go far beyond the firm.

Unilateral transfers consist of U.S. government grants (foreign aid), U.S. government pensions paid to foreign residents, and private remittances to foreigners. As noted earlier, the unilateral transfers account represents international monetary flows that are unrelated to any production. These payments are specifically excluded from GDP but, nevertheless, represent international monetary transactions that really do take place.

The Capital Account

Table 7–2 shows the international *flows* of U.S. capital. Thus, a negative item represents an outflow of capital from the United States while a positive item represents an inflow to the United States. (Prior to 1960, the U.S. international accounts were kept in a quite different form than in the three decades since.) Essentially, there are two key distinctions: (1) U.S. assets abroad and (2) foreign assets in the United States.

U.S. assets abroad consist of U.S. official reserves, other U.S. government assets, and U.S. private assets. Official assets consist of holdings of gold, special drawing rights,[5] foreign currency holdings, and the U.S. reserve position (the amount of paid-in reserves) at the International Monetary Fund (IMF). Other U.S. government assets represent disbursements on loans by U.S. agencies (Export-Import Bank, Agency for International Development, Department of Agriculture, etc.) that are due for repayment and so are regarded as assets. These two categories are often prompted by automatic, nonbusiness related factors.

The category of greater interest to business is U.S. private assets. These assets fall into two broad categories:

1. *Equity* investment in the form of direct purchases of foreign assets, purchases of equity securities, and reinvestment of interest and income earned from existing foreign assets.
2. *Credits,* either in the form of purchases of debt securities or bank lending.

These types of asset acquisition are more similar to domestic economic activity. Although the items have a negative sign in Table 7–2, that merely signifies the direction of the monetary flow. There is nothing truly negative about these flows. Indeed, they set up future inflows of investment income on the current account.

Foreign assets in the United States measure the inflow of foreign capital to the United States. There are two distinctions under this category. Foreign official assets represent acquisition of U.S. assets, particularly Treasury securities, by foreign governments, usually in conjunction with foreign exchange intervention. (When a foreign monetary authority—say, the Bundesbank—intervenes to defend the dollar, it typically buys dollars and then invests the dollars in U.S. government securities held on account by the Federal Reserve Bank of New York.) Other foreign assets are the mirror image of U.S. private assets. They represent foreign equity investments in the United States and foreign credits (including foreign purchases of U.S. Treasury securities).

The increase in foreign assets in the United States is often viewed pejoratively reflecting an unfortunate confusion. The inflow of capital does imply an obligation of repayment and a debtor status for the nation. There are times in any business, however, when increased debt is desirable; it provides more resources for the firm to utilize to earn a profit. Similarly for the economy as a whole, increased foreign capital provides more resources to supply macroeconomic demand. More basic is that the increase in foreign assets in the United States is usually a response to a deficit on current account.

Statistical Discrepancy

The current account and the net of U.S. assets abroad less foreign assets in the United States fail to balance—a stark reminder that there is a limit to the ability to capture all the international monetary flows. The *statistical discrepancy* measures this difference. Essentially, it measures the amount of unreported international monetary flows, including a great many frankly illegal transactions.

Thus, the balance of payments in its most complete form is brought into balance by the following equation:

$$\text{Current Account} = \text{Capital Account} + \text{Statistical Discrepancy}$$

As noted several times in the preceding discussion, the existence of foreign exchange values to the dollar introduces a complication to international monetary flows. This topic is taken up next.

FOREIGN EXCHANGE RATES

International economic relations involve commercial and financial transactions between U.S. residents and residents of foreign nations. Foreigners determine their demand and supply of goods and services on the basis of their own currencies. Thus, for the exchanges to take place, there has to be a conversion of the foreign currency into U.S. dollars.

From the end of World War II to the spring of 1973, *foreign exchange rates*—the rate at which currencies exchanged for one another—were fixed and could fluctuate only within narrow ranges. Since 1973, the U.S. dollar, along with most major currencies, has "floated" in much wider ranges. This has added a fresh arena of financial market uncertainty and created opportunities for speculation and trading. It has made the understanding of foreign exchange fluctuations important to nonfinancial managers whose business has an international dimension. Alan Block would be intimately involved with these fluctuations as he manages the international finances of his firm. In firms without the services of a specialist like Block, attention to foreign exchange fluctuations would be a responsibility of the domestic finance managers.

Table 7–3 shows exchange rates for the U.S. dollar against six foreign currencies for the years 1967–1992. (The rates are shown in foreign currency units per dollar, except for the British pound, which is conventionally shown as cents per pound.) The United States and these six countries are referred to as the "Group of Seven" or "G-7" countries. They constitute the largest developed economies involved in international commerce. Two facts can be readily seen from the table:

1. There has been considerable variation in the foreign exchange value of each currency against the dollar during the period of flexible exchange rates.

2. The fluctuations of the various currencies against the dollar have not been consistent from currency to currency.

Some currencies, such as the German mark and Japanese yen, have shown more consistent *appreciation* against the dollar than currencies, such as the British pound or French franc, which have shown frequent swings from *appreciation* to *depreciation* and back again:

- *Appreciation* means that a unit of foreign currency has become worth more in dollar terms. For instance, the German mark appreciated between 1973 and 1975, as it moved from 2.6715 marks per dollar ($0.3743 per mark) to 2.4614 marks per dollar ($0.4063 per mark).

- From the perspective of the dollar, *depreciation* was occurring; a dollar bought fewer marks.

A number of forces affect the foreign exchange value of a currency. The most fundamental point, however, is that *the foreign exchange value of any currency is a result of the demand and supply for the currency in international commerce.* Foreigners wish to hold the U.S. dollar in order to (1) buy U.S.-produced goods and services or (2) to invest in U.S. assets. The intensity of demand for

TABLE 7–3 Foreign exchange rates (currency units per U.S. dollar, except cents per U.K. pound).

March	Canada (Dollar)	France (Franc)	Germany (Mark)	Italy (Lira)	Japan (Yen)	United Kingdom (Pound)	Trade-Weighted* U.S. Dollar Value March 1973 = 100
1973	0.9967	4.5156	2.8132	568.17	261.90	247.24	100.0
1967	1.0789	4.9206	3.9865	624.09	362.13	275.04	120.0
1968	1.0776	4.9529	3.9920	623.38	360.55	239.35	122.1
1969	1.0769	5.1999	3.9251	627.32	358.36	239.01	122.4
1970	1.0444	5.5288	3.6465	627.12	358.16	239.59	121.1
1971	1.0099	5.5100	3.4830	618.34	347.79	244.42	117.8
1972	0.9907	5.0444	3.1886	583.70	303.13	250.34	109.1
1973	1.0002	4.4535	2.6715	582.41	271.31	245.25	99.1
1974	0.9780	4.8107	2.5868	650.81	291.84	234.03	101.4
1975	1.0175	4.2877	2.4614	653.10	296.78	222.17	98.5
1976	0.9863	4.7825	2.5185	833.58	296.45	180.48	105.7
1977	1.0633	4.9161	2.3236	882.78	268.62	174.49	103.4
1978	1.1405	4.5091	2.0097	849.13	210.39	191.84	92.4
1979	1.1713	4.2567	1.8343	831.11	219.02	212.24	88.1
1980	1.1693	4.2251	1.8175	856.21	226.63	232.46	87.4
1981	1.1990	5.4397	2.2632	1138.58	220.63	202.43	103.4
1982	1.2344	6.5794	2.4281	1354.00	249.06	174.80	116.6
1983	1.2325	7.6204	2.5539	1519.32	237.55	151.59	125.3
1984	1.2952	8.7356	2.8455	1756.11	237.46	133.68	138.2
1985	1.3659	8.9800	2.9420	1908.88	238.47	129.74	143.0
1986	1.3896	6.9257	2.1705	1491.16	168.35	146.77	112.2
1987	1.3259	6.0122	1.7981	1297.03	144.60	163.98	96.9
1988	1.2306	5.9595	1.7570	1302.39	128.17	178.13	92.7
1989	1.1842	6.3802	1.8808	1372.28	138.07	163.82	98.6
1990	1.1668	5.4467	1.6166	1198.27	145.00	178.41	89.1
1991	1.1460	5.6468	1.6610	1241.28	134.59	176.74	89.8
1992	1.2085	5.2935	1.5618	1232.17	126.78	176.63	86.6

Source: Board of Governors, Federal Reserve System.

*Weights are 1972–1976 global trade of each of the G-10 countries (with which the U.S. trades, Belgium, Netherlands, Sweden, and Switzerland in addition to countries included in this table).

these goods, services, and assets determines the intensity of demand for the dollar and, thus, its foreign exchange value.

The determinants of foreign exchange value are numerous and complex. Four sets of variables, however, deserve special consideration: (1) the pace of economic activity, (2) interest rates, (3) inflation rates, and (4) political conditions:

1. *Economic activity* in the two nations affects the relative demand for imports and the ability of a country to export. When economic activity in

the United States slumps (1980–1982), import demand is likely to fall off, lessening the demand for the foreign currency, resulting in dollar appreciation. On the other hand, when U.S. economic growth is strong (1984–1989), import demand is likely to rise, so the demand for the foreign currency will increase resulting in dollar depreciation.

2. *Interest rates* have a direct effect on exchange rates because of international investment flows. Foreign investors will be attracted to investment in U.S. assets when interest rates are high, so demand for the dollar will increase leading to appreciation. Conversely, if U.S. interest rates are low relative to other countries' interest rates, there will be a flight from dollar-denominated assets and the dollar will depreciate.

3. *Inflation* exerts a more complex effect. Modestly rising inflation is likely to lead to a domestic monetary policy tightening with higher interest rates. However, to the extent that the higher interest rates merely reflect the higher inflation premium, foreign investors are likely to be shy of investing in fixed interest rate assets. The decision to invest—and, so, the demand for the dollar—will depend on foreign investors' relative expectations about inflation in the United States compared to their expectations about inflation in their own countries.

4. The *political* concerns relate to foreigners' confidence that the political system in a country will be stable enough to ensure that they can convert their future returns back to their own currency. Fortunately, this has seldom been a concern of U.S. dollar holders (except, perhaps in the final days of the Nixon administration). It is a concern that does arise in other even quite developed countries.

The key point is that a manager like Alan Block needs to take a great deal of macroeconomic information into account in managing a firm's foreign exchange exposure.

The last column in Table 7–3 shows an index (March 1973 = 100) of the *trade-weighted value of the U.S. dollar.* This is a convenient way of summarizing the dollar's foreign exchange value against a range of currencies. Each currency is weighted in an index according to that nation's share of the U.S. total trade (exports plus imports) with all 10 nations. Figure 7–2 shows a plot of this index, providing an account of the dollar's foreign exchange movements since floating exchange rates began.

By early 1973, the dollar had already undergone a 20 percent *devaluation.* In the days of fixed exchange rates, changes in a currency's foreign exchange value resulted from explicit policy changes. (*Depreciation,* on the other hand, is a continuous, market-driven process.) The dollar appreciated through 1976, as the U.S. economy recovered from its worst post-World War II recession. The

FIGURE 7–2 Trade-weighted U.S. dollar foreign exchange value.

March 1973 = 100

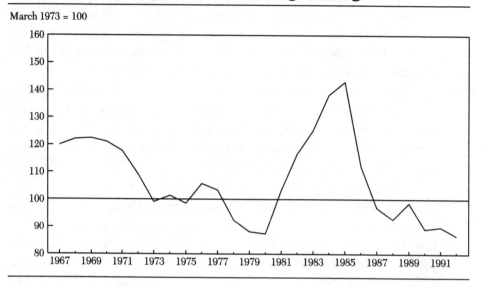

persistent inflation and erosion of confidence during the late 1970s and the two recessions of the early 1980s led to a fairly steady depreciation through 1980.

With recovery in 1983, and the ensuing increased foreign demand for U.S. Treasury securities—coinciding with the sharp widening in the federal budget deficit—the dollar appreciated strongly. One consequence of the appreciation of the dollar was a falloff in demand for U.S. exports, which had become very expensive in foreign currency terms, and a soaring demand for foreign imports, which had become cheap in dollar terms. Ultimately the plunging current account deficits (see Table 7–1) caused both foreigners and U.S. international investors to look for a realignment of exchange rates.

The dollar reached its peak foreign exchange level in February 1985. Subsequently, aided by coordinated efforts of the central banks, the dollar declined to a level that permitted a narrower current account deficit. In 1992, the dollar was some 13 percent below its 1973 level and, in fact, at the end of 1993 was still nearly 5 percent below that level.

Fluctuations in an economy's foreign exchange rate are likely and are beyond the control of any corporation, let alone a particular manager. The key point for a manager is to be aware of the forces that shape foreign exchange values and to be prepared to react to them.

SUMMARY

Thus far in this text, the discussion of domestic as well as international economic relationships has been at a highly aggregate—macroeconomic—level. In Part Two, we will look at the *microeconomic* underpinnings of economic relationships. An explanation of the reasons for trade falls properly in microeconomics, but it can be briefly touched on here.

Different nations are endowed (blessed or cursed) with different combinations of the factors of production. For instance, among developed nations, the United States has an abundance of fertile land, whereas Japan has an abundance of highly educated workers. Thus, the United States specializes in the production of grains and harvests far more corn and wheat in a good year than it can consume, so it exports the excess. Similarly, Japanese workers are admirably suited to the production of high-tech electronic equipment. They manufacture far more than is absorbed by their domestic market, hence, the renowned state of Japanese electronics exports.

Although the United States also produces high-tech electronics and Japan produces (albeit much more inefficiently) grain in the form of rice, a general rule can be stated:

> A nation will specialize in the production of a good that requires a great deal of its abundant resource(s). The nation will export the surplus (over and above what is profitably required to satisfy domestic needs). The nation will import goods and services that use a great deal of the resource(s) in tight supply. Thus international trade in goods and services supplements the resource endowments of a nation.

In this way, *micro* economics underlies many of our *macro* economic relationships.

PART TWO

MICROECONOMICS

UNDERSTANDING
8 THE MARKET
PROCESS
The Basic Elements of Supply and Demand

Macroeconomics, the subject of Part One in this book, is the study of the aggregate economy. Beginning with this chapter, we turn our attention to microeconomics: the study of buyers and sellers in individual markets within the larger economy. As this book is being written, American industry is in the throes of change. Words such as "restructuring," "rationalizing," "rightsizing," and "reengineering" are being used to describe this change. But they all add up to the same thing: Companies are refocusing their efforts around their "core competencies" while stripping away layers of management, reducing work forces, and challenging their remaining workers to do more work with less resources. The macroeconomic forces of the 1990–1991 recession caused part of this change. But much of it is because of the microeconomic forces of increasing competition (both domestic and international), technological advancements, and shifts in consumer tastes and preferences. As a result of this downsizing, American managers of the postwar era are being tested as they have never been before in their ability to deal with the basic microeconomic problem: the allocation of scarce resources among competing uses.

In economic analysis, scarcity is defined as a situation in which resources are limited relative to the demand for their use. Whenever scarcity exists, choices must be made about how to allocate resources among competing uses. Managers of companies are continually making decisions about the allocation of scarce resources. From an operational standpoint, dealing with the condition of scarcity means managing within the confines of an annual budget. From a

143

planning perspective, dealing with scarcity means the making of strategic decisions about what markets to compete in and how much of the total budget to allocate to each of these markets.

MANAGEMENT DECISIONS ABOUT THE ALLOCATION OF SCARCE RESOURCES

There are two basic types of management decisions about the allocation of scarce resources: One concerns a company's output of goods and services; and the other involves its input of labor, materials, and plant and equipment. The key questions that must be answered in making the output decision are:

> Should our firm be in the market for a particular good or service? What should the extent of our participation be in a particular market? That is, are we going to be a major player or are we going to be content to have only a small part of the market?

Some examples of the output decision that have been reported in the popular press in recent years follow:

Entering into Markets

- PepsiCo, the parent company of Pepsi-Cola, adopts a strategy to make and sell snacks and fast foods as well as soft drink beverages. Currently, about two-thirds of its revenues are derived from its food business (for example, Frito-Lay, Kentucky Fried Chicken, Pizza Hut, and Taco Bell).
- Computer Associates, a leading producer of software applications for mainframe computers, decides to enter the market for PC software applications by offering a personal finance program for the PC that will compete directly against such popular packages as "Quicken."
- Wal-Mart, the retail merchandising giant, decides to build and operate a chain of supermarkets similar in size and price structure to its main line of business.
- General Motors, Ford, and General Electric decide to compete in the revolving credit card business, following the path of another major manufacturing and service company, AT&T.

Exiting from Markets

- IBM decides to sell its typewriter business to a group of private investors and its copier business to Kodak.

- Sears decides to discontinue selling its products through its catalogue, the very channel of distribution that established it as the leading retail merchandising company in the United States.
- After some years of trying to establish itself in the orange juice market, Procter & Gamble decides to stop making Citrus Hill orange juice.
- Tandy, one of the pioneers in the personal computer industry, decides to sell its personal computer manufacturing facilities to AST.
- U.S. West, one of the seven regional Bell operating companies, sells its finance company to the Nationsbank Corporation.

Expanding or Contracting in a Particular Market

- Anheuser-Busch, the leading producer of beer in the United States, announces its intention of increasing its market share from 45 percent to over 50 percent.
- NEC announces its intention of becoming a major player in the U.S. personal computer market. At the time of its announcement, its share in this market was only about 1.5 percent.
- American Airlines decides to exit from certain short distance routes in the western region of the United States because of intense price competition from Southwest Airlines.
- Sears decides to close a number of its retail stores as part of its overall effort to restore profitability in its merchandising business.

The decision concerning the utilization of a firm's inputs basically deals with questions about hiring, staffing, and capital expenditures. How many people should be hired or laid off? Should a new plant be built? Should existing plants be closed? Should work be done by outside vendors or by company personnel? How many people should be assigned to work at a particular office or plant? How much machinery and equipment should a company use relative to its labor force? That is, should it strive to be a "capital intensive" or "labor intensive" operation? As pointed out at the beginning of this chapter, in the first half of the 1990s, resource cutbacks have dominated the company input decisions appearing in the news.

BASIC PROCESSES FOR MAKING ALLOCATION DECISIONS

Three basic processes govern the way management decisions are made about what goods and services to produce, and how to combine labor, materials, and plant and equipment to produce these goods and services. These processes are (1) the market process, (2) the command process, and (3) the traditional process. Let us first look at the market process.

The *market process* relies on supply, demand, and material incentive to help managers decide how to allocate their scarce resources. A key feature of this process is the market price, which serves as a signal to companies about how to allocate their scarce resources. In the market process, a firm will produce a particular good or service if its price is high enough relative to its unit cost to enable it to earn an adequate profit. The level of market price itself is determined or at least influenced by the forces of supply and demand. This chapter deals primarily with the market process, but before continuing with this subject, we will briefly examine the command and traditional processes.

The *command process* uses the powers of central authorities to decide on the allocation of resources. In socialist or communist countries, government officials make most, if not all the decisions. In market economies such as the United States, the command process can be seen in the powers of government to spend and tax and to establish laws regulating business activities. The automobile industry provides an example of this activity. Government environmental protection laws have affected the input decisions of car makers by requiring them to equip their cars with catalytic converters. This has also affected the output decision by creating a new market opportunity for companies such as Corning Glass that manufacture these converters for the auto industry.

In the *traditional process,* the allocation of scarce resources is determined by customs and tradition. This process is prevalent in less industrialized, developing countries. For example, in India, the output decision is informed by certain religious beliefs forbidding the eating of beef. In Moslem countries, pork is not produced because religious beliefs prohibit its consumption. The consideration of a person's family, clan, or tribal relationship is often a key factor in the making of a hiring decision in developing countries. Customs and traditions can also play a role in influencing decisions in developed, industrial economies. But here, the market process is usually intertwined with the custom or tradition. For example, the success and even the survival of the toy industry and many retail establishments depend on the customs and traditions of such religious celebrations as Christmas and Hanukkah.

THE MECHANICS OF SUPPLY AND DEMAND

We begin out market analysis by first looking at demand. It is commonplace these days for companies to strive to be "market-driven" or "demand-driven." Actually, as explained throughout this chapter, they are simply responding to the forces of supply and demand in the market process. The key factors that influence the demand for a particular good or service are price, income, tastes and preferences, prices of related products, future expectations among buyers about changes in the price of the product and the number of buyers in the market. We will first focus on the relationship between price and the amount that people are willing to buy of a particular product while holding constant the other factors that we know can influence demand.

The relationship between price and the quantity demanded can be represented as a downward sloping curve, as shown in Figure 8–1(a). This curve indicates that people are willing to buy more as the price falls and less as the price rises, if other factors besides the price are held constant. A change in one or more of the nonprice factors will cause a change in the entire demand curve. Graphically, this implies a rightward shift in the demand curve if demand increases and a leftward shift if it decreases. This is shown in Figure 8–1(b).

We can illustrate the mechanics in Figure 8–1 by looking at the demand for hamburgers in the fast-food market. Assume that a typical consumer of fast-food hamburgers behaves as follows: At a price of $2.50, this consumer is willing to buy 1 hamburger per week. At $1.50, he or she is willing to buy 2; at $1.00 he or she is willing to buy 3. If there are 50 million consumers of fast-food hamburgers who react to prices in exactly the same way, the total market demand can be illustrated as shown in Table 8–1.

If any factor besides the price changes, it would cause the demand for hamburgers in the fast-food market to change, thereby shifting the demand curve either to the left or to the right. When this occurs, it means that consumers are willing to buy more or less of a product, *regardless of the price of the*

FIGURE 8–1   The demand curve.

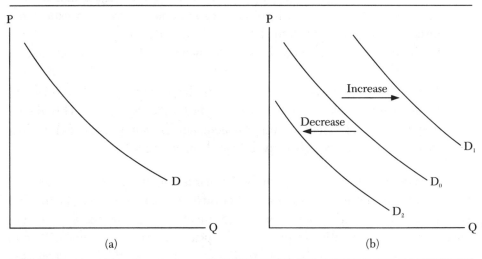

(a)   (b)

TABLE 8–1 Demand for hamburgers (weekly).

Price	Individual Demand (Typical Consumer)	Market Demand (All Consumers)
$2.00	1	50 million
1.50	2	100 million
1.00	3	150 million

product. The following examples show how changes in the nonprice determinants of hamburgers can change its demand:

1. *Tastes and Preferences.* If people become more conscious of certain *negative health effects* of eating red meat, they may be inclined to buy fewer hamburgers, no matter what their market price (leftward shift in demand curve).

2. *Income.* The impact of this factor on hamburger consumption in the fast-food market is somewhat ambiguous. Normally, we expect that changes in income would have a direct impact on the demand for any product, including hamburgers. For example, if the increase in income causes a decrease in the demand for hamburgers (because of an overwhelming shift by consumers to more desirable substitutes) then economists would consider hamburgers to be an "inferior" product.

3. *Price of Related Products (Substitutes or Complements).* If we assume hot dogs are a substitute product for hamburgers, a *rise in the price of hot dogs* would result in an *increase in the demand* for the hamburgers (rightward shift in demand curve).

4. *Future Expectations.* This factor is not expected to play a major role in influencing the demand for hamburgers. It is far more important in markets where speculation is involved. For example, if investors expect the price of a particular stock to rise in the future, they may be more inclined to purchase the stock today. This would then cause the current demand for the stock to increase.

5. *Number of Buyers.* As baby boomers, the largest age group in the United States, become older, their desire for fast food decreases. This demographic shift adversely affects the demand for hamburgers sold in fast-food establishments (leftward shift in demand curve).

We now turn to an examination of the market supply. Supply is the amount that all firms in the market want to sell at different prices, if other factors besides the price are held constant. Sellers are inclined to exhibit the opposite behavior from buyers relative to price. As the price increases, they are willing to sell more, because it would be more profitable to do so. As the price decreases,

FIGURE 8–2   The supply curve.

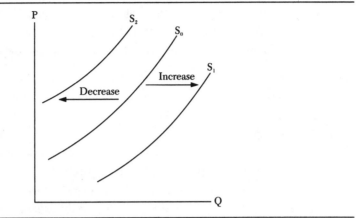

the decrease in profitability causes them to want to sell less of their product. Figure 8–2 illustrates a typical upward sloping supply curve and shows how it would shift when supply increases or decreases.

Factors other than price that influence the supply are (1) cost of production, (2) technology, (3) prices of other products that sellers could provide, (4) future expectations, (5) number of sellers, and (6) weather conditions. The following examples show how changes in each of these factors could change the supply for hamburgers in the fast-food market:

1. *Cost of Production.* The government raises the minimum wage level. This increases the wage costs of fast-food firms and causes a decrease in the supply of hamburgers (leftward shift in supply curve).
2. *Technology.* Sophisticated data networks enable fast-food chains to drastically reduce their inventories. The resulting cost savings causes supply to increase (rightward shift in supply curve).
3. *Prices of Other Products That Can Be Sold.* The increasing price (and hence profitability) of pizza prompts many hamburger franchises to devote more resources to pizza and less to hamburgers (leftward shift in supply curve).
4. *Future Expectations.* Just as in the case of demand, this factor is not expected to have much of an impact on the supply of hamburgers. (Refer back to the previous comment on future expectations and the demand for hamburgers.)
5. *Number of Sellers.* This factor's impact on supply is quite apparent. For example, suppose one of the fast-food chains decided to expand the number of its franchises in the United States. This would increase the supply of hamburgers (rightward shift in supply).

6. *Weather Conditions.* Suppose a summer drought ruins the wheat crop, which in turn raises the prices of flour and bread. The resulting increase in the cost of hamburger buns is expected to reduce the supply of hamburgers in the fast-food market (leftward shift in supply).

The workings of the market process can now be seen by combining demand and supply together. Figure 8–3(a) shows how supply and demand interact to determine the market price. The equilibrium price is indicated as P_1 and occurs at the point where the quantity that people are willing to buy is equal to that which people are willing to sell (shown in Figure 8–3(a) as Q_1). Figure 8–3(b) illustrates why P_1 is the equilibrium or market clearing price. If the price were lower than this level (shown as P'), there would be a shortage because the amount that people would be willing to buy would exceed the amount that people would be willing to sell. This shortage would cause upward pressures on the price until it reached its market clearing level, P_1. If the price were higher than P_1, shown in the figure as P'', then there would be a surplus because the quantity supplies would exceed the quantity demanded. This condition would cause price to fall until it reached the market clearing level, P_1.

CHANGES IN MARKET CONDITIONS

The notion of equilibrium price is actually only a convenient starting point in market analysis. Whenever there is a change in one of the nonprice determinants of supply or demand, market equilibrium is disturbed. Business reports

FIGURE 8–3   Market equilibrium, shortage, and surplus.

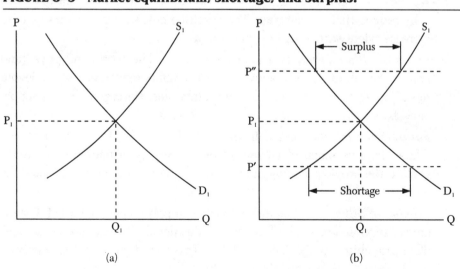

(a)   (b)

and the popular press often refer to this as a "change in market conditions." For example, Figure 8–4 shows the results of consumers deciding to eat less red meat. This change in tastes or preferences causes a decrease in demand (a leftward shift in the demand curve) for hamburgers. The market price then falls to P_2. The quantity bought and sold also falls to Q_2.

The following diagram summarizes the impact that changes in supply and demand are expected to have on market prices and the quantity bought and sold:

$D \uparrow$	$P \uparrow$	$Q \uparrow$
$D \downarrow$	$P \downarrow$	$Q \downarrow$
$S \uparrow$	$P \downarrow$	$Q \uparrow$
$S \downarrow$	$P \uparrow$	$Q \downarrow$

We have shown simple cases in which there is only one change in either supply or demand. In reality, there may be different factors causing changes in both supply and demand. For example, suppose that in the midst of an economic recovery, the number of new entrants into the restaurant and fast-food businesses increases. We assume the recovery would have a positive impact on demand for hamburgers and the new entrants would have a positive impact on the supply. Glancing at the diagram reminds us that an increase in demand causes prices to rise, while an increase in supply causes it to fall. Whether the price rises or falls therefore depends on the change in demand relative to supply. If demand increases more than supply, the price would rise. If it increases by less than supply, the price would fall.

To sort out the separate effects of supply and demand, it might sometimes be useful to start with observed changes in price and then to ask what this

FIGURE 8–4   Decrease in demand.

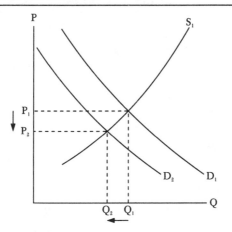

change implies about changes in supply and demand. For example, we can observe that the average price of a compact disc has fallen in recent years. At the same time, we can assume that the demand for CDs has increased because of changing tastes and preferences and because the price of CD players (the complementary product) has fallen. This increase in demand should have caused the price to rise. Since the price has fallen, it must mean that the supply of CDs has increased by more than the demand.

Another complicating feature of supply-and-demand analysis is the possibility that initial changes in one of them will eventually be followed by changes in the other. Returning to the example illustrated in Figure 8–4, if nothing else happens to disturb the market price of hamburgers at its lower level, we can expect further repercussions from the supply side of the market. That is, sellers may find their profits falling as a result of the lower prices. Some of them may start to reduce their capacity; for example, they may close down less profitable store operations. Others may simply decide to leave this market, as Tandy did in the market for PCs. When this occurs, supply will start to decrease and the market price may start to rise again (see Figure 8–5). This in turn may start to restore the profitability of those sellers remaining in the market.

Changes that first occur on the supply side of the market can also be expected to cause follow-on changes in demand. Suppose higher costs cause the market supply to decrease. This would then cause the price to rise as shown in Figure 8–5. This is accompanied by a reduction in the amount bought and sold (Q_2). At the higher price, people buy less hamburgers per time period. If the price of hamburgers remains at this higher level, it may eventually cause people who eat hamburgers regularly to start to look seriously at alternatives such as pizza, hot dogs, and tacos. As their tastes and preferences change due to the

FIGURE 8–5   Decrease in demand and follow-on decrease in supply.

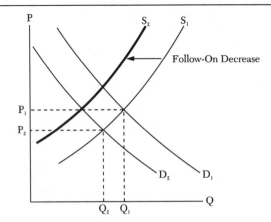

FIGURE 8–6   Decrease in supply and follow-on decrease in demand.

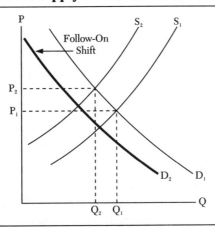

higher price, the demand itself may start to decrease. That is, people will want to buy less hamburgers regardless of the price. The initial and follow-on phases are shown in Figure 8–6.

Economic theory provides a very useful way to distinguish between the initial and the follow-on phases of the market. An initial change in supply or demand and the resulting change in market price are the components of the "short-run" market time period. Any follow-on change by either supply or demand is considered to be part of the "long-run" market time period. Table 8–2 summarizes the short- and long-run changes in supply and demand.

A word of caution to managers who would like to apply the distinction between the short- and long-run time periods in the analysis of their own markets.

TABLE 8–2   Short- and long-run changes in the market.

Initial Change (Short-Run Time Period)	Follow-On Change (Long-Run Time Period)
Increase in demand causes *price to rise*	*Supply increases* as new sellers enter the market and original sellers increase production capacity
Decrease in demand causes *price to fall*	*Supply decreases* as less profitable firms or those experiencing losses exit the market or decrease production capacity
Increase in supply causes *price to fall*	*Demand increases* as tastes and preferences of consumers eventually change in favor of the product relative to substitutes
Decrease in supply causes *price to rise*	*Demand decreases* as tastes and preferences of consumers eventually change away from the product and toward the substitutes

In actual business situations, there may not be the nice and neat changes illustrated in Table 8–2. For example, there may be an initial increase in demand resulting in higher prices and profits. But then changes in market conditions may cause a decrease in demand, and firms hoping to enter the market to take advantage of high demand, prices, and profits may find themselves in an adverse situation. Therefore, before entering a market, it is wise to assess how sustainable the higher demand actually is. For example, during the 1980s, the fast-food business grew at a double-digit rate. Then in the early 1990s, the rate of increase slowed to about 5 percent per annum. If you entered the fast-food market at this time expecting sales to continue growing at double-digit rates, you would have been sorely disappointed.

We should offer another cautionary note. If you identify an attractive market that has price and profit potential, so will others. If your firm and many others all enter the market at the same time, your combined actions may well increase the market supply sufficiently to cause the market price to collapse. A remark once made by a manager in the personal computer industry exemplifies this situation: "In the early days of the PC business, it was like all the competitors were sitting around sipping out of straws from a swimming pool filled with champagne. Now, it's so crowded that no one can get near the pool."

DIFFERENT MARKET TYPES

In applying the knowledge of supply and demand to business decisions, it is important for managers to understand that competition among firms occurs in different types of market environments. Essentially, these different market types determine the extent to which individual firms can exert control over the market price. In the most extreme case, many small firms sell the same product, and consequently, they have virtually no control over the market price. Instead, they must act as "price takers," selling at the price dictated by the interplay of supply and demand. This type of market is called perfect competition.

On the other side of the spectrum of "market power"—the power to determine a product's price—is a monopoly market. There is only one seller in this market and its singularity enables it to wield a considerable amount of market power. Somewhere in between the two extremes are markets that economists call oligopoly and monopolistic competition. In these markets, sellers exercise varying degrees of control over price because of their relative size or because they have successfully differentiated their products from their competitors. However, this market power is kept in check by other competitors in the market. Let us now take a closer look at each of these four basic market types.

Perfect Competition

This market has the following characteristics: (1) a large number of relatively small buyers and sellers, (2) a standardized product, (3) easy market entry or exit, and (4) complete information by all participants about the going market price. Because of these characteristics, firms in this type of market have no power whatsoever over the market price. Instead, price is determined by the interactive forces of supply and demand. Characteristic 1 means that each firm is so small that it is unable to control price by either increasing or decreasing its own supply in the market. Characteristic 2 means that no firm can charge a higher price by saying that its product is superior to the rest of the competition. Each seller offers the same product. Characteristic 3 means that if for any reason sellers are enjoying very high profits because of the high market price, entry into the market by newcomers will quickly reduce the price as well as profits. Characteristic 4 means that no seller can exert a higher price because of the ignorance of the lower price offered by other sellers in the market.

Agricultural commodities (wheat, corn, pork bellies, coffee beans, etc.), financial instruments (U.S. government securities, corporate stocks and bonds, currencies traded in the foreign exchange market, etc.), and precious metals are all good examples of the products exchanged in perfectly competitive markets. A key characteristic of all these products is price volatility. Indeed, their prices move by the hour or even by the minute as those who trade in these commodities shift their supply and demand. These shifts are often based on speculative perceptions of future price movements or news flashes such as rumors of the assassination of a head of state or the outbreak of fighting in some part of the world. Headline news is constantly being flashed by such news agencies as Reuters. Also, a television set tuned to CNN often sits alongside the many computer screens of financial traders.

Monopoly

A monopoly market has the following characteristics: (1) one seller, (2) a product that is usually unique or has no close substitutes, and (3) legal barriers that often block market entry and exit. The market power of a monopoly stems from its being the only seller. Companies protected by government patent laws, regulated public utilities, and cable TV companies are good examples of this type of market. Since the government controls entry or exit, the monopoly is protected as long as the government allows. A regulated monopoly such as the local gas or electric utility can establish its own pricing structure, but it must first obtain approval from a regulatory commission. The pricing policy of firms that sell patent-protected products does not have to follow any government oversight. But as will be seen in greater detail in subsequent chapters, unregulated monopoly pricing is still subject to the laws of demand.

If the monopoly sets a price that is too high, the resulting number of units sold could be too few to be profitable. Furthermore, even a monopoly cannot always prevent a substantial drop in demand because of the introduction of competing substitutes. For example, although Polaroid continues to enjoy a monopoly in the making of instant developing cameras (thanks to a successful lawsuit against Kodak), the demand for this type of camera has fallen off because of the success of the one-hour photo developing process and the growing use of video cameras. These new competitors have in effect broken Polaroid's monopoly and have constrained its ability to raise the price of its products.

Monopolistic Competition

This market is characterized by (1) a large number of relatively small buyers and sellers, (2) a differentiated product, (3) relatively easy market entry and exit, and (4) complete information about market price. It essentially differs from perfect competition in characteristic 2. For the most part, buyers and sellers must adhere to a price determined by the interaction of supply and demand. But those sellers who can differentiate their products from their competitors are able to set their prices at levels above everyone else.

The best examples of monopolistic competition can be found among small, retail enterprises. For example, there may be many dry cleaners in a town all offering essentially the same service. However, one may offer faster service on certain items; another may be conveniently located next to a train station or a municipal parking lot. Still another may simply offer a higher quality service. Each of these differences might enable a firm to charge a higher price than that of the other competitors. However, in these markets, the price differences—if any—are usually slight. Even though a particular firm may achieve considerable product differentiation, the ease of entry into this market makes it difficult for any one competitor to sustain such differentiations. For example, recall the first video rental store that opened in your town or neighborhood. Compare its market power (if it is still in business) today with that time. The increasing number of video rental stores, including national chains such as Blockbuster Video, make it extremely difficult for any one establishment to exercise market power.

Oligopoly

Oligopoly is characterized by (1) a relatively small number of large sellers, (2) either a standardized or a differentiated product, (3) relatively difficult market entry, and (4) complete information about market prices. Quite often, an oligopoly might have a few large sellers that earn the majority of a market's total revenue, with a larger number of smaller "niche" companies making up the difference. Entry of newcomers into this market is usually difficult because there may be high start-up costs, well-established brand names, or distribution systems that effectively prevent new entrants. The best examples of oligopolistic markets can be found in the manufacturing, communications, and transportation sectors. Table 8–3 shows examples of oligopoly markets in the United States.

The pricing of a product is often done by one of the competitors, called the "price leader." Once the leader sets the price, everyone else usually follows. If this pricing discipline is not observed, price wars may break out. This happened in the airline industry during the summer of 1992. American Airlines tried to play the role of the price leader by establishing a simplified fare structure. Many of the other large airlines did not want to go along with this and continued to offer a wide array of tickets at severely discounted rates. American Airlines retaliated. In the end, many fares were so low that the entire industry, particularly American Airlines, lost a considerable amount of money. More will

TABLE 8–3   Examples of oligopoly markets in the United States, 1989, 1990, or 1991.

Fed Cattle Producers (SIC 0210)*: 1990		High Fructose Corn Syrup (SIC 2046): 1991	
IBP	32.8%	ADM	30.7%
ConAgra	26.8	Staley	24.0
Cargill	21.6	Cargill	18.4
Other	18.8	CPC	11.0
		American Maize	9.0
Antilock Brake Manufacturers (SIC 3714): 1989		Roquette	5.4
		Coors	1.5
Kelsey Hayes	86.6%		
ITT Teves	7.9	Cereal (SIC 2043): 1990	
Bendix	3.1	Kellogg's	38.0%
Bosch	1.5	General Mills	24.1
Delco Moraine	.9	General Foods	11.1
		Quaker Oats	7.4
Car Rental Companies (SIC 7514): 1991		Ralston Purina	6.2
		Other	13.2
Hertz	29.3%		
Avis	25.1		
Budget	19.3		
National	15.9		
Dollar	5.5		
Other	4.9		

Source: Market Share Reporter, Detroit, Gale Research, Inc., 1992 Second Edition.
*Standard Industrial Classification Code Number.

be said about all four types of markets in Chapter 11 when we examine the pricing and output decisions of firms in each type of market.

THE IMPORTANCE OF UNDERSTANDING THE FORCES OF SUPPLY AND DEMAND

Knowledge of market supply and demand helps managers to assess their company's competitive environment. The following examples illustrate recent shifts in demand that have presented different sets of opportunities as well as threats to the firms in these markets:

1. *In the Beverage Industry.* The increase in the demand for "new age" soft drinks, juices, and bottled waters. Among other things, this has prompted Pepsi-Cola to produce a "clear" cola drink.
2. *In Retail Merchandising.* The shift by consumers from full-service department stores to discount or "everyday low price" stores, warehouses, and shopping clubs. This has benefited chains such as Wal-Mart, K-Mart and Home Depot, while hurting traditional full-service department stores such as Sears.
3. *In the Computer Industry.* The shift from centralized, mainframe computing, to decentralized computing using local or wide-area networks of personal computers or workstations. This has helped companies such as Sun Microsystems and Hewlett-Packard who were early entrants into the workstation market. This has hurt IBM, a late entrant into the workstation market.
4. *In the Fast-Food Industry.* The demographic shift whereby the age group that most frequently patronizes such staples as McDonald's and Burger King has now moved into the age grouping that still wants speed and convenience but also a more traditional sit-down meal. This has benefited chains such as Chili's and Bennigan's and has adversely affected chains such as McDonald's. In response to this shift in demand, Burger King now offers table service for its evening meals in some of its locations.
5. *In the Music Industry.* The rapid growth in popularity of compact discs, which has all but eliminated the polyvinyl long-playing record. Sales of this item are now confined to specialty shops in large urban areas.

The preceding examples indicate that changes in demand can be caused by gradual demographic shifts, or they may be caused by rapid shifts in the whims of consumers or the introduction of new technology. It is easy to apply 20-20 hindsight in pointing out these examples, but they suggest that the managers who are first to recognize and adjust to such market changes will be the most successful.

Companies that do not anticipate or adapt to market changes are bound to be hurt. One such company is the Digital Equipment Company (DEC). As reported in the *New York Times* (Dec. 23, 1992), an important reason for DEC's poor performance in the late 1980s and early 1990s was, "Its engineers decided what products to make, leaving the marketing and salespeople the job of finding customers." One industry analyst was quoted as saying, "These products were literally thrown over the wall to people who were told to sell them." In an attempt to become a quicker respondent to changes in customer demand, DEC announced at the end of 1992 that it was grouping itself into 9 units. Five of these units would focus on certain industry groupings such as health care, the military, financial services, and communications. Four other units would focus on selected lines of business such as PCs, printers, storage systems, and maintenance.

Schwinn is another company severely hurt by its inability to understand market forces. The sadly ironic part about this case is that it has the most recognizable and respected brand name in the bicycle industry. It enjoyed its most prosperous period in the 1950s and early 1960s, when millions of baby boomers dreamed of getting a Schwinn Phantom Racer for Christmas. Throughout the late 1970s and the 1980s, Schwinn completely missed the growing trend toward mountain bikes. Furthermore, it was inadequately prepared to meet the onslaught of cheaper bikes manufactured in low-wage Asian countries. In these regards, Schwinn failed to understand the forces of *both* demand and supply in its business. Schwinn's experience shows that product differentiation is not enough to offset new market entrants (particularly lower priced ones) and substantial shifts in consumer tastes and preferences. In 1992, it filed for bankruptcy protection and began negotiating to sell most of its assets, including the use of its treasured name, to other companies. In 1993, under new management, Schwinn offered a revitalized line of bikes, including the popular mountain bike.

Sometimes, changes in market conditions affect, not the demand itself, but rather the channels through which sellers meet customers' demands for goods and services. Managers must be equally aware of this variation on a theme if their companies are to survive. A good example of this is the case of Avon. "Ding-Dong, Avon Calling" . . . sorry nobody home! Beginning in the 1970s, there was a dramatic increase in the number of women entering the workforce. Avon continued to use its door to door sales representatives as its major channel of distribution. Finally in the late 80s, Avon was forced to supplement its traditional way of doing business with such methods as direct-mail contacts that solicited 800 number responses and the setting up of corporate lunches or meetings to sell Avon products to the growing number of women in the workforce.

PepsiCo is another example of a company having to adjust to changing demand via distribution channels. In mid-1993, it began an effort to offset the decline in the rate of growth in the fast-food market by experimenting with different ways to sell the products of its three fast-food subsidiaries: Taco Bell, Pizza Hut, and Kentucky Fried Chicken (KFC). For example, it is starting to use double drive-throughs in selected locations. It has also started selling tacos and pizzas from carts located in such places as stadiums and county fairs. Taco Bell and Pizza Hut outlets are also being set up in supermarkets. PepsiCo is even placing Taco Bell carts in some of its KFC and Pizza Hut establishments in Mexico to give the Mexicans a chance to try American-style tacos.

Failure to be completely market focused is found not only among American companies. A recent article in *The Wall Street Journal* (Dec. 30, 1992) points out how Samsung, South Korea's largest company, is starting to send its managers on 1-year paid leaves of absence around the world to learn more about the tastes and preferences of its international customers. It is doing this because "like all Korean companies, [it] is struggling with a tougher international environment. A generation of Korean managers came of age thinking that *if they build it, they could sell it* [emphasis added]. Now, the companies, sandwiched between low-wage workers in Malaysia or China on one side, and U.S. or Japanese high technology on the other, have lost market share."

An understanding of the factors that change market supply is just as important for managers as the factors affecting market demand. In particular, it is important for managers to anticipate changes in market supply by assessing the reaction of actual and potential competitors in markets where demand has undergone a sustained change. Earlier in this chapter, we stated that existing firms in markets that are extremely profitable because of rising demand will eventually find increased competition from new entrants and the increased production capacity of existing sellers. Indeed, those managers who complain about increasing competition from new entrants might well consider the alternative: If the market in which they are competing is unprofitable or not profitable enough, then who would want to remain or enter?

One of today's most prominent entrepreneur/executives, William Gates of Microsoft is far from resting on his company's recent successes. Fully aware of the limits to growth in the market for PC operating software, Gates is increasing his company's efforts in the development of software for multimedia applications and interactive television. He is also working to develop software that will link all the different office hardware (computers, printers, fax machines, voice and data storage, and transport devices) into one seamless digital network.

Sometimes, a company ignores competitive threats from new entrants into the market because it is so large it does not view these entrants as serious threats . . . until it is possibly too late. A good example of this is the case of

United Parcel Service (UPS) in the early 1990s. Up through the mid-1980s, the ubiquitous brown trucks dominated the package delivery industry. But beginning in the second half of that decade and continuing into the next, other companies have seriously threatened UPS's dominance. Between 1987 and 1991, the annual increase in package volume for Roadway Package System was about 35 percent. The rate of increase for Airborne Express during the same time period was slightly over 30 percent; for Federal Express it was over 10 percent. The volume for UPS increased at an annual rate of only about 5 percent. Still worse, UPS's profit margin slid from a high of about 7 percent in 1987 down to about 4 percent between 1990 and 1993. To counter the growing threat from its competitors, UPS has had to be much more market focused and efficient. For example, it began to shift its focus from residential deliveries (its traditional core business) to commercial deliveries, the segment of the market that commands a higher profit margin. It has also begun utilizing the latest technology such as the connecting of its delivery trucks to the central office via a wireless network.

EVOLUTION OF A MARKET STRUCTURE

In actual business situations, it is quite possible for a market to evolve from one market type to another for various reasons. For example, the deregulation of the telecommunications industry helped to change the long-distance market from a monopoly to an oligopoly. The deregulation of the airline industry was intended to increase the degree of competition in this business. In terms of the market categories used by economists, we can say that the expectation was that the airline industry would evolve from "regulated oligopoly" to unregulated "monopolistic competition." In recent years, however, as weaker airlines have dropped out of this business, the airline industry is beginning to look more like an unregulated oligopoly.

Government involvement is not the only factor that changes a market structure. Sometimes, the first entrepreneur to start a particular type of business—the first jewelry store in a shopping center, the first pizzeria or video store in a town—enjoys a temporary monopoly. As others realize how profitable this business can be, they begin to enter the market. Thus, a monopoly evolves into monopolistic competition.

International competition can also change the nature of a market. For years, economic textbooks described the American automobile industry as an oligopoly dominated by the big three companies, General Motors, Ford, and Chrysler. Today, with Japanese auto makers accounting for about 30 percent of the U.S. car market, this industry looks much more like monopolistic competition than an oligopoly.

The implications of the evolution of a market structure for decision makers in businesses is that they must be prepared to compete under different conditions as market structure changes. For example, when AT&T lost its government-protected monopoly, it had to reduce the number of its employees and to focus its pricing and product strategies much more closely to the needs of the market. When the airlines lost the security of a government-regulated fare structure, they had to be much more aware of the different sensitivities of passengers to the fare structure and to be much more wary of debilitating price wars among the competition. The huge losses that the major airlines continue to report year after year indicate that they have not yet learned how to make money in an unregulated market environment.

SUMMARY

Managers who strive to be market-driven or market-focused must have a thorough understanding of the basic mechanics of supply and demand. In particular, they must know all the possible factors that can cause shifts in supply and demand, both in the short term and over the long run. As much as possible, they should try to anticipate these shifts so they can better prepare their own companies for the changing competitive environment. We have pointed out in this chapter that companies have different degrees of market power, depending on the type of market in which they are competing. However, no company—with the possible exception of those completely protected by the government—can escape the market power of supply and demand.

9 CONSUMER RESPONSE

Analyzing Market Demand

Imagine these scenarios:

- You are an executive for a major computer company. Frustrated by the growing number of low-priced competitors, you decide in one fell swoop to introduce an entirely new, low-priced line of computers. To your surprise, the demand is so great that your production people cannot keep up with orders. Customers have to wait weeks and sometimes months for delivery.

- You are an executive for a major retail merchandising chain. Frustrated by the growing strength of low-priced competitors, you decide to go head to head against these companies by adopting an "everyday low price" (EDLP) policy. At the same time, you announce that your stores will begin carrying name-brand appliances and consumer electronics. To your surprise, there is some confusion and disbelief among your customers. They find it difficult to accept that your prices are indeed the lowest. Furthermore, even though your prices in most products are among the lowest, the increase in the volume of sales is not enough to offset the decrease in prices.

- You are the CEO of a major airline. The current economic recession has decreased the demand for air travel. As a result, you decide to build air traffic by offering very low airfares between major destinations. In doing so, you also hope to increase your demand by taking a certain amount of the shrinking market for air travel from your competitors. However, your major competitors quickly match your price cuts, and everyone in the industry suffers from the reductions.

163

Do these stories sound familiar? They should. The first case describes essentially what happened to Compaq in the fall of 1991 when it decided to launch its "Prolinea" line of low-priced computers to compete with the PC clones from Asia. The response was so great for the new computers that Compaq first had trouble meeting demand. The second case depicts Sears, back in 1988, when it decided to confront the growing threat from EDLP stores such as Wal-Mart, K-Mart, Target, and Circuit City. According to reports in the popular press, Sears' everyday low prices received an "everyday cold shoulder" from customers (Gannet News Service, Jan. 4, 1990). The third case involved the major U.S. airlines during the summer of 1992. Northwestern Airlines began by announcing drastically reduced fares but was quickly matched by the other airlines, thereby offsetting the benefits of a price reduction to Northwestern as well as all the other airlines that lowered prices.

These examples illustrate the importance to managers of understanding consumer response to price changes. In the first case, the response was greater than anticipated. In the second case, it was less. In the third case, the response was less than anticipated because competitors matched the price cut. If management had fully anticipated these outcomes, perhaps other decisions would have been made. For example, Compaq might have increased its production capacity before cutting its price to ensure that it could meet the higher demand. Sears might have even reconsidered its "EDLP" policy had it known how ineffective its price reductions were going to be. Had Northwestern known how closely and quickly the other major airlines were going to match its price cuts, it might have tried a different approach to stimulate demand.

This chapter presents a detailed look at the responsiveness of consumers to price changes. It will also look at how consumers respond to changes in other factors affecting demand, such as income and prices of substitute products. The key focus of this chapter, however, will be on price elasticity. If we look at the key factors that influence demand, then we can see that price is the variable subject to the greatest amount of management control. Consumers are free to choose whatever they wish. Managers can only hope to influence consumer tastes and preferences by advertising and promoting their product. People's incomes are affected by the macroeconomy and by such structural factors as labor productivity. Certainly, a manager cannot control the prices charged by companies selling competing products, the number of buyers in the market, or the future expectations of consumers.

DEMAND ELASTICITY

Demand elasticity can be defined as "the responsiveness of buyers to changes in price." It is also referred to as "price elasticity" or "price elasticity of demand."

As discussed in the previous chapter, the amount that people are willing to buy of a good or service and its price are inversely related. That is, consumers will buy *more* as the price of a good or service *decreases* and will buy *less* as the price *increases*. Compaq, Sears, and Northwestern could therefore assume that they were going to sell more when they lowered their prices. But what they hoped, but did not know for certain, was whether the increase in unit sales was going to be sufficient to offset their price reductions. From the seller's standpoint, therefore, it is important to know the extent of the consumer response relative to price changes.

Suppose at a price of $6, consumers buy 100 units per time period of a particular product. The total revenue earned by sellers is determined by the unit price multiplied by the quantity purchased. Thus, at a price of $6, sellers receive a revenue of $600. Suppose now that the price falls to $5 and as a result, consumers increase their purchases to 200 units per time period. In terms of total revenue, this price reduction will benefit the sellers because the total revenue will increase to $1,000 ($5 × 200). But what if the price reduction from $6 to $5 causes the quantity demanded to increase to only 110 units? This will hurt sellers, because their revenue will fall to $550 (see Table 9–1 for examples of demand schedules).

In Table 9–1, each demand schedule has the same set of prices. The only difference is the responsiveness of the buyers to the different prices. Demand 1 has the more responsive set of buyers; when the price falls from $6 to $5 to $4, the increase in the quantity demanded is more than enough to compensate for the decrease in price. Hence, total revenue (TR) increases. When these same reductions in price occur in Demand 2, the increase in quantity is not enough to compensate for the price reduction and so total revenue falls. However, you can see that when we start with the lower price and then proceed to increase its value, the opposite holds true for the direction of change in total revenue. That is, total revenue decreases in the case of Demand 1 and increases in the case of Demand 2. In Demand 3, the change in the quantity demanded is just enough to offset the change in the price. Thus, total revenue is unchanged, regardless of the direction of change in price.

TABLE 9–1   Three demand schedules.

Demand 1			Demand 2			Demand 3		
P	Q	TR*	P	Q	TR	P	Q	TR
$6	100	600	$6	100	600	$6	100	600
5	200	1,000	5	110	550	5	120	600
4	300	1,200	4	120	480	4	150	600

*TR = total revenue.

TABLE 9–2   Price changes, elasticity, and changes in total revenue.

	Elastic	Inelastic	Unitary
Price ↑	Total Revenue ↓	Total Revenue ↑	No Change
Price ↓	Total Revenue ↑	Total Revenue ↓	No Change

Table 9–2 summarizes the relationship between elasticity, price changes, and changes in total revenue. It shows that when the price decreases and the total revenue increases, consumers are so responsive that their increase in purchases is more than enough to compensate for the price reduction. This type of response is called "elastic" and also implies that when the price increases, the negative response by consumers is large enough to more than offset that increase. Thus, sellers end up generating less total revenue. A decrease in price accompanied by a decrease in total revenue indicates an "inelastic" demand. When the price changes and there is no change in total revenue, demand is called "unitary elastic."

We have just discussed the concept of elasticity in terms of the impact that price changes will have on total revenue earned by the sellers. Elasticity can also be measured in a more precise way by comparing the degree of responsiveness among buyers to changes in price. This measure, called the "elasticity coefficient," involves the percentage change in quantity demanded relative to the percentage change in price. That is:

$$\text{Elasticity coefficient} = \frac{\text{Percentage change in } Q_D}{\text{Percentage change in } P}$$

The computational formula for the elasticity coefficient can be expressed as:

$$E = \frac{Q_2 - Q_1}{Q_1} \div \frac{P_2 - P_1}{P_1} \ .$$

where E = the elasticity coefficient
Q_1 = the original quantity demanded
Q_2 = the new quantity demanded
P_1 = the original price
P_2 = the new price

If the percentage change in the quantity demanded exceeds the percentage change in price, the elasticity coefficient E will have a value greater than one. (Actually, the value of the elasticity coefficient is always going to be negative because the change in price is always accompanied by a percentage change in quantity demanded in the opposite direction. For purposes of analysis, we drop the negative sign and consider only the absolute value of the coefficient.) This, by definition, is an elastic demand. If the percentage change in the quantity demanded is less than the percentage change in price, then E will be less than one. This, by definition, is an inelastic demand. If E is equal to one, demand is unitary elastic.

We can illustrate the computation of the elasticity coefficient by using some of the numbers in Table 9–1. Moving from $6 to $5 in Demand 1 in this table, we see that the percentage increase in quantity is 100 percent (200 − 100/100). The percentage change in price is −16.67 percent (5 − 6 divided by 6). Thus, E is equal to 100 divided by −16.67 or −6. Using the same formula for Demand 2, we see that the decrease in price from $6 to $5 indicates an elasticity coefficient of −.6.

Although the criterion for determining the degree of elasticity is clear enough, there is an inherent ambiguity in the elasticity coefficient formula itself because percentages are involved. If we used the same price and quantities but instead increased rather than decreased the price, we would find for example that Demand 1 would produce a coefficient of −2.5. Although it is still greater than one and therefore is considered to be elastic, there is quite a difference in the magnitude of the coefficient between the increase and the decrease in price. This is because the base from which the percentage changes are measured depends on the direction of change of the price and quantity. Given the two prices $6 and $5 and the accompanying quantities demanded of 100 and 200, the increase in price from $5 to $6 would involve the base price and quantity of $5 and 200 units of output respectively. A decrease in price from $6 to $5 would utilize the base numbers $6 and 100 units of output.

To handle this inherent ambiguity, we employ a formula that adjusts for the difference in base numbers. This formula is expressed as follows:

$$E = \frac{Q_2 - Q_1}{(Q_1 + Q_2)/2} \div \frac{P_2 - P_1}{(P_1 + P_2)/2}$$

By dividing the change in quantity and price by the respective *midpoints* between the changes, this formula provides a common base from which either percentage increases or decreases can be calculated. Thus, for any two prices and quantities, the elasticity coefficient would remain the same, no matter which direction the price changed. For example, in Demand 1, between $6 and $5, the elasticity coefficient is −3.67. In Demand 2, it is −.52. In Demand 3, the elasticity coefficient is −1, thereby explaining why economists call this type of demand "unitary elastic."

Economic textbooks generally use the formula involving the midpoints of the changes between price and quantity. In our experience, however, business managers generally discuss price and quantity changes from given starting points because people naturally think about percentage changes in this manner. In any case, the ambiguity of comparing elasticity coefficients between a price increase and a price decrease is usually not a problem in actual business situations because managers usually consider price changes in a predetermined direction. In all three examples cited at the beginning of this chapter, the companies were contemplating price reductions. We can imagine that the managers responsible for making the decision were mainly concerned with whether or not to proceed with the price cuts and the extent of these reductions. An example of a company considering only a price increase is the case of General Motors in June 1993. At that time, it was reported in the business press that other car companies were raising the prices of a number of their 1993 models. The managers of General Motors had to decide whether to raise the prices of their cars and trucks to match their competitors. Their decision was to hold prices constant until September when the model year ends for all automobile manufacturers.

FACTORS THAT DETERMINE PRICE ELASTICITY

Although it is to a manager's advantage to have an accurate measure of elasticity, in actual business situations it can be extremely helpful just to know whether demand is elastic or inelastic. For example, in the case of Sears, it would have been useful for its management to have known simply whether the demand by its customers was elastic or inelastic (for instance, whether or not the absolute value of E was greater or less than unity) without even knowing the exact magnitude of the coefficient. If the demand had been elastic, Sears would have at least increased its revenue as a result of its EDLP policy. As a guide for determining whether the response by consumers to price changes will be elastic or inelastic, managers can analyze certain characteristics of the products that they are selling.

Four key characteristics of a product influence its elasticity: (1) the degree to which it is viewed as a "luxury" or a "necessity," (2) the number of substitutes that are available to buyers, (3) the price of the product in relation to buyers' incomes, and (4) the amount of time allowed for buyers to react to price changes. Table 9–3 shows how these factors influence elasticity.

A certain amount of subjectivity is involved in using these characteristics to determine price elasticity. For example, some people might consider a camcorder to be a luxury, while others (for example those with young children) might consider it a necessity. Some might consider a photo camera to be a

TABLE 9–3 Determinants of elasticity of market demand.

Elastic	Inelastic
1. Luxury	1. Necessity
2. Many substitutes available	2. Few substitutes available
3. Price is a large part of income	3. Price is a small part of income
4. Long-run time period	4. Short-run time period

substitute for this product, while others might believe there is no substitute for full-motion video with sound. For some, the $600 average price of a camcorder might be a very large part of income, while for others this might be a minor item in the household budget. The best we can do, then, is to assume that a product's characteristics apply in general to the consumers of a particular good or service. We can also use the preceding characteristics in comparing the elasticity among products. For example, given two products, a camcorder and milk, we can say that the former is more price elastic than the latter. A camcorder is more of a luxury than milk, there are more substitutes, and its price represents a larger part of household income.

As far as the market time period is concerned, the longer the time period, the more elastic the response by consumers is assumed to be. This is because with the passage of time, we assume that people may tend to change their tastes and preferences or to find substitutes for the product whose price has changed. This reasoning is based on the concept of the short-run and long-run market time periods discussed in the previous chapter.

The demand for oil offers a good example of short- and long-run elasticity. When OPEC conspired to raise the price of oil in 1973 and again in 1979, American consumers responded by reducing their purchases by a relatively small amount. One economic study at that time pointed out that the short-run elasticity of demand for gasoline was about $-.10$, a coefficient indicating a very inelastic demand. In the 1980s, however, American consumers had changed their pattern of consumption by car pooling, driving their cars at lower speeds, using more fuel-efficient automobiles, and turning their thermostats down. American businesses complemented this response by using more fuel-efficient machinery. Thus, the long-run response to increased oil prices was much more elastic than the short-run response.

The time factor also works in cases where the price of a product has fallen. For example, the price of a fax machine has fallen considerably over the past several years. As the price fell, it is reasonable to assume that certain people bought a fax machine simply because of its lower price. This would be a short-run response to the price change. As time passed, the lower price began to change people's notions of a fax machine as primarily an office tool. We can guess that many consumers started to think, "At the lower price, perhaps we can justify buying one for the home." Moreover, as these consumers learned that more of their friends and family were buying fax machines for home use, their desire to buy a fax was heightened further. Thus, the long-run change in consumer preferences or habits results in an even greater response to the price reduction.

ELASTICITY OF A PRODUCT VERSUS ELASTICITY OF A BRAND

When examining the elasticity of demand for a product, it is important to distinguish between the responsiveness of consumers to changes in a given product category and the responsiveness relative to a particular brand name within the category. As you might expect, responsiveness is generally greater for a brand than for the product category for the simple reason that competing brands within the category offer consumers more substitutes.

For example, if Philip Morris lowered the price of its Miller Lite beer, we would anticipate a relatively elastic response in the quantity purchased because of the increase in consumption from those who regularly drink this brand, as well as some additional purchases from those who drink other brands but are enticed by the price reduction in Miller Lite. (This example assumes that the sellers of the competing brands do not match the Miller Lite price cut.) On the other hand, a decrease in the average price of beer would probably generate a less elastic response because consumers might not view such substitutes as wine, soft drinks, or bottled water as being close alternatives to beer.

THE PRICE RANGE FACTOR

In determining the degree of price elasticity, it is also important to consider the range in which changes in price and quantity occur. Suppose we extend the changes in price and quantity shown in Demand 1 in Table 9–1 in exactly the same increments. That is:

P	Q	TR
$6	100	$ 600
5	200	1,000
4	300	1,200
3	400	1,200
2	500	1,000
1	600	600

As you can see, as the price drops from $6 down to $1 the pattern of change in total revenue changes. Down to $4, revenue increases, implying an elastic response. Between $4 and $3, there is no change, implying unitary elasticity. As the price drops below $3, the same incremental response of 100 units results in a decrease in total revenue. In general terms, at higher levels of price, price decreases produce *elastic* responses in quantity demanded; at lower levels of price, price reductions are accompanied by an *inelastic* response. There is no magic in this observation; it is all in the arithmetic of the elasticity formula and in the demand schedule itself.

The formula for determining elasticity utilizes the *percentage* change, not the *absolute* change, in quantity demanded relative to price. In the upper half of the price range (the lower half of the range of quantity), any decrease in price is bound to be relatively small in percentage terms because the base price is relatively high. By the same token, the corresponding increases in quantity must be relatively high in percentage terms because the base quantities from which the percentage is calculated are relatively low. This is illustrated in Figure 9–1, which shows that the upper half of the demand line is elastic, while the lower half is inelastic. At the halfway point, the demand is unitary elastic. In fact, as long as the demand is a straight line, as in Figure 9–1, we can state that it will have an elastic half and an inelastic half, with unitary elasticity occurring right in the middle.

If the demand curve is not linear, then the relationship between the range of prices and elasticity does not hold. Figure 9–2 illustrates two possible nonlinear demand curves. Figure 9–2(a) shows a demand curve that is relatively inelastic in the upper range of price and relatively elastic at the lower range. This is exactly the opposite from the relationship exhibited by a linear demand curve. This could well be the shape of a demand curve for airline

FIGURE 9–1 The elasticity of a linear demand curve.

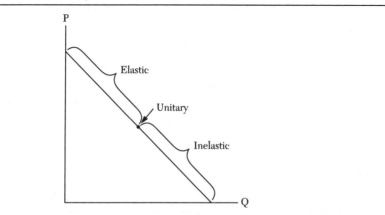

FIGURE 9–2   Examples of nonlinear demand curves and their elasticities.

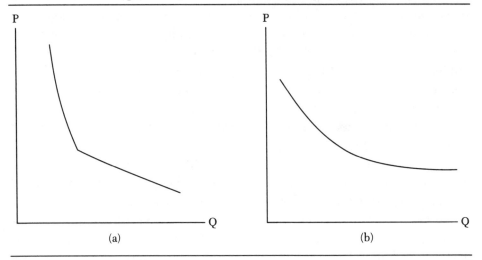

(a)   (b)

travel. In this industry, the upper range of price represents the demand by business travelers, the less price-sensitive segment of the air traffic market. The lower range includes primarily those who travel for personal reasons. These buyers are much more sensitive to price changes. To verify this picture, we need only to note how much lower the price is for an airline ticket for a trip involving a stay over a Saturday night compared with the same trip without this element. Most business travel is done during the week and business travelers (especially frequent travelers) usually want to get home for the weekends if their schedules permit this. We do know that some companies try to save money by having their employees stay over the weekend. However, the added cost to those traveling, in terms of lost personal time, can be quite high.

A nonlinear demand of the type shown in Figure 9–2(b) could also indicate a situation in which prices declining below a certain level cause a certain burst in demand. For example, people might respond in a linear fashion to reductions in the price of a color television. As the price falls into the inelastic range, we would expect total revenue in the industry to fall. However, suppose the price falls to such a low point that people now consider having more than one (perhaps three or four) TVs in the house. This could have the effect of suddenly turning the lower inelastic range into an elastic one.

OTHER TYPES OF ELASTICITY

In addition to price elasticity, there are two other important types of elasticity that economists track very closely: "income elasticity" and "cross-price elasticity." These elasticities measure the responsiveness of demand to changes in income and the price of substitute goods, respectively.

Income Elasticity

When income rises, it is reasonable to expect that consumers will buy more of a particular product, and they will buy less when their income falls. In fact, goods and services that exhibit such a relationship are called "normal." However, where there is an inverse relationship between changes in income and consumer demand, the products are called "inferior." Examples of inferior products or services are certain less expensive cuts of meat, laundromat services, and home baking products. As people's incomes rise, they start to replace these products with their higher priced substitutes. For example, they might start to buy better quality steaks; they might perhaps buy a washing machine or use a dry cleaning and laundry service; and they might buy more products from a bakery.

Income elasticity is measured in the same way as price elasticity. The percentage change in the quantity demanded is compared with the percentage change in income. That is:

$$E_1 = \frac{\text{Percentage change in income}}{\text{Percentage change in } Q_D}$$

We can categorize the results of this computation as follows:

- If the income elasticity coefficient is positive, it indicates that changes in quantity demanded and income move in the same direction. Products with coefficients of this magnitude are called "normal."
- If the income elasticity coefficient is negative, it indicates that changes in quantity demanded and income move in the opposite direction. Therefore, the product is "inferior."
- If the income elasticity coefficient is greater than one, it indicates that demand is very sensitive to changes in income. In this case, we can refer to the product as a "luxury" or "superior" product.

Knowledge of a product's income elasticity can help managers in several ways. First, it would alert them to the impact on demand caused by movements in the macroeconomy. A recession can be expected to reduce the demand for normal or superior products. In an economic recovery or expansion, these same products should experience rising demand. For example, during the sustained economic expansion of the 1980s, companies that sold luxury consumer products with high-status designer names did very well. In the 1990s, however, many of the same companies have been experiencing sluggish sales because of the slowdown in the economy.

To offset the impact of the business cycle on product demand, a manager might do well to select a portfolio of goods and services with a variety of income elasticities. Thus, in a recession, the demand for a company's inferior or low-income-elasticity products will be sustained and may even increase. In expansionary economic times, the company's high-income-elasticity products would take the lead in sales.

Cross-Price Elasticity

Cross-price elasticity is a measure of the responsiveness of consumers to changes in the price of a particular good, relative to changes in the price of substitute or complementary products. Knowledge about cross-price elasticity with respect to substitute products is particularly useful to assess the impact on sales of changes in a competitor's prices. For example, what impact will a reduction in the price of Microsoft's "Word" have on the sales of "Word Perfect"? To minimize the cross-price elasticity of a product with respect to changes in the price of a substitute, companies spend considerable sums on advertising designed to establish or strengthen brand loyalty. There appears to be increasing cross-price elasticity in consumer goods markets, as evidenced by the growing market share of lower-priced, private-label consumer products. This is becoming quite worrisome for the makers of leading premium brands of consumer products such as Procter & Gamble, Colgate-Palmolive, and Philip Morris. (For more on this, see the special Autumn/Winter, 1993 issue of *Fortune* entitled "The Tough New Consumer.")

The cross-price elasticity of a product with respect to complementary products is also important for managers to understand. For example, a seller of computer products can reduce the price of its PCs to stimulate demand for its software. If the profit margin is high for the product whose demand is affected by the cut in the price of the complementary product, then this pricing tactic is particularly appealing. For example, a clothing store might reduce the price of its men's suits to stimulate the demand for high-profit margin items such as ties, shirts, and socks. Furthermore, the degree of complementarity between suits and the fashion accessories can be stimulated by the "friendly persuasion" of the salespersons.

PRICE ELASTICITY AND MARKET TYPE

In the previous chapter, we briefly described four basic types of markets used in economic analysis. The market in which a firm competes has a significant impact on the price elasticity of its products. In the case of perfect competition, each firm has no market power and basically acts as a price taker. In terms of price elasticity, this means the firm can sell as much as or as little as it wants but must sell the product at the going market price. This particular type of demand is called "perfectly elastic," and is illustrated in Figure 9–3(a).

A firm that has a monopoly for a particular good or service must deal with a relatively inelastic demand mainly because its customers are not expected to have very many alternatives. Electric utilities and pharmaceutical companies that have patents on lifesaving drugs are two examples of firms that face a relatively inelastic demand. This type of demand is illustrated in Figure 9–3(b). In the extreme case, a firm in this market category could have a demand for its product that is "perfectly inelastic." As seen in Figure 9–3(d) this means that consumers would be willing to buy a certain amount of a product, no matter what its price.

FIGURE 9–3   Price elasticity.

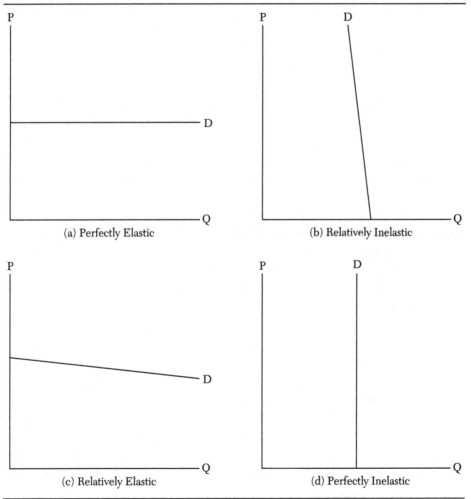

(a) Perfectly Elastic

(b) Relatively Inelastic

(c) Relatively Elastic

(d) Perfectly Inelastic

Firms that operate in monopolistically competitive markets have a demand that is somewhere in between the perfectly elastic demand of perfect competition and the relatively inelastic demand of a monopoly. Each firm in this type of market has some amount of market power because it can differentiate its products from the competition. However, because consumers have so many alternatives, the demand for a particular firm's product tends to be quite elastic. Figure 9–3(c) illustrates this possibility.

The demand elasticity of a company in an oligopoly is difficult to determine because much depends on the reaction of its competitors to price changes. The price wars that occur from time to time in the airline industry offer a good example of this factor. Suppose an airline decides to cut its prices on certain routes and times of the year to increase its demand by vacation travelers. The demand for air travel by this segment of the market is considered to be elastic, so the airline anticipates an increase in revenue as a result of these price cuts. If these cuts are matched by competing airlines, however, the cross-price elasticity may be sufficient to offset the price elasticity of the airline that initiated the price actions. As a result, the airline's elastic demand could turn out to be inelastic.

KEY ASSUMPTIONS IN THE USE OF PRICE ELASTICITY

In applying the concept of price elasticity to business decisions, managers need to recognize that other factors do not always remain constant while price is changing. For example, suppose you are the manager of a chain of multiplex cinemas. You observe that at the 6:00 P.M. shows during the weekdays, attendance is very poor. You analyze the demand for this "product" and conclude that it is probably elastic. There are many substitutes for this product such as renting a video, watching TV, and eating dinner. The price of admission can be considered a relatively small part of a person's income, but this product is not a necessity. Because of this assessment, you decide to cut the price of admission for the weekday 6:00 P.M. show by 50 percent, from $7.00 down to $3.50.

Now suppose at the same time that you cut this price, all the local video rental stores decide to offer substantially reduced rates on videos rented between Monday and Thursdays. The big chain, Blockbuster Video, even decides to offer a $1.50 credit toward the weekend rental of a video for each video rented during the rest of the week. Suppose also that your price cut was made in June, when people begin to spend more time outdoors. Still worse, suppose that the competing movie theaters also start to lower their prices. As you can imagine, because all these other factors are changing as you cut your price, the anticipated increase in revenue either will not materialize or will be much smaller than you hoped.

THE ESTIMATION OF ELASTICITY

It would be ideal if a manager knew precisely how responsive consumers are to changes in price and other factors that influence demand. Market research tries to provide managers with this information through the use of surveys and focus groups. However, people are not always truthful about how they would respond to these changes. Companies have been known to charge different prices for the same product in different segments of the market to compare consumer reactions. One well-known catalog company unfortunately received some bad publicity when certain consumers began to compare their catalogs with copies sent to other customers and found the same items being offered at different prices. A spokesperson for the company explained that it had been the company's intention to observe the different responses to the prices rather than to mislead or cheat its customers.

Economists try to complement the effort of market researchers by estimating the demand for a particular good or service using a statistical technique called regression analysis. Data from surveys or compiled from historical records are used to estimate the quantitative impact of changes in price and other factors on the demand for a product. For more information on this subject, refer to any managerial economics, econometrics, or forecasting textbook.[1]

SUMMARY

This chapter has examined in greater detail the concept of market demand introduced in Chapter 8. In particular, it focused on the concept of elasticity, the measure of the quantitative impact that changes in price and other factors have on the demand for a particular good or service. Price elasticity is the most important type of elasticity because managers have the most direct control over price in influencing market demand. The degree of price elasticity determines whether firms can expect higher or lower revenue as a result of price changes.

Economists employ a specific measure called the elasticity coefficient for assessing consumer responsiveness to changes in price and other factors. However, various situations in the business news suggest that it would be very beneficial for managers to know ahead of time simply whether the response by consumers to price changes will be elastic or inelastic. We will say more about consumer response to price changes in Chapter 11, when we discuss the pricing and output decision.

10 PRODUCER RESPONSE

Analyzing Cost

> Question: "How much is 1 + 1?"
> Answer from an engineer: "2."
> Answer from a marketing person: "3."
> Answer from an accountant: "How much do you want it to be?"

You probably have heard this joke or one of its many variations. But its point is very pertinent to the topic of cost analysis. While engineers are assumed to strive for precision and marketing people to engage in hyperbole, accountants have been known to use their skills to present their company's financial position in the best possible light. Another humorous statement, attributed to noted accounting professor and author Abraham Brillof, also exemplifies this particular impression. "A company's financial statement," Brillof quipped, "is like perfume; it should be sniffed but not swallowed." Our intention is not to malign the accounting profession. But it is true that a company's financial condition, particularly in terms of its costs of doing business, is subject to a certain degree of interpretation even without falsifying or distorting the numbers.

There are two main branches in the field of accounting, financial accounting and managerial accounting (also referred to as cost accounting). The jokes and stereotypes about accountants allude to both fields. Financial accountants are concerned primarily with presenting a picture of the company's financial condition to the outside world (bankers, investors, and suppliers), while managerial accountants measure and interpret a company's cost of doing business in ways that will help its managers make the best possible decisions. Financial accountants' interpretations of cost are subject to oversight by such bodies as the

178

Financial Accounting Standards Board (FASB) and the Securities and Exchange Commission (SEC). Moreover, the work of financial accountants is carefully monitored by auditors, both inside and outside the company. A financial accountant's failure to present an accurate and truthful picture of a firm's costs, revenues, and profit could be damaging to those who have either invested in or loaned money to the company. Managerial accountants are not bound by FASB and the SEC. However, if they provide an inaccurate or less-than-truthful picture of cost to a company's managers, this misrepresentation could lead to bad business decisions that would hurt everyone in the company as well as the outside creditors and investors.

This chapter deals with the analysis of cost from the viewpoint of economics. The economic analysis of cost is closely related to managerial accounting. The primary objective of both the economist and the managerial accountant in the analysis of cost is the same: to provide managers with information about the cost of doing business that will help them to make decisions in the company's best interest. Economists tend to be a bit more abstract than managerial accountants in their analysis of cost. For example, managerial accountants delve into considerable detail about such issues as the appropriate methodology for allocating overhead cost and the tracking of cost variances. Economists tend to deal simply with general categories such as fixed and variable costs. They also analyze cost on the assumption that what is budgeted is actually incurred and do not deal with cost variances. However, many of the terms and concepts used by the two fields of study are essentially the same. Whenever appropriate, we will discuss certain concepts in managerial accounting that are related to the economic analysis of cost.

Our presentation of the economic analysis of cost begins with the concept of relevant cost. We will then show how this concept applies to the break-even problem. This will be followed by an examination of the economic analysis of a firm's short- and long-run cost structure. The chapter concludes with a review of ways in which companies try to improve their cost structures.

HOW MUCH DOES IT REALLY COST TO PRODUCE A GOOD OR SERVICE?

Regardless of whether accountants or economists are analyzing a company's cost of doing business, you may be wondering why determining cost should involve any ambiguity at all. After all, is it not a matter of simply totaling up all the costs required to produce a company's goods and services? Well, consider the case of Joe Jones, just your ordinary guy who enjoys fishing as a hobby. One day, after returning from what he thought was a most successful fishing trip, his wife, Jennifer, presents him with the following report. In computing the cost per fish, she assumed that Joe goes fishing 15 times per year and catches an average of 20 fish per trip.

Cost per Fish Caught by Joe Jones

Boat (cost: $45,000, usable for 15 years, 15 trips per year)	$200.00
Boat fuel (per trip)	45.00
Annual dock fees and boat insurance (prorated on a per-trip basis)	300.00
Travel expenses to and from the lake (100 miles @ $ .275 per mile: Gas, oil and tires, $.20/mile; depreciation and insurance, $.075/mile)	27.50
New fishing equipment purchased this year (prorated over 15 trips)	20.00
Annual fishing license	40.00
Bait and miscellaneous expenses	30.00
Food	50.00
Beverages	35.00
Money lost playing poker on the trip	50.00
Total cost per trip	$797.50
Average number of fish caught per trip: 20	
Cost per fish	$ 39.87

She then proceeds to tell him that his hobby is far too expensive, because they could buy a fish at the market for a lot less than $39.87. Her recommendation is that he simply stop fishing. What do you think of her analysis? It should be evident from this example, that the "cost" of a particular product or activity is subject to different interpretations. For example, suppose Joe were a better fisherman and caught 30 fish per trip. Dividing $797.50 by 30 gives us a cost per fish of $26.58.

Regardless of Joe's abilities as a fisherman, the cost figures themselves can be looked at in a number of different ways. In fact, when we use this example in the classroom, we rarely find two students with the same answer. Their answers differ because they can never agree about what cost items to include and how they should be included. For example, some believe that the cost of the boat should be included, while others do not. Some believe that the dock fees, boat insurance, and fishing license should be prorated over the number of fishing trips taken per year, while others believe that they should not even be included in the cost calculation.

DISTINGUISHING BETWEEN RELEVANT AND IRRELEVANT COST

In analyzing the cost of a particular activity such as Joe's fishing trip, economists recommend that only those costs relevant to the decision at hand should be considered. A cost is deemed to be relevant if it will be affected by the choice of alternatives being considered in a decision. In Joe's case, his alternatives are either to continue fishing or to stop. The relevant costs are only those that he would incur if he continued to fish, that is, those costs he could avoid by not continuing to fish. Costs not affected by the outcome of his decision are considered to be "irrelevant." Two commonly used ways to determine which costs are relevant are the "sunk" versus "incremental" and the "fixed" versus "variable" criteria.

A sunk cost is a prior expenditure that is not affected by any decision concerning a future course of action. Based on the definition of relevant cost, sunk cost is clearly irrelevant. The opposite of sunk cost is incremental cost. This type of cost is considered to be relevant because it is defined as a cost that is associated with any decision about a future course of action. Fixed cost is the cost that does not change with the level of activity or output. A variable cost is one that does change with the level of activity or output. Fixed cost is considered irrelevant, while variable cost is considered relevant.

Using either the sunk versus incremental or the fixed versus variable criteria, we can then determine which of Joe's costs are relevant to his decision to continue or to stop fishing. If we assume that he already owns his boat and fishing equipment and paid for his license and dock fees at the start of the fishing season, then all these costs can be considered "sunk" and therefore irrelevant to his decision. The depreciation and insurance on his car are fixed costs. They do not change no matter how much he drives. The food and beverages can also be considered fixed if he basically consumes the same amount whether at home or at the lake. If we assume that he plays poker every weekend and manages to lose $50 every time he plays, this cost can be counted as fixed. If he wins, then it would not even be a cost. If Joe consumes more food and beverages while on a fishing trip than at home, the additional amount would be considered a relevant cost. Thus, we are left with the following relevant costs:

Car: gas, oil, tires (100 miles @ $.20/mile)	$100.00
Boat fuel	45.00
Bait and miscellaneous items	30.00
Food and beverages (assuming that he consumes $25 worth of food and $25 of beverages more on his fishing trip than at home)	50.00
Total relevant cost	$225.00
Relevant cost per fish (assuming 20 fish per trip)	$ 11.25

Whether a cost is sunk or fixed depends on the time perspective of the analysis. For example, suppose Joe had already purchased the boat with his own savings. Then the cost of the boat would be considered sunk. If he borrowed the money and is making a monthly payment of $400 on his boat loan, this payment would be considered a fixed cost. In either case, the costs would be considered irrelevant because neither would be affected by his decision to stop or to continue fishing.

OPPORTUNITY COST

Another criterion for identifying a relevant cost is to use the concept of opportunity cost. Opportunity cost is the amount or subjective value sacrificed when choosing one activity over the next best alternative. You might recall from your Economics 101 classes the example of "guns versus butter" often used to illustrate this concept. For any nation with a fixed amount of resources, the opportunity cost of producing guns is the amount of butter that is forgone whenever resources are allocated to the production of guns. The opposite would hold true for the production of butter. Similar consequences hold for businesses and households.

Imagine that Joe earns his living as the owner-operator of a fishing supply business. Suppose he loves to fish so much that he is willing to close his store during the height of the fishing season to pursue his hobby. The amount of income that he forgoes by not keeping his store open would be the opportunity cost of fishing. For economists, this cost is as real as the out-of-pocket expenses associated with his fishing activities.

REPLACEMENT VERSUS HISTORICAL COST

The distinction between replacement cost and historical cost is also useful in helping to determine which costs are relevant. The general rule among economists and managerial accountants alike is to always use replacement cost in determining the relevant cost of a particular business activity. For example, suppose that during the fishing season, Joe used various hooks, flies, and other fishing paraphernalia from his store inventory valued at $150, the amount that he actually paid to his suppliers. Now suppose that at the start of the next fishing season, he required a whole new supply of this paraphernalia. Because of rising costs in the industry, he would have to pay his suppliers $200 for the same amount of fishing accessories. However, Joe still has inventory in his store that he bought for $150. If he uses the old inventory, how much will it cost him—$150 or $200? Economists and managerial accountants would answer $200, the replacement value of the inventory, because by using the $150 worth of previously purchased inventory, Joe incurs a cost of $200 to replace it in his store.

Note that the economist's or managerial accountant's use of replacement rather than historical cost contrasts to some extent with the conventions of financial accounting. According to "Generally Accepted Accounting Principles" (GAAP), a company must use historical cost in computing the value and use of its inventory. Replacement or market value is used only if it is lower than the historical cost.

TIME AS A FACTOR IN THE DETERMINATION OF RELEVANT COST

The time period in which a firm's cost structure is being considered is very important in determining which costs are relevant to a particular business decision. In the example of Joe and his fishing decision, the season had already begun when Jennifer began to question the economics of his hobby. Thus, we assumed that Joe had already incurred such costs as the purchase of the boat, the payment of dock fees, insurance, and the fishing license. If Joe and Jennifer were calculating the cost of fishing *before* he began to pursue this hobby, all these costs would be relevant to the decision. Furthermore, if enough time were allowed for him to make certain adjustments after incurring these costs, they might still be considered relevant. For example, once he stopped fishing, he might be able to sell his boat and dock space. (If he sold the boat for less than he paid for it, the difference would still be considered a sunk cost.) If his fishing license is transferable, he might even be able to sell the remaining time for its use to another fisherman.

In the economic analysis of cost, the time factor is handled by dividing time periods into two basic types: the short run and the long run. Recall that this distinction was also used in the analysis of supply and demand and price elasticity. In the short run, we assume that there are certain resources such as land, factory space, and machinery that cannot be changed within the time period allowed. The cost of using these resources is either sunk or fixed. Thus, there will always be certain costs that are irrelevant to a short-run decision. Long-run analysis assumes that there is enough time for managers to vary the costs of utilizing all their resources. Consequently, all long-run costs are either incremental or variable and therefore relevant to a particular business decision.

ARE THE SUNK OR FIXED COSTS EVER RECOVERED?: BREAK-EVEN ANALYSIS

What is to be done about those costs that are not relevant to a decision? After all, even if they are ignored, they must still be paid for. But this, in fact, is the logic of designating a cost as irrelevant. By definition, an irrelevant cost is one that must be incurred, regardless of the alternative selected by the decision maker. The question of how this cost is recovered is a separate issue altogether. To understand this aspect of the problem, we turn to a commonly used technique called break-even analysis.

Break-even analysis is perhaps the most widely used application of the concept of relevant cost. You will find information on this subject in books on finance, accounting, and marketing as well as economics. This analytical technique addresses the basic question: "How many units of a particular product does a company have to sell to cover all its costs of production 'break even'?" Another name for break-even analysis is "cost-volume-profit analysis." This label describes the break-even problem more explicitly. That is, given the company's fixed and variable *cost,* how much *volume* does it have to sell to break even? Moreover, once it passes the break-even point and becomes profitable, how much *profit* will it earn as its volume increases?

Suppose Joe's wife Jennifer decides to open a seafood store. (Included in her store's offering will be the fish that Joe catches.) How many pounds of seafood per month must she sell to break even? To answer this, we first divide her monthly costs into their fixed and variable components. Fixed cost is presented as a total figure, while the variable cost is shown on a per-unit basis. Variable cost per unit is also referred to as average variable cost (AVC):

Monthly Cost of Operating a Seafood Market

Total Fixed Cost		Variable Cost per Unit (Average Variable Cost or AVC)	
Rent	$1,200	Average wholesale price per	
Utilities	400	pound of seafood	$3.00
Wages	2,350		
Interest payment on loan	1,500		
Insurance	400		
Miscellaneous	150		
Total	$6,000		

To find the break-even point, we use the following equation:

$$Q_{BE} = \frac{TFC}{P - AVC}$$

where
Q_{BE} = the break-even quantity of product sold
TFC = total fixed cost
P = selling price of the product
AVC = average variable cost of the product
$P - AVC$ = "contribution margin" per unit of product sold

FIGURE 10–1 Break-even analysis.

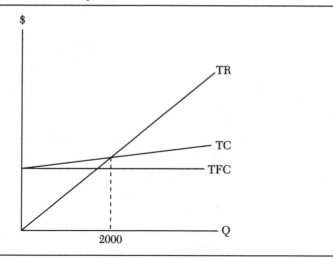

Let us assume that the average retail price of her seafood is $6.00 per pound. Using this price and the break-even formula, we find that Jennifer needs to sell 2,000 pounds of seafood per month to break even ($6,000/$3.00 = 2,000).

The logic of break-even analysis is very straightforward. The amount by which the selling price exceeds the average variable cost is called the "contribution margin" per unit of product sold. When the amount of product sold reaches the point where the total contribution margin covers all the fixed costs of a product, the firm breaks even. The break-even concept can also be shown graphically. In Figure 10–1, the break-even point occurs when the firm's total cost line crosses the total revenue line.

Although our example is quite simple, we do not want to imply that break-even analysis applies only to small and uncomplicated business operations. To be sure, larger and more complex businesses might have a more difficult time dividing their costs into fixed and variable components, particularly when fixed and variable costs have to be determined for many different products. But no matter how complicated the situation, there still remains the basic concept of generating enough sales so that the contribution margin covers fixed cost. Moreover, an extension of break-even analysis called "operating leverage" provides considerable insight into the strategy and operations of big and small businesses alike.

Operating leverage is the relationship between a firm's fixed and variable costs: the greater the fixed cost in relation to variable cost, the higher the degree of operating leverage. Consider two products—"A" and "B." Each sells its product at the same price but has a different degree of operating leverage:

	Product A (High Leverage)	Product B (Low Leverage)
Total fixed cost (TFC)	$10,000	$3,000
Average variable cost (AVC)	$2.50	$4.00
Price (P)	$5.00	$5.00
Contribution margin (CM)	$2.50	$1.00
Break-even quantity (Q_{BE})	4,000	3,000

As you can see, more units of Product A have to be sold than of Product B for a firm to break even. Although Product A's contribution margin is higher than Product B's ($2.50 versus $1.00), it is not enough to compensate for its considerably higher fixed cost. Once the two products reach their respective break-even points, however, Product A becomes a much more profitable product to sell than Product B. Beyond the break-even point (once its fixed cost has been covered), each unit of Product A that is sold adds $2.50 to bottom-line profit. Only $1.00 of profit is added after Product B reaches its break-even point. Figure 10–2(a) and (b) shows this difference in graph form.

You can also see in Figure 10–2 that a high degree of operating leverage is a two-edged sword. If the break-even points of Product A and Product B are not attained, the company that sells Product A stands to lose relatively more. Thus, the high-leverage approach to running business is considered riskier than the low-leverage approach. But as is usually the rule in business, greater risks are associated with greater rewards. In the case of high operating leverage, the downside risk of losing relatively more than with the use of low operating leverage is made up for by the upside potential of relatively higher profits.

FIGURE 10–2 High and low leverage.

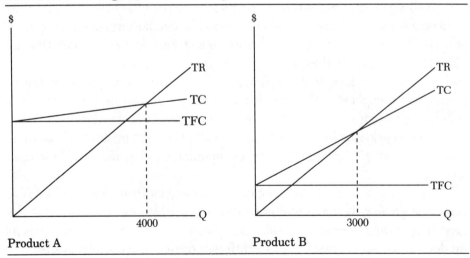

Product A   Product B

The degree of operating leverage can also be measured by looking at the percentage change in profit relative to the percentage change in sales volume. That is:

$$\text{Degree of operating leverage} = \frac{\text{Percentage change in profit}}{\text{Percentage change in quantity sold}}$$

The formula used to actually compute this measure can be expressed as follows:

$$\text{Degree of operating leverage} = \frac{Q(P - AVC)}{Q(P - AVC) - TFC}$$

where Q = quantity sold
  P = price
  AVC = average variable cost
  TFC = total fixed cost

When actually computing this measure, the quantity sold must be greater than the break-even level. In this example, we can compute the degrees of operating of Product A and Product B by using $Q = 5{,}000$, a level at which both products are earning a profit:

Product A

$$\text{Degree of operating leverage} = \frac{5{,}000\ (5.00 - 2.50)}{5{,}000\ (5.00 - 2.50) - 10{,}000} = 5$$

Product B

$$\text{Degree of operating leverage} = \frac{5{,}000\ (5.00 - 4.00)}{5{,}000\ (5.00 - 4.00) - 3{,}000} = 2.5$$

Our computations confirm what we already knew: Product A's degree of operating leverage is greater than Product B's. More precisely, Product A's leverage is twice as big as Product B's. A 1 percent increase in quantity sold would result in a 5 percent increase in Product A's profit. A 1 percent increase in quantity sold would increase Product B's profit by only 2.5 percent.

In our view, the value for managers of understanding operating leverage is not just in the "number crunching," but also in application of the concept to business strategy and tactics. For example, during the 1980s, General Motors invested billions of dollars to install and use state-of-the-art robotics as well as to expand its production capacity. These large investments increased its operating leverage significantly by adding a greater amount of depreciation to its fixed costs. This should have put GM in a position to earn substantial profits once it passed its break-even point.

Unfortunately for GM, strong competition from Japanese automakers as well as from Ford and Chrysler prevented it from selling enough vehicles to take advantage of its higher operating leverage. Indeed, we believe that the huge losses suffered by GM in recent years partly reflect its being on the left side of the break-even point of a high operating leverage situation. Presumably, the massive layoffs and plant closings that GM intends to implement in the 1990s will lower its operating leverage and dampen the losses that would result if it continued to fall short of its break-even point. (Ideally, GM should generate a greater volume of sales so it can surpass its break-even point, whatever its degree of operating leverage happened to be, but that is another story altogether.)

The concept of operating leverage does not only apply to manufacturing situations. Consider the case of the cellular or wireless communications market. Currently, each geographical market is restricted to only two competitors, one of which is the company that also provides local telephone service. Let us consider the case of one particular geographical market in which Company "A" and Company "B" are competing. Company A employs a greater direct sales force to sell its services than Company B. Company B relies more on indirect sales channels such as retail electronics stores to sell its services. Using a direct sales force incurs a greater fixed cost (e.g. salaries and benefits, support staff, office space etc.) than using the indirect channel of independently owned and operated establishments. However, the commission paid for a sale made through an indirect channel is considerably higher than for a sale made by a company's own salesperson. This is because a company's salesperson receives a base salary as well as commission for bringing new customers on to its wireless network. An independent dealer receives only a commission from a cellular phone company for signing up a customer.

From a marketing standpoint, a firm such as Company A chooses this to use a direct sales channel because it helps them to maintain closer control over the quality of the sales effort and the integrity of the way special promotions are handled. However, from an economic standpoint, this implies that the direct sales force has to generate relatively higher volumes of sales compared to indirect sales in order to give the company the full benefit of the higher leverage operation.

LIMITATIONS OF BREAK-EVEN ANALYSIS

This review of break-even analysis should give you a good idea of how the knowledge of a firm's fixed and variable costs can help in the making of certain business decisions or in the analysis of particular manufacturing or marketing strategies. However, as useful as this technique can be, it is still subject to several shortcomings. First, break-even analysis selects only one price for a particular product and then proceeds to determine how much a firm has to sell at this price to break even. In order to consider the possibility of different amounts demanded by consumers at different prices (i.e. the price elasticity of demand), a whole schedule of prices and break-even points would have to be constructed. In other words, break-even analysis determines how much a firm with a given price and cost structure NEEDS TO SELL in order to break even. But it does not provide any indication how many units it WILL ACTUALLY sell. Second, and more important, this analysis assumes that a firm's average variable cost is constant. Under certain circumstances, it quite possible for a firm's average costs to either decrease or increase as more of a good or service is produced. To understand why, we turn now to the economic analysis of short-run cost.

THE ECONOMIC ANALYSIS OF SHORT-RUN COST

Table 10–1 presents a typical short-run cost schedule used in economic analysis. The amount of output produced is shown in column 1. The total cost data are shown in columns 2, 3, and 4. Data on cost per unit are shown in columns 5 through 8. The various cost measures are defined and related to each other in the following manner:

Total cost:	$TC = TFC + TVC$
Average fixed cost:	$AFC = TFC/Q$
Average total cost:	$ATC = TC/Q$
Average variable cost:	$AVC = TVC/Q$
Marginal cost:	$MC = \Delta TVC/\Delta Q = \Delta TC/\Delta Q$
Average total cost:	$ATC = AFC + AVC$

As shown in Table 10–1, the economic analysis of cost, unlike break-even analysis, does not assume that average variable cost remains constant over the range of output produced. In this table, as the firm begins producing its output, average variable cost decreases, reaches a minimum point at 4 units of output, and then starts to increase. This pattern of behavior also holds for average total cost. However, average total cost reaches its minimum at 6 units of output.

The key to understanding why the average variable and average total costs change in this manner lies in understanding the changes that occur in marginal cost. Marginal cost, shown in column 8 of Table 10–1 is defined as the change in total variable cost divided by the change in output. It can also be defined as the change in total cost divided by the change in output because the fixed-cost component of total cost does not change. Notice that as production begins, it starts to decrease. At three units of output, it reaches a minimum and then begins to

TABLE 10–1   Measures of total and average cost.

(1) Quantity of Output [Q]	(2) Total Fixed Cost [TFC]	(3) Total Variable Cost [TVC]	(4) Total Cost [TC]	(5) Average Fixed Cost [AFC]	(6) Average Variable Cost [AVC]	(7) Average Total Cost [ATC]	(8) Marginal Cost [MC]
0	100	0	100	—	—	—	
1	100	56	156	100.00	56.00	156.00	56
2	100	106	206	50.00	53.00	103.00	50
3	100	154	254	33.33	51.33	84.67	48
4	100	205	305	25.00	*51.25*	76.25	51
5	100	263	363	20.00	52.60	72.60	58
6	100	332	432	16.67	55.33	*72.00*	69
7	100	416	516	14.29	59.42	73.71	84
8	100	519	619	12.50	64.87	77.37	103
9	100	646	746	11.11	71.77	82.88	127
10	100	801	901	10.00	80.10	90.10	155

increase. Graphs of the cost data in Table 10–1 are presented in Figure 10–3 and enable us to see the pattern of change of the different measures of cost as output increases. They also help us to visualize the impact that marginal cost has on the average variable and average total costs.

Using either the data in Table 10–1 or the graphs in Figure 10–3, we can observe the following about marginal cost's impact on average variable cost:

- When marginal cost is less than average variable cost, average variable cost decreases.

- When marginal cost is greater than average variable cost, average variable cost increases.

- When marginal cost is equal to average variable cost, average variable cost neither decreases nor increases. (In the context of the numerical example provided here, this corresponds to the point of its minimum value.)

The same statements can be made about the impact of marginal cost on average total cost.

The reason marginal cost has this particular effect on both average variable and average total cost is the mathematical relationship between *any* marginal and average values. As a simple example, consider a bowler whose season's average is 190. Suppose he bowls 170 in a particular game. What will this "marginal" score do to the season's average? Of course, it will decrease the average. If instead, the score of this one game is 250, it will increase the season's average. If, by chance, the game's score is exactly 190, then the season's average will neither increase nor decrease.

FIGURE 10–3   Changes in cost as output increases.

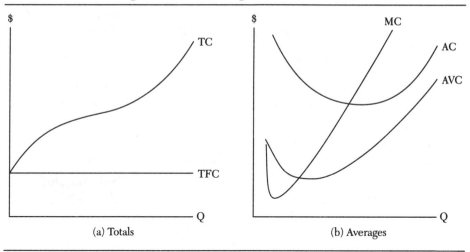

(a) Totals   (b) Averages

Now that we have elaborated on the impact that marginal cost has on average variable and average total cost, we still need to explain the behavior of marginal cost itself. Break-even analysis assumes that marginal cost is constant. Why does economic analysis assume that marginal cost decreases and then at some point starts to increase as more of a good or service is produced? To answer this question, we need to review a concept referred to in economic theory as the "returns to a variable input." In the short run, a firm must work with a certain fixed amount of resources or "inputs" such as land, factory or office space, machinery, and equipment. As additional amounts of variable inputs such as labor hours and raw materials are combined with the fixed inputs, more output is produced. At first, additional units of the variable inputs are assumed to result in *increasing* amounts of additional output (also called "marginal product"). But eventually, the additional inputs are expected to result in *decreasing or diminishing* marginal product. We can show this with a simple numerical example.

Suppose one person, working with a fixed amount of factory space and machinery, produces 100 units of output. Now suppose further that this person is joined by another worker. The two of them working together as a team produce 250 units of output. From the standpoint of the additional output contributed by each worker, the marginal product of the first worker is 100 and the marginal product of the second worker is 150. This is an example of "increasing returns" to the variable input, labor. As the two workers are joined by still more people, sustained efforts to work as a team may cause the marginal product of the additional workers to continue increasing. At some point, however, the marginal product resulting from the additional workers will start to diminish because of the limits imposed by the fixed inputs. Belief in this inevitable decline in additional output is so strong that economists stated it in the form of the *law of diminishing returns.* This law states that "as additional units of a variable input are added to a fixed input, at some point, the additional output or marginal product will start to diminish."

To explain the relationship between returns to a variable input and marginal cost, we have extended the example in the previous paragraph into the schedule of numbers shown in Table 10–2.

In this example, we assume that each worker is paid $15 per hour. Recall that the marginal cost is defined as the change in total variable cost relative to the change in output. Labor is the only variable input in this example, and it costs the firm $15 per hour to employ each worker. Thus, the wage rate is, in fact, the change in total variable cost. The change in output resulting from the additional worker is each person's marginal product. Therefore, we can say that:

$$MC = \frac{\Delta TVC}{\Delta Q} = \frac{\text{wage rate}}{MP}$$

The relationship between the returns to the variable input and marginal cost can be summarized as follows:

- When a firm experiences *increasing* returns to its variable input (when its marginal product increases), its marginal cost will *decrease.*
- When a firm experiences *decreasing* (or *diminishing*) returns to its variable input (when a firm's marginal product decreases), its marginal cost will *increase.*
- When a firm experiences *constant* returns to a variable input (when its marginal product neither increases nor decreases), its marginal cost will be *constant* over the range of output produced.

Figure 10–4 compares the shapes of the total and average cost curves in economic analysis with those in break-even analysis. By utilizing a constant

TABLE 10–2 Output per hour (assuming a wage rate of $15/hr.).

Labor	Output	Marginal Product	Marginal Cost
0	0		
1	100	100	$.15
2	250	150	.10
3	350	100	.15
4	400	50	.30
5	425	25	.60

FIGURE 10–4   Cost structures used in break-even and economic analysis.

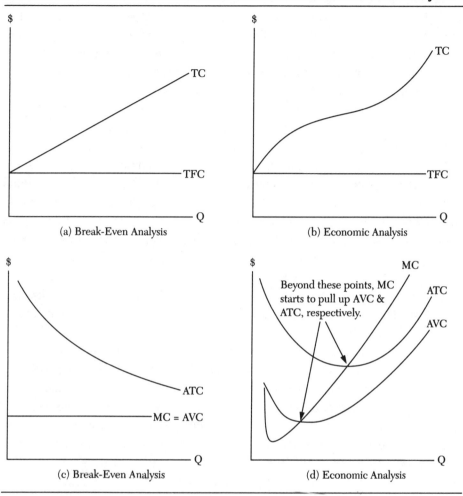

(a) Break-Even Analysis   (b) Economic Analysis

(c) Break-Even Analysis   (d) Economic Analysis

marginal cost, break-even analysis implicitly assumes that the firm experiences constant returns to its variable inputs over the range of output considered. By utilizing a marginal cost curve that decreases and then increases, economic analysis implicitly assumes that the firm experiences increasing returns and then diminishing returns to its variable inputs.

The linear total cost structure used in break-even analysis and the nonlinear structure used in economic analysis have differing patterns of change in per unit costs. In the linear case, both the marginal cost and average variable cost are constant, and of the same magnitude. (In cost accounting, this constant average variable cost is sometimes referred to as "standard variable cost." Cost accountants then determine the extent to which the actual variable cost differs from the standard variable cost.) Average total cost is not constant. It decreases as output increases because of its average fixed-cost component. The term sometimes used in business in reference to a decreasing average fixed cost is the "spreading out of overhead cost." Theoretically, average total cost can continue to decrease as output increases. But as seen in Figure 10–4, it actually starts to level off because there is less and less overhead cost to spread over the increasing number of units of output produced.

In the nonlinear case, marginal cost starts out below average variable and average total costs. For this reason, both average total cost and average variable cost decrease as production begins. Average total cost also decreases for the same reason that it decreases in the linear total cost example. That is, its average fixed-cost component is decreasing (see Table 10–1, column 5). As marginal cost increases, it eventually equals and surpasses the value of average variable cost. When this happens, average *variable* cost starts to increase. As marginal cost continues to increase, it first equals and then surpasses the value of average *total* cost. At this point, average total cost starts to go up as well. In effect, the rising value of marginal cost has caused average variable cost to increase to such an extent that it offsets the decreasing average fixed-cost component of average total cost. This particular point can be verified by studying the schedule of numbers in Table 10–1.

In addition to the law of diminishing returns, there are other possible reasons for the expected increase in a firm's marginal cost (and hence average variable and average total costs) as more of a good or service is produced. For example, to produce more output, a firm may have to pay overtime wages so employees will work longer hours. The higher levels of output may increase maintenance costs or alternatively increase the frequency of breakdowns of machinery and equipment. Finally, if a firm is not careful, running an operation at full capacity can affect the quality of the product, leading to increasing defects and returned products. This, too, will make the production of additional units of output *increasingly* more costly. The nonlinear cost structure is an integral part of the economic analysis of pricing, output, and competition, as will be described in Chapter 11.

THE ECONOMIC ANALYSIS OF LONG-RUN COST

In the economic analysis of the long run, a firm is assumed to have enough time to change all its resources. Economists also assume that the firm has enough time to adopt new technology; to learn new and better ways to produce its goods and services; and to organize itself more efficiently. In this section, we review the various ways that a firm can take advantage of this flexibility to reduce its costs over the long run.

Economies of Scale

Economies of scale is defined as the "decrease in the unit cost of production as a firm increases all its inputs of production." This phenomenon is illustrated in Figure 10–5.

In this figure, we see that the average total cost curve labeled "Plant 1" represents a certain amount of capacity. At its most efficient point, a firm with this plant capacity is able to produce Q_1 units of output at a unit cost of AC_1. "Plant 2" represents a greater production capacity because it is positioned to the right of Plant 1. But in addition, it is located on a lower level than Plant 1, signifying that over a certain range of output, the larger plant is able to produce greater amounts of output at a lower average cost than the smaller one. The graph in Figure 10–1 shows that at its most efficient level of production, Q_2, Plant 2 is able to produce the output at roughly two-thirds the average cost of Plant 1 when it operates at its most efficient level, Q_1.

The key factors that can cause a firm to experience economies of scale are listed in Table 10–3. Not every firm benefits from all these factors when it increases its scale of production. For example, firms that have a high level of debt will usually not be able to borrow at the lowest possible interest rate. Furthermore, size may not always offer the firm a cost advantage. Firms that are very large may become bureaucratic and inflexible, with management coordination and control problems. They might also experience a disproportionate increase in staff and indirect labor. The resulting increase in these types of cost may cause the average total cost to rise. These possibilities are listed in Table 10–3 under

FIGURE 10–5 Economies of scale.

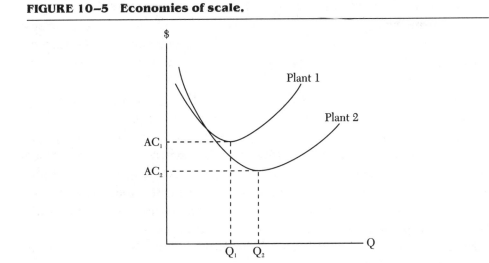

TABLE 10–3   Factors affecting economies and diseconomies of scale.

Reasons for Economies of Scale	Reasons for Diseconomies of Scale
Specialization in the use of labor and capital	Disproportionate rise in transportation costs
Indivisible nature of many types of capital equipment	Input market imperfections (e.g., wage rates driven up)
Productive capacity of capital equipment rises faster than purchase price	Management coordination and control problems
Economies in maintaining inventory of replacement parts and maintenance personnel	Disproportionate rise in staff and indirect labor
Discounts from bulk purchases	
Lower cost of raising capital funds	
Spreading of promotional and research-and-development costs	
Management efficiencies (line and staff)	

Source: Paul Keat and Philip Young, *Managerial Economics* (New York: Macmillan, 1992), p. 316.

the heading "Reasons for Diseconomies of Scale." If such diseconomies should occur, we can expect the cost curves illustrated in Figure 10–5 to shift upward and to the right. Figure 10–6 shows a long-run average cost curve reflecting both economies and diseconomies of scale.

Technological Innovation

Managers of a firm may seek to reduce the long-run costs of production by introducing new technologies. Such efforts may be the result of a firm's own research and development or may be from the purchase of technology developed by other firms' long-run investment of time and money in research and development. In either case, the new technology can be expected to increase the productivity of the firm's resources, which in turn leads to a reduction in its unit cost of production.

From the start of the industrial revolution in the United States in the early nineteenth century to the midpoint of the twentieth century, much of the technology that helped to increase productivity came in the form of labor-saving machinery. In the second half of this century, the growing use and importance of the computer began to change the very way in which productivity could be improved. At first, computers could be seen to increase productivity by automating certain administrative tasks, just as machines help to automate certain manual tasks in an assembly. For example, the data-processing capabilities of computers enabled companies to automate many routine clerical jobs such as accounts payable and inventory control.

FIGURE 10–6   Long-run average cost curve.

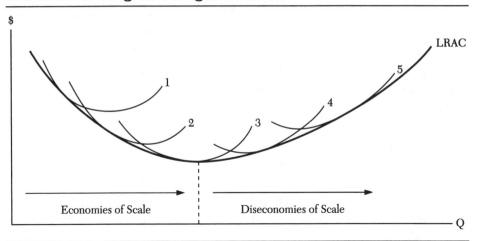

But very soon after the full-scale use of computers in large companies became the norm, managers began to realize that the tremendous amount of information about a company's activities that computers could store, analyze, and provide became in and of itself an important resource for improving a company's productivity. This was especially true in the late 1980s as companies shifted from centralized mainframe computers to decentralized personal computers and workstations tied together in networks. As a result, many more people in a company have direct control as well as access to this information. Moreover, this information is not only being made available in the form of descriptive reports, but also in the form of "expert systems." For example, credit card companies have developed an expert system to help their staff evaluate the creditworthiness of credit card applicants or approve the use of a card for a particular purchase. Manufacturing companies have developed expert systems to help maintenance personnel diagnose equipment problems.

Economies of Scope

In the long run, it is also possible for managers to identify ways to take advantage of "economies of scope." This cost-saving phenomenon occurs when it is possible to produce two or more products together at a lower per-unit cost than for each product separately. A key factor in this form of cost savings is the sharing of a company's fixed cost by multiple products. For example, certain neighborhood video rental stores are now starting to sell compact discs. These CDs are displayed on racks that occupy otherwise unused floor space in the stores. The use of this retail establishment's "excess capacity" in this manner reduces the average total cost of selling each of the products.

Another way that a company can utilize economies of scope is to produce goods or services that require similar skills and experience. For example, when PepsiCo expanded into the snack and fast-food business, it was able to utilize its background in one type of fast-moving consumer item (soft drinks) to another (chips, pizza, tacos, and fried chicken). The product development, channels of distribution, and marketing know-how are very similar in these two product groups.

The Learning Curve

As pictured in Figure 10–7, the learning curve shows that a firm's unit cost decreases as its total cumulative output increases. Its rationale is that old adage, "You improve with practice." Over the long run, as a firm produces more of a good or service, its workers are expected to get better at what they are doing. This increase in labor productivity will then decrease the unit cost of production. But other people besides the direct labor involved in the production process are also expected to improve with practice. For example, researchers may find less costly substitutes for raw materials currently used; engineers may develop more efficient production processes or product designs.

The learning curve has played an important part in the strategic approach called "learning-curve pricing." This approach advocates that a firm should set its price at a relatively low level to stimulate demand, even though there is the possibility that it will earn minimal profit or even incur a loss. The greater demand will accelerate the learning effects that accompany the higher accumulated volume of production. As the company's costs are brought down the

FIGURE 10–7   The learning curve.

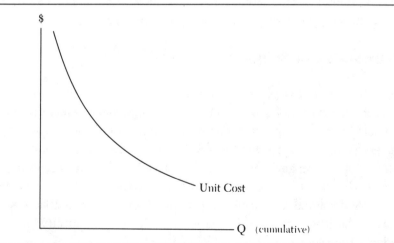

learning curve, the company will start to become profitable. The Boston Consulting Group was the first to conceptualize the learning curve as a strategic weapon. Japanese companies that manufacture such products as copiers, televisions, and computer chips used this strategy to their advantage when entering the U.S. market.

New Approaches to Manufacturing

Manufacturing in the United States has recently begun to move away from the reliance on mass production to a system that is referred to as "lean" or "flexible" manufacturing. This new system has enabled Japanese companies to achieve substantial improvements in productivity and cost efficiency. In these times of increasing global competition, American companies are hoping that the use of flexible manufacturing will also help them to attain similar results. Thomas Klier of the Federal Reserve Bank of Chicago describes the new approach to manufacturing as a

> . . . lean production system which emphasizes quality and speedy response to market conditions while utilizing technologically advanced equipment and a different organization of the production process.[1]

The advantages of the lean manufacturing system can be better appreciated by comparing it with the old system of mass production. Henry Ford was the first to use mass production in the automobile industry. He was so successful that this approach to manufacturing is often referred to as the "Fordist model" or the "Fordist system." Essentially, Ford's system involved the use of interchangeable parts and a moving assembly line. Workers were highly specialized and were expected to do one or two tasks over and over again. The management structure of this manufacturing process was hierarchical, and the management style was authoritarian. This system enabled the Ford Motor Company to achieve significant economies of scale. As reported by Thomas Klier, between 1909 and 1916, the price of a Model T Ford fell by 60 percent.

The Fordist model of manufacturing worked very well in the United States up until the early 1970s. It provided low-priced, standardized products to consumers who had growing purchasing power, a strong demand for goods and services, and fairly homogeneous tastes. However, the Fordist model had certain inherent weaknesses. Its reliance on specialization and standardized, interchangeable parts caused companies to be inflexible and unresponsive to changes in market demand. Its need to keep the assembly line running regardless of problems encountered in the manufacturing process forced companies to rely heavily on buffer stocks of inventories. These buffer stocks were set up at various stages of the production process and were quickly incorporated into the assembly line whenever a defective part was discovered. As a result, managers never had any incentive to investigate the reasons for the defects. Furthermore, the added cost to a firm of carrying large buffer stocks was another major disadvantage of the Fordist model.

Two postwar developments exposed the weaknesses of the Fordist approach. First, Japanese manufacturers and their use of lean manufacturing became formidable competitors in the U.S. market, because this new approach enabled the Japanese to make superior quality products at lower costs. Second, the tastes and preferences of American consumers became more diverse and less predictable. Thus, mass production became less useful as mass marketing gave way to niche marketing.

Lean manufacturing utilizes a "just in time" approach to inventory control. By keeping a minimum amount of inventory on hand, management requires workers to deal with quality problems immediately. This also reduces costs by eliminating the expenses associated with carrying the higher level of inventory. In lean manufacturing, workers also perform a greater and more diverse number of tasks. For example, in the automobile industry, a worker who installs wheels and tires is also expected to perform maintenance and cleaning duties and to monitor the quality of the operations. An increasing number of American and European companies have begun to adopt lean manufacturing to reduce their costs and remain competitive with Japanese manufacturers.

RECENT EXAMPLES OF WAYS TO MANAGE COSTS

On any given day, the business news of any major newspaper or periodical provides numerous examples of ways that businesses have been trying to cut or control their costs. For example, "Company News" is a daily column in the *New York Times*. On July 13, 1993, half the news items in that day's column concerned the issue of cost (see Figure 10–8).

Managers can cut or control costs in many ways, some of which are exemplified in Figure 10–8. These examples and others can be categorized into the approaches discussed on the next several pages.

The Budgetary Approach

This approach usually takes on an air of crisis for a company's management team, with the financial people taking the lead role as the messengers of gloom. For example, halfway through the fiscal year, the "bean counters" notice that operating departments are far over budget. Actual costs must then be brought into line with the budgeted amounts. Another possibility is that the company's revenue is falling far short of the forecasted amount. Ways must then be found to cut costs to compensate for the revenue shortfall. This approach to cost cutting usually entails the identification of items in the budget that are most amenable to quick changes. Travel is restricted or frozen; training classes are canceled; coffee and doughnuts are no longer provided at meetings.

The Input Reduction Approach

This approach has captured most of the headlines in today's news about cost reductions. Plant closings, layoffs, early-retirement offerings are all part of this. "Doing more with less" is an often-used phrase for this effort by companies to reduce their costs. For specific examples of this approach, just turn to any newspaper or periodical's coverage of the business news, including "Company News" (Figure 10–8).

The Input Cost Approach

The reduction of wage costs is a good example of this approach. As illustrated in the news item about Northwest Airlines (see Figure 10–8), management sometimes is able to extract wage concessions from workers in exchange for such things as shares of stock and seats on the board of directors. However, the news item about Sabena Airlines in this same news column shows that management can also implement wage cuts unilaterally.

Besides lowering the cost of labor, managers can work to reduce input costs by putting pressures on their suppliers or by searching thoroughly for the least costly suppliers. Managers of large companies with suppliers that depend on them heavily for business or who have the resources to conduct a global search for their suppliers are most likely to utilize this approach to cost cutting. An additional way for managers to reduce the cost of their inputs is to lower overhead costs by moving into offices with lower rents and maintenance costs.

The Input Substitution Approach

Managers can reduce costs anytime they can find cost-effective substitutes for their inputs. By cost-effective, we mean the cost of the input relative to its productivity. For example, an American manufacturing company that considers building a plant in a foreign country to take advantage of its low wages must also consider that country's labor productivity. If labor productivity is too low, it could offset any of the cost savings that result from the low wages.

FIGURE 10–8   Cost-cutting in the business news.

COMPANY NEWS

NORTHWEST ATTENDANTS TO VOTE ON REVISED PACT

 The International Brotherhood of Teamsters, which represents 9,000 Northwest Airlines flight attendants, said yesterday that its members would vote next week on a revised contract agreement with the airline. "This agreement assures that employees get back what they invest to save their jobs," the union's president, Ron Carey, said in a statement.

→ Cost

The union is negotiating with the company to make several adjustments to reflect gains made by the International Association of Machinists and Aerospace Workers. In exchange for wage concessions, the teamsters' union said, members will receive shares of Northwest stock, a provision regarding flight attendants' average salaries and control of three seats on the 15-member board.   (Reuters)

BANC ONE WINS F.D.I.C. CONTRACT TO MANAGE 5,000 LOANS

The Banc One Corporation of Columbus, Ohio, said yesterday that it had been awarded a three-year management contract from the Federal Deposit Insurance Corporation to manage about 5,000 commercial mortgage loans, valued at $1.7 billion. The Banc One Management and Consulting Corporation of Dallas, a unit of Banc One, the nation's eighth-largest banking company, will service the assets.

→ New Product

The loans are mostly commercial mortgage loans from various failed banks and savings and loans. Banc One Management will collect payments on the loans, administer escrow accounts, prepare documentation, remit funds to the F.D.I.C. or trustees and work out problem loans. The company said it was not assuming any credit risk related to the assets in the transaction.   (Bloomberg Business News)

CHEMICAL IS SAID TO BE IN TALKS TO BUY SHELL OIL CARDS

 The Chemical Banking Company is in discussions to buy the Shell Oil Company's charge card portfolio, industry sources said. Chemical is seeking to acquire four million accounts from Shell, the sources said. Chemical would convert Shell card holders into Visa or Mastercard holders. The Shell card is used for buying gasoline and other products at the company's service stations.

→ Product Acquisition

The deal would double Chemical's portfolio of credit card accounts to eight million, making the New York banking company the sixth-largest bank card issuer, as measured by number of accounts. Chemical officials would not comment about the plan but said the bank had talked to oil companies, auto makers and airlines about ventures to "co-brand" their private-label charge cards.   (American Banker)

ELECTRIC BOAT TO LAY OFF 800 TO MEET JOB-CUTTING GOAL

Electric Boat, based in Groton, Conn., said yesterday that it would lay off up to 800 workers in the next month to achieve its previously announced goal of cutting 1,500 jobs this year. The submarine builder had hoped to use attrition to take care of most of the reductions.

→ Cost

Electric Boat, a division of the General Dynamics Corporation, has been steadily cutting its work force in the last several years because of declining orders for submarines. Notices will be handed out between July 26 and Aug. 9. Electric Boat employs about 19,000, including fewer than 13,000 at its Groton shipyard.   (AP)

ANDREA IN DISTRIBUTION DEAL FOR NOISE-REDUCTION KITS

The Andrea Electronics Corporation of Long Island City, Queens, has signed its first distribution agreement for its noise-reduction products. Technology Services Group Inc. of Lansdale, Pa., will have the right to distribute two Andrea Electronics products using its active noise cancellation technology to the seven Bell regional telephone companies for use in public telephones. The agreement requires Technology Services to buy $10 million in noise-reduction kits in three years to keep its distribution rights. Andrea's stock soared $9.825 a share yesterday, to $38.50, on the American Stock Exchange, where its 33.3 percent gain was the best of the day.   (Bloomberg Business News)

→ Product Distribution

FIGURE 10–8 (Continued)

COORS PLANS TO CUT WHITE-COLLAR STAFF BY 20%

The Adolph Coors Company, the nation's third-largest brewer, said yesterday that it would cut its white-collar work force by 500 employees, or 20 percent, through early retirement, attrition or layoffs. Beginning in early August, employees will have 90 days to decide on accepting buyout packages, the spokesman said. If the total does not reach 500, the company will start layoffs. Coors, based in Golden, Colo., employs more than 11,000.

Coors also said it planned to farm out its marketing services by forming an independent company, Front Range Communications. The new company will offer 100 jobs to employees leaving Coors. (Reuters)

⟶ Cost

BELGIAN AIRLINE PLANS TO CUT WAGES BY UP TO 15%

The national airline of Belgium, Sabena S.A., announced wage cuts yesterday of up to 15 percent to stave off collapse and warned that many European airlines would face similar decisions soon. Smarting from a price war among European competitors and an industrywide crisis, the carrier's board approved measures to provide savings of five billion Belgian francs, or about $141 million, in the next three years.

The carrier's chief executive, Pierre Godfroid, said the fare war in Europe had wreaked havoc with Sabena and called on the European Community to curb the price cutting before companies go broke. Sabena also cited currency devaluations and political upheaval in Central Africa, one of Sabena's key regions. Sabena is owned by the Belgian Government and Air France. (AP)

⟶ Cost

DUTY FREE SHARES GO SOUTH ON REPORT OF BORDER SALES

Duty Free International Inc. stock fell by almost 24 percent yesterday, after the company said sales along the Canadian border might be down 10 to 15 percent from a year earlier. Its shares plunged $6.125, or 28.9 percent, to $19.875. It was the worst decline among New York Stock Exchange issues yesterday.

The company, based in Ridgefield, Conn., sells duty-free luxury merchandise along the Canadian and Mexican borders and to diplomats. Duty Free said that if the weakness in sales continued, earnings for the quarter ending July 31 would be between 28 cents and 31 cents a share, down from 35 cents a share for quarter a year earlier.
(Bloomberg Business News)

⟶ Demand

TASTY BAKING SETS SPINOFF OF PRINTING SUPPLIES UNIT

The Tasty Baking Company of Philadelphia said yesterday that its board had approved the spinoff of its Phillips & Jacobs Inc. printing supplies subsidiary to shareholders. Shareholders of record on July 21 will receive two shares of the new company for every three shares of Tasty Baking common stock held. The spinoff of Phillips & Jacobs Inc., based in Pennsauken, N.J. will be effective on Aug. 1. Phillips & Jacobs stock has been approved for trading on Nasdaq. (Reuters)

 Product Spinoff

ALLIED SIGNAL FORMS NEW BRAKING SYSTEMS UNIT

Allied Signal Automotive announced the formation of a new business unit, Allied Signal Braking Systems, combining the company's automotive brake and friction materials operations. Stephen Rabinowitz, vice president of Allied Signal Friction Materials, was named president of the new unit, which will be based in Drancy, France. Allied Signal Automotive, based in Southfield, Mich., is a subsidiary of Allied Signal Inc. of Morristown, N.J. (AP)

⟶ Cost

Cost-effectiveness is also a key to making decisions about the substitution of capital for labor. For example, a large financial services company converted the storage system for its records from microfilm to CD-ROM. At first, some managers resisted this move because of the cost of the conversion itself. They quickly realized, however, that the new system would increase the productivity of those involved in maintaining it to such an extent that it would eventually be less costly to run. Once again, it is not just the cost, but the cost relative to the output that is important.

The "Not-Made-Here" Approach

If it can be determined that an outside supplier or service vendor can perform an activity for less than it would cost a company, it would make sense for a company to utilize these outside resources. This has long been a practice in manufacturing activities. But there is also a growing amount of outsourcing in service activities. For example, an increasing number of companies are now contracting such firms as IBM and EDS to operate their data-processing facilities.

The Suggestion Box Approach

Sometimes, the best ways to reduce cost come from suggestions from employees, particularly those who work directly in the production process. For example, the story is told by those in the soft drink industry that an engineer in a bottling plant figured out that the empty space between the "fill-level" of a 12-ounce aluminum can and its top provided the opportunity for a potential savings in raw material cost. The engineer saw that by crimping the top of the can, a smaller lid could be used. Today, this reduction in the lid size enables soft drink bottlers to save substantial amounts in the cost of aluminum.

The Strategic Approach

In June 1993, the American Express Company appointed Jeffrey E. Stiefler to be its president. An article in the *New York Times* (June 30, 1993) reported:

> [Mr. Stiefler] will oversee IDS, an investment and insurance sales company, and the American Express Bank. . . . He will also oversee corporate efforts in technology, quality, and reengineering—in other words *cost cutting* [emphasis added].

One of the main reasons for Mr. Stiefler's promotion was the success he had as head of IDS in the development and implementation of a strategic plan.

As stated in this same news article, the strategic effort began by addressing the following question: "What sort of company could put IDS out of business and how [can] IDS become that company?" Answering these questions led IDS to make many changes in its operating procedures, its technology, and the way it pays its sales force. These changes included many of the cost-cutting areas discussed in this chapter.

This article about Mr. Stiefler and American Express underscores the strategic approach to managing a company's cost structure. Ideally, the management of a company's costs should not be a series of ad hoc cost-cutting measures. Rather, it should begin with a comprehensive analysis of cost as part of a long-run plan to beat the competition. Michael Porter, a professor at Harvard University, has been instrumental in promoting the use of cost analysis in the development of a company's strategic plan.[2] Basically, Porter's concept is for a company to divide its production activities into a complete "production-cost chain." Figure 10–9 shows such a chain for a manufactured product.

Porter's idea is that managers should try to compute the costs of each of these activities for their competitors as well as for their own company. They then must find ways to exercise a cost advantage over the competition in as many of these activities as possible. In our view, this is what Jeffrey Stiefler was doing at American Express's IDS.

COST, REVENUE, AND THE BOTTOM LINE

As important as it is to manage a company's costs, it is even more important to manage costs relative to its revenue. It would be obviously imprudent if management efforts to reduce cost led to an even greater reduction in revenue. It would be equally foolish if a decision not to spend a certain amount of money

FIGURE 10–9 The complete production cost chain.

←	The complete production-cost chain						→
					Manufacturer's selling price		Price paid by/Cost to the final user
Supplier- related activities ← →	↑ ←	Manufacturing-related activities			→	↑ ←Forward channel→ activities	
Purchased Materials, Compo- nents, Inputs, and Inbound Logistics	Production Activities and Opera- tions	Marketing and Sales Activities	Customer Service and Outbound Logistics Activities	General Adminis- trative Activities	Profit Margin	Wholesale Distributor and Dealer Network Activities	Retailer Activities

Source: Adapted from Arthur A. Thompson & John P. Forby, *Economics of the Firm,* Englewood Cliffs, N.J., Prentice Hall, 1993, p. 232.

prevented the company from earning an even greater amount of revenue. In other words, a thorough economic analysis involves considering the benefits as well as the costs of a particular decision. American Express provides an excellent example of considering cost in relation to benefits.

In the mid-1980s, the executives of American Express's Travel Related Services (TRS) realized that rising mailing costs were making it increasingly expensive to use a billing method referred to in the credit card industry as "country-club billing." The name is derived from the often-used practice in country clubs of mailing all the chits that members have signed during the month as proof that they actually incurred these expenses. Every month, American Express cardmembers were sent a carbon copy of all the slips that they actually signed when purchasing something from the service establishment. Not only did these slips increase the weight of the monthly statement, but they were also very expensive to retrieve, collate, and stuff into the envelopes.

The obvious solution would have been to drop the use of this billing method. MasterCard and Visa had already stopped country-club billing and provided only a line-item listing of the service establishments and the amount of the charges in their monthly statements to cardholders. The problem is that American Express used this billing method as a way of differentiating itself from its competitors. If it did away with country-club billing there would be one less reason for customers to perceive the American Express card as a premium product that required a higher annual fee than either MasterCard or Visa. Today, American Express continues to use country-club billing. However, it also uses state-of-the-art optical scanning and storage technology to reduce the administrative costs of this billing method. Instead of receiving the actual carbon copies of their record of charges, American Express card members now receive electronic reproductions of these records.

Another example of the way costs can be analyzed relative to revenue is the case of Western Digital Corporation, the fourth largest maker of hard disk drives in the United States. In the early 1990s, the company's profits and shareholder returns were hurt by a fierce price war in the industry. In mid-1993, Charles A. Haggerty, formerly of IBM, was appointed president to help the company turn around its sagging fortunes. According to an article in the *New York Times* (July 6, 1993) one of the first things that Haggerty did was to cut costs by "[paying] down debt to a manageable but still heavy level, cut selling and administrative expenses, reduce the head count from 7,500 to 6,300 and the customer list from 450 to at most 50."

What we find interesting is the cost-cutting step involving a reduction of Western Digital's customer list. On the surface, it would seem that less customers would mean less revenue and possibly less profit. But the move was made because it cost the company more to deal with these companies than the revenue these accounts brought in. Mr. Haggerty was quoted in the *New York Times* as saying, "It was too expensive for us to deal with them." As you might expect, the new "short list" of customers includes most of the major makers of personal computers such as Apple, Dell, and IBM.

Cutting costs with a close eye on the impact on revenue can also be illustrated with Procter & Gamble's new strategy to deal with serious price competition from generic brands. To ready itself to match the price cuts of the generics while still meeting profit targets, P&G is cutting promotional spending, eliminating weaker brands, and working to reduce manufacturing and administrative costs. This appears to be the typical list of steps that a company might take to reduce costs with one exception: cutting promotional spending.

For a company such as Procter & Gamble, promotional spending has always been a vital way of maintaining the premium image of products, with their higher prices and gross profit margins. Procter & Gamble started reducing its promotional costs in 1991. But by 1993, it became a crucial part of its overall policy of reengineering. Promotional costs involve discounts, fees, and allowances that manufacturing companies offer to retailers and wholesalers. According to *Business Week* (July 19, 1993), P&G began to realize that these types of promotions were not cost-effective. This is the basic argument from the company's point of view:

> It shifts some of the manufacturer's profits to the retailer. It often requires extra spending on special packaging and handling. Because it causes wild swings in production—creating spikes when promotions are high and troughs, when discounts are eliminated—it raises manufacturing costs. And worst of all, since it has Dawn dish detergent selling for $.99 one week and $1.89 the next, it makes consumers even more price sensitive.[3]

In effect, what the managers of P&G believe is that the revenues that promotions generate are not high enough to justify the costs. Competitors are watching closely to see if this is in fact the case.

Dell Computer Corporation, one of the fastest growing companies in the personal computer industry, provides a final example of why cost management should be closely tied to as many different aspects of a business as possible, particularly revenue and profit. Dell's strategy is a textbook example of the low-cost approach. By operating in low-rent office space, buying rather than making most of its PCs, and generally being tightfisted about all its operations, Dell has been able to undercut its rivals, particularly Compaq and IBM.

Unfortunately for Dell, in trying to keep its costs down, it also neglected to build the internal support structure required of a rapidly growing company. Michael Dell, the 28-year-old founder and CEO of the company that bears his name, perhaps described his company's situation best. According to Dell, "The fundamental problem is that the success of our marketing engine has produced more size and complexity than our support processes could keep up with" (*New York Times,* July 15, 1993). *Business Week* reported that Dell's growth problems have forced Michael Dell to work quickly to hire new managers with extensive experience in large companies (at the salary levels of large companies) and to install the types of systems and management controls that usually take a long time to develop (*Business Week,* July 12, 1993).

SUMMARY

It is critical for managers to understand how cost is measured, how cost changes both in the short run and the long run, and how the analysis of cost can be included in a company's overall strategic plan.[4] It is equally important for managers to recognize that cost must ultimately be considered in relation to such benefits as revenue and profit. In Chapter 11, we explain how cost is part of the "three C's" (cost, customers, competition) involved in the making of pricing and output decisions.

11 PUTTING IT ALL TOGETHER

Revenue, Cost, Price, and Profit

One of the most important business decisions that a manager must make is the pricing of a good or service. The ability of a firm to sell its product at a price that generates a desirable level of profit depends to various degrees on all the economic factors presented thus far in this book, particularly in the microeconomic chapters. To appreciate fully the significance of the pricing and output decision and how it involves all aspects of economic analysis, consider this question: "What do the following six firms and the selected products that they sell (noted in parentheses) have in common?" In answering this question, keep in mind the time frame of roughly 1988 to 1993:

- IBM (mainframe computers).
- Kodak (photographic film).
- Procter & Gamble (soaps and detergents).
- Apple (personal computers).
- Sears (retail merchandising stores).
- Merck (innovative, patent-protected drugs).

There may be a number of answers to this question, but we believe a key element all six have in common during this time period is their difficulty in either raising or maintaining the prices of their products, thereby resulting in an erosion of their profit margins. The managers of these products might not want to lower their prices, but they really have no choice; it all has to do with the changing economics of their business:

- *IBM*. IBM's most profitable product has been the mainframe computer. New technology has made it possible for personal computers or workstations tied together in networks to have the same computing power as the mainframe at a much lower cost. Prices of its mainframe computers have been falling while unit sales have slowed. Meanwhile, it is struggling to make a profit in the personal computer market and to gain market share from the leaders in the workstation market, Sun Microsystems and Hewlett-Packard.

  Basic Economic Changes. Shift in buyer tastes and preferences; increasing competition from other firms; technological innovations; introduction of substitute products.

- *Kodak*. Kodak is facing increasing price competition from Fuji and the potential threat of electronically recorded and stored images (the "filmless camera"). Consumers have also been increasing their use of video cameras for ordinary events as well as for special occasions. And to top it off, in mid-1993, Sony announced that it had developed a product that converts video recordings to still images. All these factors have severely hurt Kodak's core business: the manufacturing of photographic film and paper.

  Basic Economic Changes. Shift in buyer tastes and preferences; increasing price competition from major competitor; introduction of substitute products.

- *Procter & Gamble*. There has been a steady shift among buyers to private label consumer products. Part of this willingness by consumers to use the lower priced generics has been prompted by the sluggish economy and the end of the economic boom of the 1980s. All this has made it difficult for P&G to charge premium prices for its brand-name items, including soaps and detergents.

  Basic Economic Changes. Shift in buyer tastes and preferences; slowdown in the macroeconomy.

- *Apple*. The introduction of Microsoft's "Windows" gives users of IBM-compatible PCs an operating system that has the look, feel, and ease of use of Apple's Macintosh. As a result, Apple can no longer use this differentiation to justify the higher price of its personal computers.

  Basic Economic Changes. Introduction of a substitute product; intense price competition among sellers offering very similar products.

- *Sears*. There has been a substantial growth in "EDLP" (every day low price) national chains, particularly Wal-Mart and K-Mart. This has pushed Sears from first to third in total retail sales in the United States. In addition, warehouse stores, specialty catalogues, and specialty chains such as Circuit City, Home Depot, and Builder's Square, have cut further into

Sears' market share. Home shopping by television also looms as a potential threat to Sears as well as the entire retail merchandising industry.

Basic Economic Changes. Increasing competition from firms that compete aggressively on the basis of location, focused product categories, and price.

- *Merck.* Growing competition from generic drug manufacturers and the increasing market power of buyers such as health maintenance organizations make it difficult to raise prices and also cause some price reductions in certain products. There has also been an increasing number of "me-too" drugs that have been produced by the major drug companies. These are patented drugs that essentially provide the same therapy for a given condition. In addition, the publicity stemming from the federal government's efforts to reform the U.S. health care industry acts as a dampener on price increases.

  Basic Economic Changes. Increasing competition from firms that compete aggressively on the basis of price; changing consumer tastes and preferences; potential government regulatory actions.

In this chapter, the basic concepts and method of analysis of the microeconomic theory of the firm are used to explain the elements that go into a firm's pricing and output decisions. We strongly believe that this theory provides a solid foundation on which to build the analysis of these all-important decisions for any type of business, including those described here.

Our presentation begins with an analysis of a firm that operates in a perfectly competitive market. We then proceed to explain how the pricing and output decision is made in the other three market types: monopoly, monopolistic competition, and oligopoly. We conclude this chapter with a brief discussion of selected pricing strategies and tactics that can be seen as extensions of the microeconomic theory of the firm.

KEY ASSUMPTIONS USED IN THE MICROECONOMIC THEORY OF THE FIRM

Before discussing the pricing and output decision in the four types of markets, it is important to point out two key assumptions used in the economic theory of the firm:

1. The firm's primary objective is the short-run maximization of profit. If it cannot earn a profit, then the managers of a firm try to minimize its losses.

2. The opportunity cost of producing a particular good or service is included in the cost of doing business.

The term "short-run maximization" means that the firm tries to earn as much profit as it can, given the existing number of its competitors and its set of fixed and variable resources. We realize that in the short run, firms may strive primarily to increase revenues and market share. Once they establish a sizable presence in the market, they may then focus on profit maximization. But in economic theory, foremost in the minds of the managers of a firm is the pursuit of short-run profit.

The economic theory of the firm also assumes that a firm's opportunity cost is included in its cost structure. Chapter 10 defined opportunity cost as "the amount or subjective value sacrificed when choosing one activity over the next best alternative." In this chapter, the firm's opportunity cost is based on the amount that the firm could earn by selling the most profitable alternative compared with the one currently being produced. For example, suppose a firm is producing low-fat low-cholesterol frozen dinners, but it could be earning a certain amount of profit by producing frozen orange juice instead. The profit that is forgone by not producing the orange juice and producing instead the frozen dinners must be included in the production cost of the frozen dinners.

In actual business practice, the use of a financial "hurdle rate" is akin to the use of the opportunity cost concept in the economic theory of the firm. For example, a manager may want to invest company funds in a new venture. In developing the financial justification for this venture (often referred to by managers as "the business case"), the manager proposing the venture would have to show that its return on the company's investment exceeds some predetermined rate (for example, 14%). This rate is usually determined by the company's chief financial officer (CFO). It represents what the CFO believes is the return that a company could earn if it invested its money in another manner besides the proposed venture. It could also include a certain percentage above this amount for the perceived risk that a project entails. For example, if the firm could conceivably earn 7 percent in a safe financial investment and the project is considered to be extremely risky, another 7 percent might be added, giving a total required rate of return of 14 percent. If the projected rate of return on the investment in this venture exceeds the hurdle rate (for example, 16%), then the project is deemed financially sound. What the manager advocating this venture would be saying to the CFO is that the return on this project exceeds the opportunity cost of the investment funds.

Because opportunity cost is assumed to be embedded in the firm's cost structure, a firm that breaks even in economic analysis is actually earning an accounting profit that is just enough to compensate it for its opportunity cost. For example, suppose you are a manager of a supermarket and decide to leave your job to go into business for yourself as the owner and operator of a restaurant. In so doing, you give up $50,000 a year in salary and benefits. If you earn an accounting profit of $50,000 from the operation of the restaurant, you will have made just enough to compensate for the $50,000 opportunity cost of leaving your job. Because economic analysis includes the $50,000 of opportunity cost in the total cost of operating a business, the revenue needed to earn an accounting profit of $50,000 is actually just enough to break even. As will be explained later in this chapter, another term for economic breakeven is "normal profit."

In analyzing a firm's pursuit of short-run profit, the economic theory of the firm posits that its managers must address three basic questions:

1. Should our company be in this business? That is, should we be selling this particular product at all?
2. If so, how much should we produce?
3. Assuming we are able to set the price, what price should we charge?

The third question is qualified by the assumption that the firm is indeed able to set its own price. Those firms operating in perfectly competitive markets cannot set their own price. Therefore, this question does not apply to them.

THE OUTPUT DECISION OF A FIRM IN A PERFECTLY COMPETITIVE MARKET

In economic analysis, the type of market in which a firm is competing affects its ability to determine its price. In the extreme case of perfect competition, the managers of a firm have no power to set price and must sell their product at the price determined by the market forces of supply and demand. In effect, they do not have to make a pricing decision because they act as "price takers." They only have to decide how much output to produce. A review of the characteristics of a perfectly competitive market, first presented in Chapter 8, shows why this is so:

1. A perfectly competitive market consists of so many buyers and sellers that no one can set the price by controlling the supply or the demand. At the opposite extreme, a seller without competition could control the price by keeping the supply at a level relative to demand that would support the desired price. A single buyer would also have considerable power to set the price by dictating the demand for the product relative to the available supply.
2. In a perfectly competitive market, there is no way sellers can exercise any product differentiation. They all sell a standardized product. Any attempt by a seller to raise the price would simply result in a complete switch by customers to other suppliers because all are selling the same product.

3. There is complete information about the market price by all buyers and sellers. Sellers cannot offer any special discounts to selected buyers nor can they raise the price to take advantage of those buyers unaware of what the other competitors are charging.

4. There is easy entry and exit among buyers and sellers in a perfectly competitive market. As we will explain later, this ensures that firms will have a difficult time earning extraordinary profits in the long run.

The Total Cost-Total Revenue Approach

With this background in mind, let us assume that a typical firm is operating in a perfectly competitive market with the same short-run cost schedule first used in the previous chapter. Total fixed cost, total variable cost, and total cost are shown in Table 11-1. Let us further assume that supply and demand establish a market price of $105. Given this information, should the profit-maximizing firm be in this business? If so how much should it produce? In answering these questions, we should actually consider the latter question first. In fact, if the answer to this question is "zero," then we will have answered the first question as well.

Inspection of the numbers in Table 11-1 shows that the firm would do best by producing 8 units of output. We arrive at this answer simply by comparing the firm's total revenue with its total cost and selecting the output level that maximizes the difference between these two variables. Hence, we can refer to this method of finding the answer as the "total revenue-total cost approach." At output level 8, the firm earns a maximum profit of $221, given its costs and the going market price of $105. In fact, we can say that this amount is "economic"

TABLE 11-1   Total cost, total revenue, and total profit.

(1)	(2)	(3)	(4)	(5)	(6)	(7) Total Profit
Q	TFC	TVC	TC	P	TR	(or loss)
0	100	0	100	105	0	100
1	100	56	156	105	105	(51)
2	100	106	206	105	210	4
3	100	154	254	105	315	61
4	100	205	305	105	420	115
5	100	263	363	105	525	162
6	100	332	432	105	618	198
7	100	416	516	105	735	219
8*	100	519	619	105	840	221
9	100	646	746	105	945	199
10	100	801	901	105	1050	149

*Profit maximizing output level.

or "above normal" profit since it is actually more than enough to justify the firm being in this business. This is because opportunity cost is assumed to be included in the firm's cost.

If the firm's revenue is just enough to cover its total cost, it breaks even in the economic sense of the term. That is, it will have earned enough revenue to cover both its out-of-pocket cost plus the amount of profit forgone in its next best business activity. Given the cost data in Table 11–1, the firm would earn a normal profit (break-even or zero economic profit) if the market price is $72. At this price, the best that the firm could do would be to produce 6 units of output. At this level, its total revenue would be $432, the same as its total cost.

If the market price were $60, then the firm would suffer a loss. The firm could minimize its loss if it produced 5 units of output. At this level, its total revenue is $300, its total cost is $363 and its total loss would be $63. Does this mean that the firm should not be in this business? Well, that depends. In the short run, we know there are certain fixed costs that the firm would incur, regardless of the level of output. This means that even if the firm produced no output, perhaps by shutting down its factories, it would still have to pay for such things as insurance, security, certain utilities, administrative salaries, and interest on loan payments. It could go out of business completely or at least divest itself of all assets relating to this particular production activity, but this takes time and is considered in economic analysis to be a long-run change. Therefore, even though it is incurring a loss, it may well pay for the firm to continue producing in the short run as long as its operating losses are less than its fixed cost. In this example, we can see that this is in fact the case. If the firm simply shuts down, it would be losing the amount of its total fixed cost: $100. However, by operating and selling 5 units of its product for the going market price of $60, it would lose a smaller amount: $63. At the market price of $60, the managers of this firm are faced with the short-run decision of shutting down operations and losing $100 or operating and losing $63. The rational manager would certainly choose the latter alternative.

Marginal Revenue-Marginal Cost Approach

A more commonly used approach in economic analysis to determine how much a firm should produce involves the use of marginal analysis. This type of analysis can be defined as "the consideration of small changes around some given point."[1] Marginal analysis applies the following rule to the optimal level of output: *A firm that wishes to maximize its profit or minimize its loss should produce at the point where its marginal revenue is equal to its marginal cost.*

This "*MR = MC* Rule" can be easily applied to the data presented in Table 11–2. In this case, however, a small adjustment to the rule must be made. Quite

TABLE 11–2 Marginal revenue, marginal cost, and profit.

(a) P = $105

(1)	(2)	(3)	(4)	(5)	(6)	(7)
						Marginal Profit
Q	**AFC**	**AVC**	**ATC**	**MC**	**P = MR**	**(or Marginal Loss)**
0	—	—	—			
1	100.00	56.00	156.00	56	105	49
2	50.00	53.00	103.00	50	105	55
3	33.33	51.33	84.67	48	105	57
4	25.00	*51.25*	76.25	51	105	54
5	20.00	52.60	72.60	58	105	47
6	16.67	55.33	*72.00*	69	105	36
7	14.29	59.42	73.71	84	105	21
8	12.50	64.87	77.37	103	105	2
9	11.11	71.77	82.88	127	105	(22)
10	10.00	80.10	90.10	155	105	(50)

(b) P = $72

(1)	(2)	(3)	(4)	(5)	(6)	(7)
						Marginal Profit
Q	**AFC**	**AVC**	**ATC**	**MC**	**P = MR**	**(or Marginal Loss)**
0	—	—	—			
1	100.00	56.00	156.00	56	72	16
2	50.00	53.00	103.00	50	72	22
3	33.33	51.33	84.67	48	72	24
4	25.00	*51.25*	76.25	51	72	21
5	20.00	52.60	72.60	58	72	14
6	16.67	55.33	*72.00*	69	72	3
7	14.29	59.42	73.71	84	72	(12)
8	12.50	64.87	77.37	103	72	(31)
9	11.11	71.77	82.88	127	72	(55)
10	10.00	80.10	90.10	155	72	(83)

(c) P = $60

(1)	(2)	(3)	(4)	(5)	(6)	(7)
						Marginal Profit
Q	**AFC**	**AVC**	**ATC**	**MC**	**P = MR**	**(or Marginal Loss)**
0	—	—	—			
1	100.00	56.00	156.00	56	60	4
2	50.00	53.00	103.00	50	60	10
3	33.33	51.33	84.67	48	60	12
4	25.00	*51.25*	76.25	51	60	9
5	20.00	52.60	72.60	58	60	2
6	16.67	55.33	*72.00*	69	60	(9)
7	14.29	59.42	73.71	84	60	(24)
8	12.50	64.87	77.37	103	60	(43)
9	11.11	71.77	82.88	127	60	(67)
10	10.00	80.10	90.10	155	60	(95)

TABLE 11–2 (*Continued*)

(1)	(2)	(3)	(4)	(5)	(6)	(7)
				(d) P = $51		
						Marginal Profit
Q	**AFC**	**AVC**	**ATC**	**MC**	**P = MR**	**(or Marginal Loss)**
0	—	—	—			
1	100.00	56.00	156.00	56	51	(4)
2	50.00	53.00	103.00	50	51	1
3	33.33	51.33	84.67	48	51	3
4	25.00	*51.25*	76.25	51	51	0
5	20.00	52.60	72.60	58	51	(7)
6	16.67	55.33	*72.00*	69	51	(18)
7	14.29	59.42	73.71	84	51	(33)
8	12.50	64.87	77.37	103	51	(52)
9	11.11	71.77	82.88	127	51	(76)
10	10.00	80.10	90.10	155	51	(104)

often, it is difficult to find a level of output that coincides exactly with the point where *MR* equals *MC* (unless calculus is used). If this happens, then managers must find the level of output that brings *MR* as close as possible to *MC*, without being less than *MC*. As expected, we see from the data in Table 11–2 that the "adjusted" *MR* = *MC* rule gives us the same answer as the total revenue-total cost approach. At the price of $105, the firm should produce 8 units of output. At this level of output, *MC* is $103. If the firm were to proceed to the ninth unit of output, the marginal cost of production would exceed marginal revenue (specifically, $127 > $105), leading to a marginal loss to the firm of $22 due to producing this last unit.

In Column (6) of Table 11–2, we indicate that the firm's marginal revenue is equal to the product's price. This is true only when the firm is a price taker. Because the firm can sell as much (or as little) as it wants at the given market price, the revenue from each additional unit sold is in fact the product's price. Therefore, in the special case of perfect competition, the *MR* = *MC* can also be expressed as the *P* = *MC* rule.

The price at which the perfectly competitive firm must sell its product is determined by the interaction of supply and demand. If this price is high enough, following the *P* = *MC* rule will result in economic profit. Suppose, however, supply-and-demand conditions in the market result in prices such as those specified in the example using the total revenue-total cost approach. At the price of $72, the firm that follows the *P* = *MC* rule would produce 6 units of output because at that level, price would be closest to marginal cost. And, of course, we know that it would break even. At the price of $60, the *P* = *MC* rule dictates that the best a firm could do would be to produce 5 units of output, because this level brings the price as close as possible to the *MC* of $58. At this price, it would continue to operate in the short run because its loss of $63 would be less than the loss in total fixed cost that it would incur by shutting down.

Marginal analysis gives us a better insight into why, at the market price of $60, it is better for a firm to operate than to shut down, even though it is incurring a loss. Looking at the numbers in Table 11–2(b), we see that at the output level of 5, the price exceeds the firm's average variable cost of $52.60. In effect, this means that the price is high enough for a firm to cover its operating expenses. Another way of expressing this is to say that as long as the price is higher than the firm's average variable cost, it provides a positive contribution margin.

FIGURE 11–1   Profit and loss for different market prices.

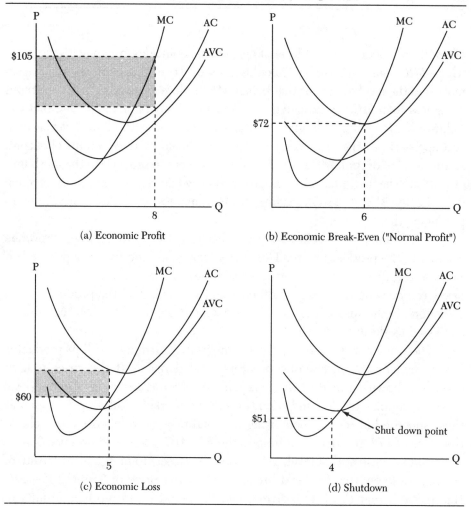

(a) Economic Profit

(b) Economic Break-Even ("Normal Profit")

(c) Economic Loss

(d) Shutdown

The discussion of break-even analysis in Chapter 10 stated that contribution margin is defined as the amount by which a firm's price exceeds its per unit or average variable cost.

A better appreciation of the contribution margin is possible by considering the market price of $51. At this price, P would be equal to MC at the output level 4. But, this would mean a negative contribution margin for the firm because $51 is less than the average variable cost of $51.25. In other words, by operating, the firm would not even be able to cover all its variable costs.

In addition to giving us a better insight into the concept of contribution margin, the marginal approach enables us to use graphs that are more efficient in illustrating the pricing and output decisions. The graphs in Figure 11–1 illustrate the numerical situations presented in Table 11–2. In Figure 11–1(a), we can easily see that the market price of $105 enables a firm to earn an economic profit. The shaded area shows the total amount of economic profit earned by the firm at this price. In Figure 11–1(b), we can see how the price of $72 leads the firm to produce 6 units of output: This output level results in the matching of its marginal cost not only with price but also with its average total cost. Therefore, only normal profit is earned. In Figure 11–1(c), we can see how the intersection of P and MC falls below the firm's average total cost, thereby causing it to lose money. The total loss is indicated in the shaded area. Because the price is greater than the average variable cost, however, the firm should continue operating in the short run.

In Figure 11–1(d), the shutdown situation is clearly revealed when the price falls below the firm's average variable cost. In fact, this figure also shows that the firm's "shutdown point" occurs when the price just equals the firm's average variable cost. At this point, the firm in the short run would lose just as much by operating as it would by shutting down.

Important Implications of the Perfectly Competitive Model for Business Managers

The significance of the perfectly competitive model for today's business decision makers is not so much in the numerical detail as it is in the model's short- and long-run dynamics. Suppose the firm finds itself in the situation represented by Table 11–2(a) and Figure 11–1(a). That is, given its cost structure and the market price of $105, it produces 8 units of output per time period and earns an economic profit of $221. In the long run, this economic profit can be expected to attract new sellers into the market and to encourage current sellers to expand their production capacity. This should lead to an increase in supply and a reduction in market price. As the price falls, economic profit becomes more difficult to earn.

In theory, the increase in supply would stop when firms in the market earn just enough to "break even" from an economic standpoint. As explained earlier, this means a firm earns just enough to offset any opportunity cost that it had to incur by not engaging in some other business activity. Thus, this break-even point is referred to in economic analysis as "normal profit" because an amount above this would induce firms to enter the market and consequently eliminate any profits above normal.

If for any reason, firms are not earning "normal profit," then we can expect some firms to eventually drop out of the market. (The popular press often refers to this situation as an "industry shakeout.") When this happens, the industry supply curve will shift to the left and the market price will begin to rise to the point that will enable the remaining firms to earn a normal profit. This situation is depicted by examples shown in Table 11–2(c) and Figure 11–1(c) where the market price is only $60. Figure 11–2(a) illustrates the changes that will occur when the price is high enough for firms to earn economic profit and Figure 11–2(b) illustrates the case when the price is so low that a typical firm will lose money (that is, not even able to achieve economic breakeven).

The short- and long-run dynamics of perfect competitiveness provide us with three key lessons for managers in highly competitive market environments:

1. *It is important to enter a growing market as far ahead of the competition as possible.*

When the market price is high enough for firms to earn an economic profit (in Figure 11–1, $105), it is because the demand is high, the supply is low, or some combination of both. It is at this time that smart managers will have their firms well established in such markets if at all possible. Very often, to be ahead of the pack requires the *entrepreneurial* skill of taking a risk before the demand has fully materialized or before the competition enters the market, rather than the managerial skill of reacting to a situation in the correct way. For example, the owner/managers of the first neighborhood video rental stores were betting that more VCRs would be sold and that more movies would become available on video. Meanwhile, because relatively few other firms were in the market, their rental prices were higher and they probably made some economic profit.

Now, it has become much more difficult to earn economic profit in this business. For one thing, there are many more video stores, including chains such as Blockbuster Video. For another, a certain saturation point has been reached by many customers who were at first eager to rent all the classics. For example, an industry survey indicates that currently about 60 percent of those who walk into a video rental store walk out without renting a tape. To offset these changes, many small video stores have either closed or have started to offer other services such as one-hour photo developing.

FIGURE 11–2 Long-run entry and exit of firms.

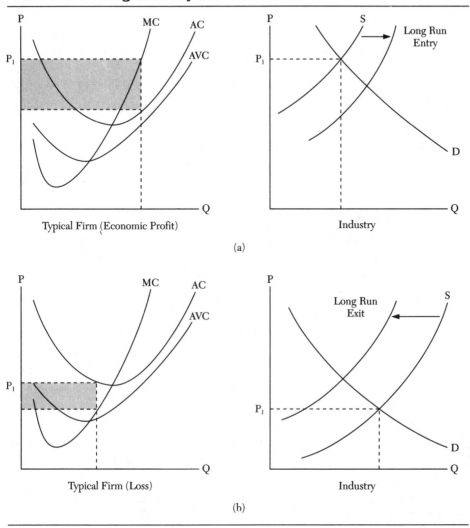

2. *No firm that is earning an economic profit can afford to be complacent or unprepared for increasing competition.*

The perfectly competitive model shows that economic profit eventually attracts new entrants and encourages investment in production and selling capacity. This will increase supply, drive prices down, and reduce economic profits. Therefore, no firm can afford to be complacent and unprepared. We found one of the best examples of this point when one of the authors was conducting a study of Korean-owned produce stores in New York City.

During an interview with one of the owners in his store in Queens, New York, we were interrupted by a customer who complained about the high prices of the produce. "Go ahead and buy your fruits from the supermarket and from my store on the same day," he retorted. "Several days later, those from the supermarket will not be fresh. However, mine will." Later, after the customer had left, he explained to us that the real reason his prices were high was because he knew that other Koreans would open up stores nearby as soon as they determined that he had a successful operation in his location. "I spent over six months driving around New York looking for the perfect location," he explained. "The most important thing I was looking for was not a location that was near a big apartment building or a subway stop. It was a spot that was as far away as possible from other Korean-owned produce stores. But I know that soon other Koreans will open up a store near mine. When they arrive, there will be fierce price competition. But I'll be ready because my prices are already higher than average."

Technically, the video rental market and the retail produce market are more like "monopolistic competition" than perfect competition because store owners do exercise some degree of control over their prices. But being prepared for the competition—most dramatically shown in the perfectly competitive model—applies to any market, even those that might be called monopoly or oligopoly. This will be seen when we discuss the other types of markets.

3. *It is impossible for a firm in a perfectly competitive market to compete on the basis of product differentiation. Therefore, the only way that it can earn or maintain a profit in the face of added supply and lower prices is to keep its costs as low as possible.*

As we showed in Figure 11–1, the representative firm earns an economic profit at the market price of $105. When the price falls to $72 (on the assumption that supply has increased), it earns only normal profit. However, if its cost structure were such that its unit cost decreased at every level of output, it could earn economic profit even at $72. Figure 11–3 illustrates this possibility. Managers seeking to accomplish this must pursue some of the methods that can be used to cut costs discussed in Chapter 10.

One way for managers to escape the pressures that a perfectly competitive market exerts on the cost structure is to try to differentiate their products from the competition. (In the jargon of the marketing professionals, the idea is to avoid operating in a "commodity-like market.") This option is discussed later in this chapter. Very often, however, differentiation only offers a company temporary relief from the competitive pressures on cost. In high-tech industries, firms are constantly keeping up and even leapfrogging the lead that one company may have in a particular technology. Microsoft's development of Windows, with its impact on Apple's ability to differentiate its Macintosh, is a good example. Companies may try to differentiate by maintaining brand loyalty, but there is increasing competition from generic and private labels. The globalization of the

FIGURE 11–3 Cost reduction and economic profit.

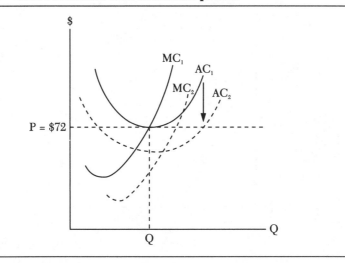

world economy is also posing new competitive cost pressures on U.S. companies as well as on companies around the world. All these factors have led experts such as Professor Michael Porter of Harvard University to state that, in the long run, the only way a company can ensure its survival is to be among the lowest cost producers. This is indeed the lesson that can be learned by understanding the perfectly competitive model.

MONOPOLY

The extreme opposite of a perfectly competitive market is one in which there is only one seller of a particular product or service. When a firm has a monopoly, it has considerable power to determine its price and output level. Some monopolies, such as public utilities, are sanctioned by the government. Government patent laws also provide companies with a monopoly for the duration of the patent on a particular product. Sometimes, circumstances allow a firm to enjoy a temporary monopoly. For example, there may be only one store in a shopping mall that sells gourmet coffee.

Whenever a firm has a monopoly in a particular market or market segment, economic theory states that it still must adhere to the $MR = MC$ rule to maximize its short-run profit. Because it is a "price maker" rather than a "price taker," we can no longer say that its price is equal to its marginal revenue. The relationship between its price and marginal revenue can best be understood using the analysis of price elasticity first presented in Chapter 8. Figure 11–4

FIGURE 11-4 Demand, marginal revenue, and total revenue of a price maker.

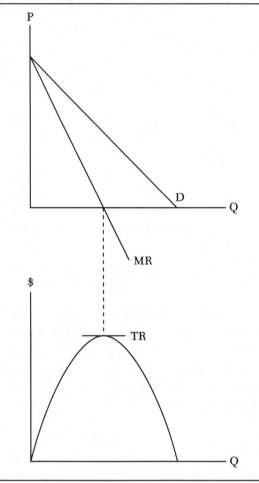

serves as a brief refresher. In this figure, the firm's marginal revenue line lies below its demand line. Furthermore, marginal revenue is positive over the elastic portion of the demand curve and negative over the inelastic portion. At the point of unitary elasticity or maximum total revenue, marginal revenue is equal to zero.

We can show how a monopoly would proceed to price its product by combining its cost structure with the type of demand and marginal revenue curve shown in Figure 11-4. For convenience, we will use the cost structure of the perfectly competitive model. This is shown in Table 11-3, along with information on price and marginal revenue. Note that we are skipping the total revenue-total cost approach and going right to the marginal revenue-marginal cost approach.

TABLE 11–3 Price, output, and profit for a monopoly.

(1)	(2)	(3)	(4)	(5)	(6)	(7) Total Profit
P	*Q*	*AVC*	*ATC*	*MC*	*MR*	(or loss)
$170	0	—	—			4
160	1	56.00	156.00	56	160	96
150	2	53.00	103.00	50	140	166
140	3	51.33	84.67	48	120	215
130	4	*51.25*	76.25	51	100	237
120	5	52.60	72.60	58	80	228
110	6	55.33	*72.00*	69	60	184
100	7	59.42	73.71	84	40	101
90	8	64.87	77.37	103	20	(26)
80	9	71.77	82.88	127	0	(201)
70	10	80.10	90.10	155	(20)	

If the data shown in Table 11–3 are available for the monopoly firm, it is a simple matter of applying the *MR = MC* rule to find the profit-maximizing price and quantity. We can see that *MR* is as close as possible to *MC* without falling below *MC* at the output level of 5. To sell five units, the firm would have to charge a price of $120. Figure 11–5 illustrates profit-maximizing levels of price and output for this firm.

As long as this firm enjoys a monopoly, it should continue selling its product for $120. It has the power to charge a higher price, but would not do so as long as its goal is to maximize its profits. As can be seen in Table 11–3, the price of $130 would result in a profit of $215, which is less than the $237 it

FIGURE 11–5 Demand, cost, and profit for a price maker.

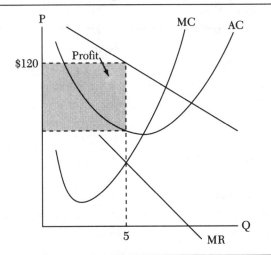

would earn by charging $120. Any changes in demand or cost would cause it to readjust its price accordingly. From a management standpoint, the most important implication of the monopoly model is that a firm in a position to be the only seller of a good or service should not charge the highest price, but the right price. And we know that the right price is the one that helps to equate the firm's marginal revenue with its marginal cost. In so doing, the firm will be able to earn the maximum profit.

Even a monopoly must be aware of the possibility of competition in various forms. To begin with, there might be competition from a substitute product. For example, Polaroid still has a monopoly on the instant developing camera. However, the increasing use of video cameras and the growing number of one-hour photo shops have greatly affected Polaroid's demand for its camera and film, forcing it to reduce prices and to constantly come up with new or improved products.

A monopoly can also be faced with a buyer that has considerable market power. An example of these "monopsonistic" firms can be found in the pharmaceutical industry. Up to now, the drug companies have enjoyed a monopoly on certain patent-protected products and as a result, they have been able to charge relatively high prices. The demand for these drugs is highly inelastic because they often provide lifesaving therapies. It is also inelastic because drugs are often prescribed by physicians who assume that the pharmaceutical costs are nearly if not completely reimbursable. These factors are all changing. Many drug companies are being faced with large customers such as health maintenance organizations, which try to be profitable by keeping their costs under control. One way to do this is to use their huge volume of purchases as leverage in negotiating with the drug companies for lower drug prices.

Finally, even companies that have a government-sanctioned monopoly cannot assume this protection lasts forever. The breakup of AT&T's telephone monopoly in the early 1980s is a good example of this. Moreover, the Federal Communications Commission (FCC) is now starting to allow competition in local telephone service. This market represents the last vestige of the monopoly telephone system and has heretofore been provided primarily by the regional telephone companies that were spun off from the original AT&T.

MONOPOLISTIC COMPETITION

Monopolistic competition is a cross between perfect competition and monopoly. It has most of the characteristics of a perfectly competitive firm: a large number of sellers, fairly easy entry and exit into and out of markets, and knowledge by all market participants about the prices being offered by the sellers. The only characteristic that makes it monopolistic is the ability of sellers to differentiate their product. For example, brand names, packaging, advertising, location, and "service with a smile" all help a product appear to be different from the competition. This differentiation enables a firm to charge a higher price than its competitors, if it so desires.

Let us assume that the data shown in Table 11–3 represents the cost and demand data for a monopolistically competitive firm. The big difference between this situation and that faced by a pure monopoly is that the monopolistic competitor cannot expect to earn an economic profit indefinitely. As soon as other firms notice that it is possible to earn an economic profit in a particular market, they will quickly try to move in. Their entry will cause the demand curve facing our representative firm to decrease (shift to the left) because the newcomers will be taking a certain amount of its business away. This is illustrated in Figure 11–6.

Theoretically, new sellers will continue to enter until it is no longer possible to earn economic profit.

The best examples of monopolistic competition are small retail businesses such as florists, pharmacies, pizzerias, restaurants, and dry cleaners. For instance, some Chinese restaurants try to offer foods from different regions of China. Others advertise that their chef comes directly from Hong Kong. Certain dry cleaners offer one-hour services or offer informal credit arrangements ("pay me the next time you come in"). The phrase found on many pizza boxes is "You've tried the rest, now try the best." Presumably, each pizzeria tries to live up to this slogan. The neighborhood pharmacist tries to get to know all his or

FIGURE 11–6   New entrants cause the demand of a monopolistic competitor to fall.

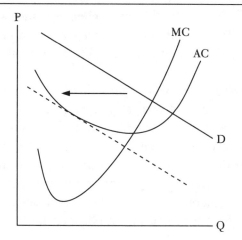

her customers by name and becomes familiar with a customer's entire family as well as all the family's doctors.

Competition among small retail businesses is fierce in the sense that there are many of them in each product or service category and entry into their markets is fairly easy. When one of the authors moved from the city into a suburban community 11 years ago, he lamented that almost no Chinese restaurants were to be found. Today, there are well over 30 Chinese restaurants within a 20-minute driving radius from his house.

The implications for managers of the monopolistically competitive firms is similar to that of the perfectly competitive ones. A firm must try to be first into a particular market. Moreover, the managers of the early entrants must never be complacent, because new entrants are always lurking around the corner, waiting to seize the economic profits of those already in the market. The main difference between perfect and monopolistic competition is the ability of firms to differentiate their products. A monopolistically competitive market offers the opportunity for firms to compete not only by trying to be the lowest cost producer but by effectively differentiating their products. If a pizzeria really serves the best pizza and its customers recognize and appreciate this, its business will continue to be strong no matter how many new pizzerias come to town. Furthermore, it may not have to lower prices in the face of added competition, as long as customers are willing to pay for the added value that they believe exists in the firm's differentiated product.

THE FIRM IN AN OLIGOPOLY

The determination of price, output, and profit is not as simple in an oligopolistic market as it is in the other three types. Firms in an oligopoly might sell a standardized product such as steel, aluminum, chemicals such as hydrochloric acid, or paper products. They might also sell a differentiated product such as beer, soft drinks, automobiles, mainframe computers, and long-distance telephone service.

The key characteristic distinguishing this market from the other three is the relatively small number of competing firms. There is no rule in economic theory that states how few the number has to be to qualify as an oligopoly. Some economists employ a criterion known as the "four-firm concentration ratio." If the top four firms in an industry or product segment have more than an 80 percent share of the total market, then we can consider it to be an oligopoly. This is the most stringent criterion. The cutoff point can be as low as 60 percent and the market might still be considered oligopolistic.

Regardless of how few firms there are in a market and what percentage of market share is held by the top firms, the most important implication for managers in an oligopoly is that the pricing practices in this type of market are informed by a condition known as "mutual interdependence." This means that ideally, each firm must set its price on the basis of its costs, demand elasticity, *and* the anticipated reaction by its competitors. In other words, assuming the data are available, just following the $MR = MC$ rule may not be enough to maximize profit.

Suppose you are a manager for Procter & Gamble and you have just hired a consultant to do an extensive study of your cost structure and the demand for your body soap products. You then decide to follow the $MR = MC$ rule and set the suggested retail price of the average size of your leading brand at $1.99. Suddenly, your main competitors, Colgate-Palmolive, Lever Brothers, and Dial, set prices for their products of comparable size and quality 10 to 15 percent lower than your price. What will you do? You may decide to fight them with more advertising and promotions. But you may also give in and drop your price closer to their level. You may even decide to do nothing because you are confident your customers have strong loyalty to your brand. The point is that you cannot price your products without explicit consideration of your competitors' reaction. This is the essence of mutual interdependence.

Generally, when mutual interdependence characterizes the pricing process in a market, all the sellers end up charging the same or close to the same price. The next time you're in the supermarket, check out the price of the pink soap pad and the blue soap pad or Hefty trash bags and Glad trash bags. The chances are that the prices within each product group will be the same. The similarity in the prices of products sold in oligopolistic markets might lead you to suspect collusion among the competing firms. If this were indeed the case, the managers of these firms would be subject to criminal investigation. But collusion is not required to have every competitor charging the same price. Here is why.

A useful device employed in economic theory to explain why mutual interdependence leads to the same price being charged among competitors is the "kinked demand curve." Figure 11–7 illustrates the essential aspects of this curve. Notice that at the given price P^*, the demand curve is "kinked" in the sense that its slope is not continuous. The portion of the demand curve above the price is much more elastic than the portion below the price. This is because at the market price, each competitor anticipates that if it increased its price, none of the other competing firms would follow. If this is indeed the case, the firm that raised its price stands to lose a considerable amount of market share. Hence, the elastic demand curve.

FIGURE 11–7   The kinked demand in an oligopoly market.

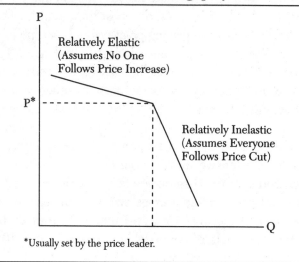

*Usually set by the price leader.

The lower portion of the kinked demand curve is rather inelastic because each competitor is assumed to anticipate that the lowering of its price would bring about retaliatory price reductions from the other competitors. The main intent of lowering prices in an oligopoly is to gain market share at the expense of the other competitors. If every firm lowers its price, none would gain very much market share. In fact, they may all end up selling about the same amount as before but at lower prices, unless their price cuts help to stimulate total market demand. This would depend on the price elasticity of the industry demand.

The kinked demand curve helps to explain why firms in an oligopolistic market tend to charge the same price. Seldom does any one competitor want to strike out on its own to either raise or lower the price. Raising the price may mean pricing the company out of the market and losing significant market share. Lowering the price entails the risk of starting a price war in which everyone loses. However, the kinked demand curve model does not explain how the market price around which the kinked curve lies is actually determined, nor does it explain why individual firms try from time to time to either raise or lower the price.

Economists have employed game theory to elucidate the dynamics of price determination in a mutually interdependent environment. Essentially, this technique involves designating the probability of certain pricing outcomes based on the assumption of one firm raising or lowering its prices relative to the possible reactions of competitors (either holding fast in its price or following suit). While game theory is an important part of the current literature in microeconomics, we believe it is a bit too theoretical to have any widespread applications in actual business situations.[2] However, the thought process involved in setting up and solving the game theory problem may very well be a part of the decision-making process for managers of oligopolistic firms.

Without resorting to game theory, we can say that the raising of price in an oligopolistic market is usually done by a price leader. Typically, this firm has the largest market share. For example, in the automobile market, General Motors has usually played this role. In the market for mainframe computers, the entire industry looked to IBM to set or raise prices, and in certain cases continues to do so. Whatever price is determined by the leader, the others either set it at the same level or perhaps slightly lower. During the years in which IBM dominated the mainframe market, the other companies generally used the IBM price as an umbrella under which they set their prices about 10 percent lower. IBM was able to maintain this "10 percent umbrella" because of its ability to lock in customers to its proprietary system of hardware and software and its backing of outstanding support and training services. Sometimes, companies in oligopoly markets that do not have the largest market share act as price leaders. For example, smaller banks outside New York City, such as Boatman's Bank in St. Louis, often initiate a change in the prime rate. Regardless of who initiates a price increase, there is no guarantee that the others will follow. Every so often, it is reported in the business news that a large steelmaker such as USX (formerly U.S. Steel) has to roll back its prices because other steelmakers did not follow. Recently in the tobacco industry, Philip Morris tried to foster an increase in the price of generic cigarettes but was unsuccessful because no other company followed its move to raise prices.

Although lowering the price can also be done by the company with the largest market share, it often is instigated by one that has a smaller share. Because it has the largest market share, the price leader usually does not want to "rock the boat" and risk eroding its profit margin by triggering a price war. Moreover, when large firms cut their prices, they leave themselves open to accusations by smaller companies of predatory pricing tactics designed to drive weaker or smaller firms out of business. This was the case in the airline industry.

In recent years, the price cutting done by the top three or four manufacturers of personal computers and the price wars of the major U.S. airlines are good examples of price reductions that can be started by any firm in the market. As this book is being completed, TWA, the eighth largest major airline in a field of ten, announced a "two-for-one" ticket policy on selected routes and times for the remaining part of 1993. Many of the top airlines quickly followed suit.

In the summer of 1992, American Airlines presumably tried to establish some kind of order in the bazaarlike atmosphere of airline ticket pricing by establishing a three-tiered pricing system. Some order was restored but not to the extent desired by American. A year later, Continental and Northwest sued

American Airlines for using this simplified pricing structure as a means of driving them out of business. A quick decision was rendered by the court acquitting American of these charges. The price cutting and all-out wars that have gone on in the airline industry in the late 1980s and early 1990s serve as a hard lesson to managers of how brutal an oligopoly can become if the kind of order represented by the kinked demand curve is not established.

A pricing action taken by Philip Morris represents an unusual tactic by a price leader. In recent years, Philip Morris and its chief competitors have observed a gradual switch among smokers away from the leading premium brands of cigarettes to generic or private labels. Part of it was a result of the general move among consumers in the value-conscious 1990s to seek out private labels or generic brands in all consumer items as a way of saving money. Part of it was because rising cigarette taxes pushed the retail price of this product to such a high level that consumers were beginning to react in a more elastic fashion than usual.

On April 2, 1993 (now dubbed "Marlboro Friday" by the popular press), Philip Morris made the decision to cut the price of its leading brand, Marlboro by an average of $0.40 a pack, a considerable amount, given that its retail price (including taxes) ranges from about $2.00 to $2.95 depending on the part of the country where it is being sold. Wall Street reacted by sending down the price of Philip Morris stock. For a while, the big question in the minds of investors and competitors alike was "Is this a temporary or a permanent price reduction?" Articles in the popular press quoted a Philip Morris spokesperson as saying the company would maintain a "wait and see" attitude. This remark prompts us to remind readers that if a large, profitable, and sophisticated company such as Philip Morris is really unsure how consumers will react to changes in price, it is indeed difficult for any company to produce quantitative estimates of price elasticity.

Part of what Philip Morris was waiting for was the response by consumers to the price reduction. But we believe that another aspect of its assessment was the reaction by its competitors. Would its action prompt an all-out price war in which every price cut is matched by a greater price cut? As it turned out, other cigarette companies reduced the price of their major brands by about the same amount as Philip Morris did, but primarily in the form of mail-in rebate coupons. In late summer of 1993, the prices of the industry brand names simply settled down to a lower level, thereby becoming more price competitive with the generics. Quarterly earnings of all the tobacco companies were hurt by the price cutting. It remains to be seen whether Marlboro Friday will help or hurt the long-term financial situation. In particular, it will be interesting to see whether the lower price will start to affect Marlboro's premium image.[3]

THE "THREE C'S OF PRICING"

We can summarize the factors that go into the pricing of a product by using what economics and marketing professors often refer to as the *three C's of pricing*: cost, customers, and competition. "Cost" refers to the firm's fixed and variable costs. "Customers" refers to the consumer demand for a firm's product. Actually, two distinct aspects of demand must be considered in the pricing decision: (1) There is the overall market demand for the product and (2) there is the demand faced by the individual firm. "Competition" refers to the actions or reactions of other firms in the market. In our economic analysis, we specified two basic ways that competition can influence a particular firm's pricing decision. One way is for competing firms to enter or exit from the market. The other way is for these firms to engage in price competition by instigating or matching price cuts.

The extent to which the managers of a firm must consider the three C's in its pricing decision depends on the type of market in which the firm is competing. The managers of a perfectly competitive firm have the simplest decision to make. Their price is determined by the market and they only have to decide whether their firm's cost structure is low enough for them to earn a profit at that price. The managers of an oligopolistic firm have the most complex pricing decision. They have to consider all three C's, including both aspects of customers and competition. The managers of a monopoly and a monopolistic competitor have decisions whose complexity lies somewhere in between these two extremes. The factors that go into the pricing decisions of managers in each type of market are summarized in Table 11–4.

TABLE 11–4 Factors that must be considered in the pricing of a product—The three C's.

Market Type	Cost	Customers		Competition	
		Total Market Demand	Demand for a Particular Firm's Product	Entry & Exit	Price Comparison
Perfect competition*	X	X		X	
Monopoly	X	X	X**		
Monopolistic competition	X	X	X	X	
Oligopoly	X	X	X	X	X

*Because firms in this market are price takers, these factors are used only to help them decide how much to produce.

**This is actually the same as total market demand because the monopoly is the sole supplier of the product.

PRICING STRATEGY AND TACTICS

Pricing is one of the most important tasks of a manager; it is also one of the most difficult. Part of the problem is that managers often deal with imperfect or incomplete data about cost and demand. For example, recall the case of Philip Morris waiting to see their customers' response to the reduced price of Marlboro. Seemingly, the lack of data on cost should not be as much of a problem. However, most companies produce more than one product, and sometimes their management information system is not set up to track and produce reports about the cost of each product. For example, the regional telephone companies are finding that increasing competition is forcing them to understand the costs of providing various telephone services in the different geographic areas that they serve. However, it is only recently that they have been developing the management information system (MIS) capability to separate out and report the cost of providing each type of service.[4] Finally, even though a company has all the information about the cost and price elasticity of a product, it might still be unsure how competitors will react to a change in its price.

Without complete information about cost and price elasticity, it is difficult for a firm to follow the $MR = MC$ rule. However, even if the profit-maximizing (or loss-minimizing) price cannot be determined, economists assume that rational managers will try to find a price that helps to at least approximate this level of profit. How do they try to do this? The following sections briefly review some useful pricing techniques that consider cost, customers, and competition but not in as thorough and precise a manner as the $MR = MC$ approach. One of the most commonly used practices is called "cost-plus pricing."

Cost-Plus Pricing

Cost-plus pricing involves the computation of the unit cost of a good or service and the markup of its price by some percentage of this cost. For example, suppose a product costs $2 per unit to produce. Suppose further that a 50 percent markup on this cost is established, thereby resulting in a $3 selling price. It is typical of firms in the restaurant and retail merchandising business to mark up from the per unit cost of goods sold rather than from the per unit total cost. For example, an upscale retail store might mark up the wholesale price of men's suits by 200 to 300 percent or women's dresses by as much as 400 percent. In setting the prices of its menu, similar markups might be taken by a restaurant based on the cost of the food.

Cost-plus pricing is a far cry from the more precise $MR = MC$ rule. If it is done well, however, it can achieve similar results because the degree to which the price of a product can be marked up from its cost depends on the degree of price elasticity. The more elastic a product, the less able a firm is to mark up its price. The less elastic it is, the more a firm should be able to mark up its price. We have found that many businesspeople, particularly in retail apparel, understand this even though they may not be familiar with the economic terms. To test your understanding of this, ask yourself what product category in a typical shopping mall enjoys the highest average markup from cost of goods sold (gross profit margin)? Answer: women's apparel. In men's apparel manufacturing, what product on the average has the highest markup? Answer: ties.

Price Skimming

During the early stages of a product's life cycle, the early entrants into the market might want to take advantage of the lack of competitors and the growing demand for the new product by charging a relatively high price. This is known as price skimming. As the market becomes crowded with more competitors and the growth in total market demand starts to taper off, firms will have to lower prices in an attempt to increase total market demand as well as to try and take market share from the other competitors. The pricing of VCRs is a good example of this particular technique. Remember when the first VCRs cost about $1,000? You can be sure that at this price the producers of this product were able to skim the cream of "early product adopters." Perhaps you were one of those who paid this price and could boast about being the first among your friends and family to have one.

Penetration Pricing

Sometimes it is beneficial for a firm to charge a relatively low price to establish itself in a market that is dominated by well-established competitors. This approach is called penetration pricing. A good example of this is the pricing of small copiers by Japanese competitors who were trying to penetrate the copier market in the United States in the 1970s. At that time, Xerox dominated the market. Not only did the Japanese enter the copier market at the low end (a segment where Xerox had little presence), but they also offered very attractive prices for their small copiers.

In the market for photographic film, Fuji has been using its lower prices to penetrate the near monopoly of Kodak in the U.S. market. And it has been very successful.[5] It is one thing, however, to lower prices to build volume, it is another to earn a profit on this volume. This is where a type of pricing called "learning-curve" pricing might be employed.

Learning-Curve Pricing

This approach assumes a company's cost of production will fall as it increases its total volume of production, because of the learning-curve effect (see Chapter 10). To accelerate the learning experience and the accompanying reduction in cost, a firm may set a relatively low price for a product. The low price will increase the amount of products sold, which in turn will enable personnel to learn how to be more efficient much faster. The manufacturers of computer chips have used this type of pricing technique in their industry.

Prestige Pricing

Sometimes, to create or maintain an aura of prestige and status for a product, sellers will try to price it as high as possible. Luxury cars, perfume, high-fashion, and designer apparel come to mind as obvious examples of products subjected to prestige pricing. But this approach may also be used for everyday consumer items such as soaps and detergents, beer, coffee, and cigarettes. Sellers of these products who use this technique refer to it as "premium pricing."

In using prestige pricing, sellers assume that buyers associate the price of the product with certain desirable characteristics such as quality and status. For example, this type of pricing would be effective if a typical buyer thinks, "If a product costs so much, it has to be good." Nonetheless, sellers cannot assume that the higher price alone will provide sufficient reason for believing it is a better product. They also have to spend substantial amounts of money to promote the image of prestige and quality for the product's brand identity. And, the product itself must actually have characteristics of quality and status.

Price Discrimination

Price discrimination occurs when a seller is able to charge different prices for the same good or service. The key is for the seller to segment customers into distinct and mutually exclusive segments, each with its own unique price elasticity. Those customers with the more inelastic demand are charged higher prices, and those with the more elastic demand are charged lower prices. In economic analysis, there are three degrees of price discrimination:

1. "First degree discrimination" occurs when a seller tries to sell a product at the highest price each buyer is willing to pay. The bargaining that is done by sellers in a bazaar or street market best exemplifies this type of pricing.
2. "Second degree price discrimination" occurs when the seller divides up the buyers into distinct groupings according to the volume of their usage.

Any firm that offers volume discounts for large purchases is engaging in this type of price discrimination. For example, electric utilities offer lower rates for customers who use large amounts of kilowatts per month.

3. "Third degree price discrimination" seeks to segment the market on the basis of differences in price elasticity and certain demographic characteristics that make it impossible for a buyer to switch from one category to another. For example, some academic journals set a higher subscription rate for libraries than for individuals. The setting of lower admission prices by movie theaters for children and senior citizens is another example of third degree price discrimination.

SUMMARY

We have tried to show in this chapter how and why an understanding of the microeconomic theory of the firm can help to sharpen a manager's pricing skills. The more information that a manager can obtain about a product's cost structure, demand, and competitive offerings, the better able he or she will be to use the $MR = MC$ rule to set a profit-maximizing price. Even without complete information about cost, customers, and competition, a thorough understanding of the theory of the firm can still help a manager to use more effectively the various pricing techniques such as cost-plus pricing and price discrimination.

Beyond the specific skills of product pricing, we have tried to show that the microeconomic theory of the firm can give a manager a heightened awareness of the unrelenting forces of competition. As shown in our discussion of the four market types, no product's price, not even those sold by a dominant oligopoly or a monopoly, is ever completely safe from competitive pressures. The manager who is aware of and prepared for this competition is the one most likely to be successful.

APPENDIX

A GUIDE TO OFFICIALLY COMPILED ECONOMIC DATA

Much of the data discussed or referred to in this book, especially the macroeconomic data discussed in Chapters 2 to 7, are compiled and presented by agencies of the U.S. government in various publications. This appendix provides a selection of samples from three of the most important sources of officially compiled data:

1. *The Survey of Current Business.*
2. *The Federal Reserve Bulletin.*
3. *The Economic Report of the President.*

There are many other sources of detailed economic and business data, but these are representative of the sources that every manager is likely to desire access to at some time.

This appendix provides brief descriptions and sample pages from each source. The examples are intended to serve only as samples of the scope and type of information provided. Seek out and use these sources as a means of exploring the raw material of economics and applying it to business management.

THE SURVEY OF CURRENT BUSINESS

The Survey of Current Business is the primary publication through which the Commerce Department presents economic and business data. It is published monthly and consists of three main parts. Each part is color-coded:

1. The *white* pages in the front contain articles (with supporting tables) on various aspects of *aggregate* economic activity, often quarterly.
2. The *yellow* pages present tables of data and charts showing the *business cycle* behavior of 250 key economic indicators that have cyclical characteristics.
3. The *blue* pages consist of tables of roughly 1,900 series covering most aspects of general business activities, as well as specific industry measures.

The National Income and Product Accounts

Each month, detailed tables of the National Income and Product Accounts (NIPA) are presented. In the first month of each quarter (January, April, July, and October), the tables present the "advance" estimate of the prior quarter's GDP. In subsequent months, the "preliminary" and "final" estimates are presented.

The example on the facing page shows the first two summary GDP tables (in current and constant dollars, respectively) for the final estimates for the second quarter of 1993. Including special charts and supplementary detail, the entire set of NIPA tables covered pages 7 through 39 in the September 1993 issue of *The Survey of Current Business*.

NATIONAL INCOME AND PRODUCT ACCOUNTS

Selected NIPA Tables

New estimates in this issue: Second quarter 1993, final.

The selected set of national income and product accounts (NIPA) tables shown in this section presents quarterly estimates, which are updated monthly. (In most tables, the annual estimates are also shown.) These tables are available on the day of the gross domestic product (GDP) news release on printouts and diskettes on a subscription basis or from the Commerce Department's Economic Bulletin Board. For order information, write to the National Income and Wealth Division (BE-54), Bureau of Economic Analysis, Washington, DC 20230 or call (202) 606–5304.

Tables containing the estimates for 1929–88 are available in the two-volume set *National Income and Product Accounts of the United States;* see inside back cover for order information. Estimates for 1989 are in the July 1992 SURVEY OF CURRENT BUSINESS (most tables) and the September 1992 SURVEY (tables 3.15–3.20 and 9.1–9.6). (Fixed-weighted price indexes for 1988 and 1989 were subsequently revised and published in the April 1993 SURVEY.) Estimates for 1990, 1991, and 1992 are in the August 1993 SURVEY (most tables) and in this issue beginning on page 29 (tables 1.15, 1.16, 3.15–3.20, 7.15, and 9.1–9.6). This month's SURVEY also contains revised alternative quantity and price indexes and the associated percent changes for 1988–92 beginning on page 40 (tables 7.1, 7.2, and 8.1) and summary NIPA series back to 1929 beginning on page 47. NIPA tables are also available, most beginning with 1929, on diskettes or magnetic tape. For more information on the presentation of the estimates, see "A Look at How BEA Presents the NIPA's" in the February 1993 SURVEY.

NOTE.—This section of the SURVEY is prepared by the National Income and Wealth Division and the Government Division.

Table 1.1.—Gross Domestic Product
[Billions of dollars]

	1991	1992	1992 I	1992 II	1992 III	1992 IV	1993 I	1993 II
Gross domestic product	5,722.9	6,038.5	5,908.7	5,991.4	6,059.5	6,194.4	6,261.6	6,327.6
Personal consumption expenditures	3,906.4	4,139.9	4,046.5	4,099.9	4,157.1	4,256.2	4,296.2	4,359.9
Durable goods	457.8	497.3	484.0	487.8	500.9	516.6	515.3	531.6
Nondurable goods	1,257.9	1,300.9	1,278.2	1,288.2	1,305.7	1,331.7	1,335.3	1,344.8
Services	2,190.7	2,341.6	2,284.4	2,323.8	2,350.5	2,407.9	2,445.5	2,483.4
Gross private domestic investment	736.9	796.5	750.8	799.7	802.2	833.3	874.1	874.1
Fixed investment	745.5	789.1	755.9	786.8	792.5	821.3	839.5	861.0
Nonresidential	555.9	565.5	547.0	566.3	569.2	579.5	594.7	619.1
Structures	182.6	172.6	173.9	174.5	170.8	171.1	172.4	177.6
Producers' durable equipment	373.3	392.9	373.1	391.7	398.4	408.3	422.2	441.6
Residential	189.6	223.6	208.9	220.6	223.3	241.8	244.9	241.9
Change in business inventories	–8.6	7.3	–5.1	12.9	9.7	12.0	34.6	13.1
Nonfarm	–8.6	2.3	–10.8	6.2	4.4	9.5	33.0	16.8
Farm	.0	5.0	5.6	6.7	5.3	2.4	1.5	–3.7
Net exports of goods and services	–19.6	–29.6	–7.0	–33.9	–38.8	–38.6	–48.3	–65.1
Exports	601.5	640.5	633.7	632.4	641.1	654.7	651.3	660.0
Imports	621.1	670.1	640.7	666.3	679.9	693.5	699.6	725.0
Government purchases	1,099.3	1,131.8	1,118.5	1,125.8	1,139.1	1,143.8	1,139.7	1,158.6
Federal	445.9	448.8	445.5	444.6	452.8	452.4	442.7	447.5
National defense	322.5	313.8	312.3	310.4	316.7	315.7	304.8	307.6
Nondefense	123.4	135.0	133.1	134.2	136.1	136.7	137.9	140.0
State and local	653.4	683.0	673.0	681.2	686.2	691.4	697.0	711.1

NOTE.—Percent changes from preceding period for selected items in this table are shown in table 8.1.

Table 1.2.—Gross Domestic Product in Constant Dollars
[Billions of 1987 dollars]

	1991	1992	1992 I	1992 II	1992 III	1992 IV	1993 I	1993 II
Gross domestic product	4,861.4	4,986.3	4,922.0	4,956.5	4,998.2	5,068.3	5,078.2	5,102.1
Personal consumption expenditures	3,258.6	3,341.8	3,302.3	3,316.8	3,350.9	3,397.2	3,403.8	3,432.7
Durable goods	426.6	456.6	446.6	447.5	459.0	473.4	471.9	484.2
Nondurable goods	1,048.2	1,062.9	1,052.0	1,055.0	1,062.9	1,081.8	1,076.0	1,083.1
Services	1,783.8	1,822.3	1,803.7	1,814.3	1,829.0	1,842.0	1,855.9	1,865.4
Gross private domestic investment	675.7	732.9	691.7	737.0	739.6	763.0	803.0	803.6
Fixed investment	684.1	726.4	696.7	724.4	730.0	754.3	773.7	790.6
Nonresidential	514.5	529.2	510.5	528.8	533.8	543.7	562.3	584.3
Structures	160.2	150.6	152.8	152.9	148.8	148.0	148.2	151.1
Producers' durable equipment	354.3	378.6	357.7	375.9	385.1	395.7	414.1	433.2
Residential	169.5	197.1	186.2	195.6	196.2	210.6	211.4	206.2
Change in business inventories	–8.4	6.5	–5.0	12.6	9.6	8.7	29.3	13.0
Nonfarm	–8.6	2.7	–9.6	7.0	5.8	7.5	29.3	17.1
Farm	.2	3.8	4.6	5.6	3.8	1.2	.0	–4.1
Net exports of goods and services	–19.1	–33.6	–15.2	–38.0	–42.5	–38.6	–59.9	–75.2
Exports	543.4	578.0	571.0	570.2	579.3	591.6	588.0	593.2
Imports	562.5	611.6	586.2	608.2	621.8	630.3	647.9	668.4
Government purchases	946.3	945.2	943.1	940.7	950.2	948.9	931.3	941.1
Federal	386.5	373.0	372.1	369.2	377.0	373.7	357.6	359.4
National defense	281.3	261.2	261.2	257.9	264.4	261.3	246.0	246.4
Nondefense	105.3	111.8	110.9	111.3	112.5	112.4	111.5	113.0
State and local	559.7	572.2	571.0	571.5	573.2	573.2	573.7	581.6

NOTE.—Percent changes from preceding period for selected items in this table are shown in table 8.1.

Special Article—Example: U.S. International Transactions, Second Quarter 1993

Each month there are a number of special articles that appear on a regular schedule in the white pages. For instance, an article on *U.S. International Transactions* appears four times a year (March, June, September, and December) providing a detailed accounting of the U.S. international transactions and the balance of payments position.

The page opposite shows the first page of the article that appeared in the September 1993 issue, presenting details on U.S. international transactions in the second quarter of 1993. Table A, shown, provides a summary of U.S. International Transactions showing most of the main items that comprise the current account. The detailed discussion and tables presented in this article covered pages 94 through 156.

U.S. International Transactions, Second Quarter 1993

By Douglas B. Weinberg

THE U.S. current-account deficit increased to $26.9 billion in the second quarter of 1993 from $22.3 billion (revised) in the first quarter (table A).[1] A large increase in the deficit on goods and services and a small increase in the deficit on investment income were partly offset by a decrease in net unilateral transfers.

In the capital account, net recorded capital inflows were $12.9 billion in the second quarter, compared with $13.4 billion in the first. Net inflows on banking transactions diminished, and inflows on official transactions picked up.

U.S. dollar in exchange markets

In the second quarter, the U.S. dollar depreciated 3 percent on a trade-weighted quarterly average basis against the currencies of the 10 industrial countries and 2 percent against the currencies of 26 countries comprising the 22 OECD countries

---

[1]. Quarterly estimates of U.S. current- and capital-account components are seasonally adjusted when statistically significant seasonal patterns are present. The accompanying tables present both adjusted and unadjusted estimates.

---

and the 4 newly industrialized countries in Asia (table B, chart 1). The dollar depreciated against the Japanese yen and major European currencies.

The dollar depreciated 9 percent against the yen in the second quarter, continuing a sharp fall begun early in the year; by mid-June, the dollar reached a new post-World War II low against the yen. The second-quarter movement was primarily influenced by market sentiment that a lower dollar-yen exchange rate was needed to reduce large surpluses in Japan's trade and current-account balances. Official intervention in the foreign exchange market during the quarter temporarily slowed, but failed to stop, the dollar's decline.

The dollar depreciated against major European currencies in the second quarter. It depreciated most against those currencies not in the Exchange Rate Mechanism (ERM), declining 4 percent against the British pound and 3 percent against both the Italian lira and the Swiss franc; it depreciated 1 percent against the currencies of countries participating in the ERM (Germany,

Table A.—Summary of U.S. International Transactions
[Millions of dollars, quarters seasonally adjusted]

Line	Lines in tables 1 and 10 in which transactions are included are indicated in ()	1991	1992	1992 I	1992 II	1992 III	1992 IV	1993 I r	1993 II p	Change: 1993 I–II
1	Exports of goods, services, and income (1)	708,489	730,460	182,211	181,454	182,038	184,759	184,071	187,810	3,739
2	Merchandise, excluding military (2)	416,937	440,138	108,347	108,306	109,493	113,992	111,530	113,125	1,595
3	Services (3)	164,260	179,710	44,836	44,507	45,350	45,018	46,463	47,227	764
4	Income receipts on investments (11)	127,292	110,612	29,028	28,641	27,195	25,749	26,078	27,458	1,380
5	Imports of goods, services, and income (15)	−723,388	−763,965	−181,507	−191,697	−192,666	−198,098	−198,793	−207,678	−8,885
6	Merchandise, excluding military (16)	−490,739	−536,276	−126,110	−133,107	−137,105	−139,954	−140,839	−147,513	−6,674
7	Services (17)	−118,378	−123,299	−30,788	−30,856	−30,069	−31,589	−31,839	−32,432	−593
8	Income payments on investments (25)	−114,272	−104,391	−24,609	−27,734	−25,492	−26,555	−26,115	−27,733	−1,618
9	Unilateral transfers (29)	6,575	−32,895	−7,389	−8,010	−7,147	−10,348	−7,586	−7,066	520
10	U.S. assets abroad, net (increase/capital outflow (−)) (33)	−59,974	−50,961	−1,029	−8,695	−10,798	−30,438	−12,358	−25,428	−13,070
11	U.S. official reserve assets, net (34)	5,763	3,901	−1,057	1,464	1,952	1,542	−983	720	1,703
12	U.S. Government assets, other than official reserve assets, net (39)	2,905	−1,609	−275	−293	−305	−737	55	55	−480
13	U.S. private assets, net (43)	−68,643	−53,253	303	−9,866	−12,445	−31,243	−11,910	−26,203	−14,293
14	Foreign assets in the United States, net (increase/ capital inflow (+)) (48)	83,439	129,579	19,834	44,450	26,450	38,845	25,718	38,292	12,574
15	Foreign official assets, net (49)	17,564	40,684	21,124	21,008	−7,378	5,931	10,929	17,839	6,910
16	Other foreign assets, net (56)	65,875	88,895	−1,290	23,442	33,828	32,914	14,789	20,453	5,664
17	Allocations of special drawing rights (62)	....	....	....	....	....	....	....	....	....
18	Statistical discrepancy (63)	−15,140	−12,218	−12,120	−17,502	2,123	15,280	8,948	14,070	5,122
19	Memorandum: Balance on current account (70)	−8,324	−66,400	−6,685	−18,253	−17,775	−23,687	−22,308	−26,934	−4,626

r Revised.
p Preliminary.

Business Cycle Indicators

This section presents economic indicators arranged with special regard to their cyclical characteristics. As discussed in Chapter 2, economic activities can be classified according to whether they lead, coincide with, or lag aggregate economic activity.

The page excerpted opposite presents the three composite indices (leading, coincident, and lagging), as well as the component series for each composite index for the latest month available (August 1993) and the 12 months preceding it. Subsequent pages provide detail on these and associated economic indicators classified by their cyclical characteristics.

BUSINESS CYCLE INDICATORS

> NOTE TO USERS: *The composite indexes of leading, coincident, and lagging indicators are scheduled to be revised in the November* SURVEY. *For more information, see the box on page C-6.*

Series originating in Government agencies are not copyrighted and may be reprinted freely. Series from private sources are provided through the courtesy of the compilers and are subject to their copyrights.

Current and historical data for the series shown in the C-pages are available on diskettes, printouts, and the Commerce Department's Economic Bulletin Board. For more information, contact the Business Cycle Indicators Branch, Business Outlook Division (BE-52), Bureau of Economic Analysis, U.S. Department of Commerce, Washington, DC 20230. (Telephone: (202) 606-5366; fax: (202) 606-5313.)

NOTE.—This section of the SURVEY is prepared by the Business Cycle Indicators Branch.

Series no.	Series title and timing classification	Year 1992	1992 July	Aug.	Sept.	Oct.	Nov.	Dec.	1993 Jan.	Feb.	Mar.	Apr.	May	June	July	Aug.

1. COMPOSITE INDEXES

The Leading Index

910	Composite index of leading indicators, 1982=100 (L,L,L)	148.9	148.9	148.6	148.7	149.4	150.5	153.1	152.5	153.2	151.6	151.9	151.4	151.5	151.6	153.1
	Percent change from previous month	.5	.1	-.2	.1	.5	.7	1.7	-.4	.5	-1.0	.2	-.3	.1	.1	1.0
	Percent change over 3-month span, AR	4.7	-1.6	-.3	1.3	5.2	12.4	8.6	7.4	-3.9	-1.6	-4.6	-.3	-.8	4.6	
	Leading index components:															
1	Average weekly hours, mfg. (L,L,L)	41.0	41.1	41.1	41.0	41.1	41.2	41.2	41.4	41.4	41.2	41.5	41.4	41.2	41.4	41.5
5	Average weekly initial claims for unemployment insurance, thous. (L,C,L) ‡.	412	417	436	455	396	373	333	364	343	376	374	390	386	399	378
8	Mfrs.' new orders, consumer goods and materials, bil. 1982$ (L,L,L)	1,106.53	91.74	91.04	91.90	93.50	95.13	98.05	98.64	98.21	96.26	96.48	94.51	94.89	94.03	94.65
32	Vendor performance, slower deliveries diffusion index, percent (L,L,L)	50.2	51.1	50.2	50.9	48.8	51.0	51.7	53.2	53.1	52.1	53.8	51.7	49.9	49.6	51.6
20	Contracts and orders for plant and equipment, bil. 1982$ (L,L,L)	520.10	43.07	42.70	43.88	43.79	42.62	47.54	45.55	49.76	47.23	46.94	48.26	51.23	50.00	52.97
29	Index of new private housing units authorized by local building permits, 1967=100 (L,L,L)	87.7	86.4	86.2	89.3	91.0	90.8	95.4	92.3	91.0	82.5	87.8	89.4	88.9	92.7	98.0
92	Change in mfrs.' unfilled orders, durable goods, bil. 1982$, smoothed (L,L,L)	-2.81	-2.94	-3.20	-3.49	-3.35	-3.47	-3.06	-2.43	-1.85	-1.99	-2.30	-2.80	-3.20	-3.07	-2.92
99	Change in sensitive materials prices, percent, smoothed (L,L,L) †	.27	.72	.52	.50	.22	-.15	-.26	-.22	-.16	-.20	-.36	-.46	-.48	-.47	-.43
19	Index of stock prices, 500 common stocks, 1941-43=10, NSA (L,L,L)	415.74	415.05	417.93	418.48	412.50	422.84	435.64	435.23	441.70	450.16	443.08	445.25	448.06	447.29	454.13
106	Money supply M2, bil. 1982$ (L,L,L)	2,387.5	2,377.3	2,378.6	2,380.8	2,378.8	2,376.8	2,373.0	2,351.5	2,340.2	2,335.3	2,327.2	2,344.4	2,349.2	2,351.3	2,346.3
83	Index of consumer expectations, U. of Michigan, 1966:1=100, NSA (L,L,L) ©	70.3	67.6	69.5	67.4	67.5	78.2	89.5	83.4	80.6	75.8	76.4	68.5	70.4	64.7	65.8
950	Diffusion index of 11 leading indicator components:															
	Percent rising over 1-month span	54.5	50.0	40.9	54.5	63.6	63.6	77.3	36.4	50.0	9.1	54.5	36.4	54.5	45.5	90.9
	Percent rising over 6-month span	67.0	59.1	63.6	77.3	81.8	81.8	72.7	72.7	45.5	22.7	31.8	45.5			

The Coincident Index

920	Composite index of coincident indicators, 1982=100 (C,C,C)	123.6	123.8	123.2	123.3	123.9	124.2	125.5	125.5	126.0	126.1	126.9	127.2	127.0	126.5	127.4
	Percent change from previous month	.1	.4	-.5	.1	.5	.2	1.0	0	.4	.1	.6	.2	-.2	-.4	.7
	Percent change over 3-month span, AR	1.5	-.6	0	.3	3.3	7.3	5.3	5.9	1.9	4.5	3.9	2.9	-1.3	.6	
	Coincident index components:															
41	Employees on nonagricultural payrolls, thous. (C,C,C)	108,519	108,605	108,615	108,674	108,789	108,921	109,079	109,235	109,539	109,565	109,820	110,058	110,101	110,312	110,273
51	Personal income less transfer payments, bil. 1987$, AR (C,C,C)	3,460.4	3,432.8	3,450.0	3,451.2	3,484.7	3,484.5	3,689.9	3,441.9	3,449.3	3,471.1	3,517.7	3,524.3	3,511.7	3,493.9	3,537.2
47	Index of industrial production, 1987=100 (C,C,C)	106.5	106.8	106.6	106.2	107.5	108.4	108.9	109.3	109.9	110.1	110.4	110.2	110.4	110.9	111.1
57	Manufacturing and trade sales, mil. 1987$ (C,C,C)	5,852,305	490,591	485,782	492,068	491,584	495,679	505,895	505,283	507,033	505,647	503,088	505,922	509,945	504,496	
951	Diffusion index of 4 coincident indicator components:															
	Percent rising over 1-month span	65.6	87.5	25.0	37.5	75.0	87.5	100.0	50.0	100.0	62.5	75.0	75.0	62.5	50.0	83.3
	Percent rising over 6-month span	89.6	100.0	100.0	100.0	100.0	87.5	100.0	100.0	100.0	75.0	75.0	100.0			

The Lagging Index

930	Composite index of lagging indicators, 1982=100 (Lg,Lg,Lg)	106.0	104.7	104.9	104.2	104.1	104.6	104.2	103.8	103.9	103.5	103.4	103.2	103.4	104.2	104.4
	Percent change from previous month	-.5	-.7	.2	-.7	-.1	.5	-.4	-.4	.1	-.3	-.2	-.2	.2	.8	.2
	Percent change over 3-month span, AR	-5.6	-5.2	-4.5	-2.3	-1.1	0	-1.1	-2.6	-2.3	-1.5	-2.7	-.8	3.1	4.7	
	Lagging index components:															
91	Average duration of unemployment, weeks (Lg,Lg,Lg) ‡.	17.9	18.3	18.3	18.5	19.2	18.4	19.2	18.7	18.3	17.5	17.4	17.6	17.6	17.9	18.3
77	Ratio, mfg. and trade inventories to sales in 1987$ (Lg,Lg,Lg)	1.61	1.60	1.62	1.60	1.60	1.59	1.56	1.56	1.56	1.57	1.58	1.57	1.56	1.57	
62	Change in labor cost per unit of output, mfg., percent, AR, smoothed (Lg,Lg,Lg)	.1	0	.2	.8	.8	-1.4	-.2	-2.2	-3.7	-4.3	-4.3	-3.7	-3.4	-2.8	-2.0
109	Average prime rate charged by banks, percent, NSA (Lg,Lg,Lg)*	6.25	6.02	6.00	6.00	6.00	6.00	6.00	6.00	6.00	6.00	6.00	6.00	6.00	6.00	6.00
101	Commercial and industrial loans outstanding, mil. 1982$ (Lg,Lg,Lg)	361,793	356,142	356,459	354,948	359,663	364,712	365,248	359,005	359,516	353,221	354,116	355,773	356,490	362,331	364,402
95	Ratio, consumer installment credit outstanding to personal income, percent (Lg,Lg,Lg)	14.27	14.24	14.26	14.17	14.01	14.05	13.46	14.23	14.24	14.18	14.01	13.96	14.04	14.18	
120	Change in Consumer Price Index for services, percent, AR, smoothed (Lg,Lg,Lg)	3.8	3.5	3.3	3.1	3.4	3.7	3.9	4.1	4.2	4.2	4.3	4.3	4.2	3.8	3.7
952	Diffusion index of 7 lagging indicator components:															
	Percent rising over 1-month span	32.1	14.3	28.6	21.4	57.1	64.3	50.0	42.9	71.4	42.9	71.4	42.9	57.1	64.3	50.0
	Percent rising over 6-month span	20.3	14.3	14.3	42.9	42.9	42.9	50.0	42.9	35.7	57.1	50.0	60.0			
940	Ratio, coincident index to lagging index, 1982=100 (L,L,L)	116.7	118.2	117.4	118.3	119.0	118.7	120.4	120.9	121.3	121.7	122.7	123.3	122.8	121.4	122.0

NOTE.—The following current high values were reached before July 1992: June 1991—BCI-106 (2,424.6); August 1991—BCI-92 smoothed (-0.83); December 1991—BCI-62 smoothed (3.1) and BCI-77 (1.66); and June 1992—BCI-99 smoothed (0.83).

See page C-6 for other footnotes.

Cyclical Indicator Charts

The yellow pages of *The Survey of Current Business* also present cyclical charts for most of the economic indicators covered in the tables. The charts generally cover 25 years and include shaded bars for the periods of officially classified business cycles.

For example, the charts on the facing page track the composite leading, coincident, lagging, and ratio of coincident to lagging indices for the period from 1956 through August 1993. (The numbers above the arrows show the months from a cycle peak or trough. For example, the −8 that precedes the 1969–70 recession for the index of leading indicators means that the index reached a cyclical peak eight months before the recession began.)

CYCLICAL INDICATORS

Composite Indexes

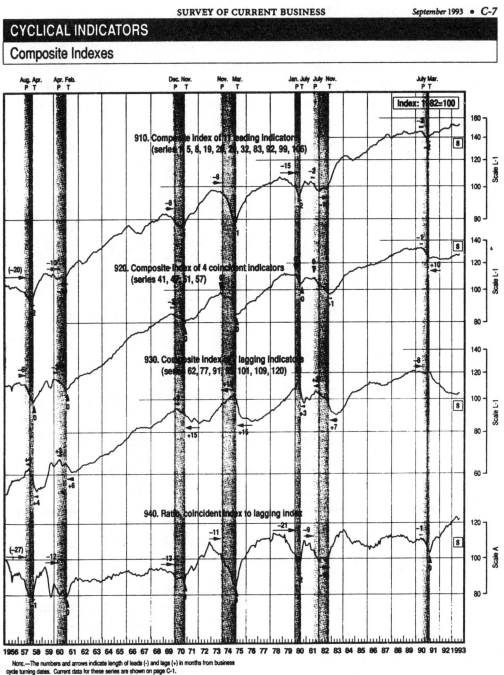

Index: 1982=100

910. Composite index of leading indicators
(series 1, 5, 8, 19, 20, 29, 32, 83, 92, 99, 106)

920. Composite index of 4 coincident indicators
(series 41, 47, 51, 57)

930. Composite index of lagging indicators
(series 62, 77, 91, 95, 101, 109, 120)

940. Ratio, coincident index to lagging index

1956 57 58 59 60 61 62 63 64 65 66 67 68 69 70 71 72 73 74 75 76 77 78 79 80 81 82 83 84 85 86 87 88 89 90 91 92 1993

NOTE.—The numbers and arrows indicate length of leads (-) and lags (+) in months from business
cycle turning dates. Current data for these series are shown on page C-1.

247

Current Business Statistics

The blue pages of *The Survey of Current Business* present monthly data on most economic series. The page excerpted presents detailed data on personal income and industrial production. A list of the major topics is presented below. This list provides a summary of most economic and business measures compiled by the U.S. government. The blue pages are an invaluable source of current data.

A. *General Business Indicators*
  (1) Personal Income (by Source and Disposition)
  (2) Industrial Production
  (3) Business Sales (Manufacturing, Wholesale, and Retail)
  (4) Business Inventories (Manufacturing, Wholesale, and Retail)
  (5) Business Inventory-Sales Ratios (Manufacturing, Wholesale, and Retail)
  (6) Manufacturers' Shipments, Inventories, and Orders
  (7) Business Incorporations
  (8) Industrial and Commercial Failures

B. *Commodity Prices*
  (1) Prices Received and Paid by Farmers
  (2) Consumer Prices
  (3) Producer Prices
  (4) Purchasing Power of the Dollar

C. *Construction and Real Estate*
  (1) Construction Put in Place
  (2) Construction Contracts
  (3) Housing Starts and Permits
  (4) Construction Cost Indexes
  (5) Real Estate

D. *Domestic Trade*
  (1) Advertising
  (2) Wholesale Trade
  (3) Retail Trade

E. *Labor Force, Employment, and Earnings*
  (1) Labor Force and Population
  (2) Employment

  (3) Average Hours per Week
  (4) Aggregate Employee-Hours
  (5) Hourly and Weekly Earnings
  (6) Employment Cost Index
  (7) Help Wanted Advertising
  (8) Work Stoppages
  (9) Unemployment Insurance

F. *Finance*
  (1) Banking
  (2) Consumer Installment Credit
  (3) Federal Government Finance
  (4) Gold and Silver
  (5) Monetary Statistics
  (6) Profits and Dividends (Quarterly)
  (7) Securities Issued
  (8) Security Markets
  (9) Stock Market Customer Financing
  (10) Bonds
  (11) Stocks

G. *Foreign Trade of the United States*
  (1) Value of Exports
  (2) Value of Imports
  (3) Merchandise Trade Balance
  (4) Export and Import Price Indexes
  (5) Shipping Weights and Value

H. *Transportation and Communication*
  (1) Transportation
       Air Carriers
       Urban Transit Industry
       Motor Carriers

CURRENT BUSINESS STATISTICS

Series originating in Government agencies are not copyrighted and may be reprinted freely. Series from private sources are provided through the courtesy of the compilers and are subject to their copyrights.

Current and historical data for the series shown in the S-pages are available on diskettes, printouts, and the Commerce Department's Economic Bulletin Board. Historical data, data sources, and methodological notes for each series are published in BUSINESS STATISTICS, 1963–91. For more information, contact the Business Statistics Branch, Business Outlook Division (BE-52), Bureau of Economic Analysis, U.S. Department of Commerce, Washington, DC 20230. (Telephone: (202) 606-5367; fax: (202) 606-5313.)

NOTE.—This section of the SURVEY is prepared by the Business Statistics Branch.

1. GENERAL BUSINESS INDICATORS

Unless otherwise stated in footnotes below, data through 1991 and methodological notes are as shown in BUSINESS STATISTICS, 1963–91	Annual 1991	Annual 1992	1992 July	Aug.	Sept.	Oct.	Nov.	Dec.	1993 Jan.	Feb.	Mar.	Apr.	May	June	July	Aug.
PERSONAL INCOME BY SOURCE																
[Billions of dollars]																
Seasonally adjusted, at annual rates:																
Total personal income	4,850.9	5,144.9	5,128.6	5,118.4	5,172.4	5,239.1	5,238.5	5,507.3	5,225.7	5,249.1	5,289.2	ʳ5,365.6	ʳ5,380.4	ʳ5,373.6	ʳ5,357.8	5,428.1
Wage and salary disbursements, total	2,815.0	2,973.1	2,954.6	2,981.6	2,976.3	3,002.5	3,021.1	3,263.9	2,970.9	2,976.3	2,975.8	ʳ3,068.3	ʳ3,093.8	ʳ3,086.0	ʳ3,101.7	3,128.8
Commodity-producing industries, total	738.1	756.5	751.6	752.0	751.3	758.8	755.6	835.4	738.7	742.7	740.8	ʳ765.2	ʳ766.7	ʳ763.3	ʳ766.4	769.7
Manufacturing	557.2	577.6	573.5	572.9	573.5	579.0	575.4	651.6	558.6	561.0	559.6	ʳ582.1	ʳ580.3	ʳ578.4	ʳ579.2	581.6
Distributive industries	648.0	682.0	676.3	685.2	685.9	688.2	695.3	746.2	681.5	684.3	683.0	ʳ704.9	ʳ713.1	ʳ709.2	ʳ713.8	721.0
Service industries	883.5	967.0	956.7	974.3	969.5	981.0	997.1	1,107.1	963.8	967.0	969.0	ʳ1,013.6	ʳ1,027.5	ʳ1,025.4	ʳ1,031.5	1,046.7
Government	545.4	567.5	569.6	570.0	569.6	574.4	573.0	575.2	587.0	582.3	583.0	ʳ584.5	ʳ586.4	ʳ588.1	ʳ590.0	591.5
Other labor income	296.9	322.7	324.0	326.0	327.9	329.8	331.5	333.1	335.8	338.5	341.2	343.9	346.6	349.3	352.0	354.7
Proprietors' income: ‡																
Farm	36.8	43.7	35.1	31.5	43.8	58.0	38.6	46.2	36.9	48.2	82.0	ʳ59.7	ʳ45.2	ʳ36.0	ʳ6.2	28.3
Nonfarm	339.5	370.6	370.1	370.5	373.2	380.7	382.4	387.8	388.4	388.7	388.2	ʳ389.7	ʳ392.7	ʳ394.8	ʳ395.1	399.8
Rental income of persons with capital consumption adjustment	-12.8	-8.9	-4.8	-42.7	-8.0	-1.8	-1.4	-.4	4.9	9.5	8.1	ʳ14.3	ʳ12.0	ʳ11.9	ʳ3.5	12.6
Personal dividend income	127.9	140.4	142.0	145.2	147.4	149.7	152.0	155.3	156.7	157.1	157.2	157.5	157.8	158.2	158.6	159.0
Personal interest income	715.6	694.3	695.2	691.9	689.6	692.2	694.8	696.6	695.7	695.3	695.2	ʳ694.1	ʳ693.1	ʳ692.0	ʳ693.0	694.5
Transfer payments to persons	769.9	856.4	861.6	864.5	872.2	879.7	872.4	880.2	892.4	892.6	898.3	ʳ901.7	ʳ904.5	ʳ912.0	ʳ913.5	918.2
Less: Personal contributions for social insurance	237.8	249.3	248.9	250.3	250.1	251.6	252.9	255.4	256.1	256.9	256.9	ʳ263.5	ʳ265.3	ʳ264.9	ʳ265.9	267.8
Total nonfarm income	4,792.0	5,080.1	5,072.5	5,065.9	5,107.7	5,160.2	5,178.9	5,440.2	5,167.4	5,179.0	5,185.1	ʳ5,283.7	ʳ5,312.8	ʳ5,315.0	ʳ5,329.0	5,377.1
DISPOSITION OF PERSONAL INCOME																
[Billions of dollars, unless otherwise indicated]																
Seasonally adjusted, at annual rates:																
Total personal income	4,850.9	5,144.9	5,128.6	5,118.4	5,172.4	5,239.1	5,238.5	5,507.3	5,225.7	5,249.1	5,289.2	ʳ5,365.6	ʳ5,380.4	ʳ5,373.6	ʳ5,357.8	5,428.1
Less: Personal tax and nontax payments	620.4	644.8	638.9	644.2	645.5	651.2	656.7	705.1	655.1	657.3	659.0	ʳ677.8	ʳ683.1	ʳ682.0	ʳ684.6	689.5
Equals: Disposable personal income	4,230.5	4,500.1	4,489.8	4,474.2	4,526.9	4,587.9	4,582.8	4,802.2	4,570.6	4,591.9	4,630.1	ʳ4,687.8	ʳ4,697.3	ʳ4,691.6	ʳ4,673.1	4,738.7
Less: Personal outlays	4,029.0	4,261.5	4,265.6	4,248.9	4,317.5	4,356.4	4,371.3	4,406.0	4,414.2	4,435.1	4,409.8	ʳ4,459.4	ʳ4,481.9	ʳ4,509.4	ʳ4,528.4	4,544.2
Personal consumption expenditures	3,906.4	4,139.9	4,145.4	4,128.7	4,197.1	4,235.3	4,249.9	4,283.3	4,290.8	4,311.6	4,286.1	ʳ4,355.8	ʳ4,358.7	ʳ4,385.3	ʳ4,403.9	4,419.5
Durable goods	457.8	497.3	496.4	502.4	503.9	515.4	508.9	525.5	531.0	508.2	506.7	ʳ526.6	532.7	ʳ535.6	ʳ536.8	537.1
Nondurable goods	1,257.9	1,300.9	1,298.4	1,307.7	1,310.9	1,328.1	1,329.0	1,337.9	1,333.7	1,345.0	1,327.2	ʳ1,342.3	ʳ1,344.1	ʳ1,348.1	ʳ1,349.1	1,350.0
Services	2,190.7	2,341.6	2,350.5	2,318.6	2,382.3	2,391.7	2,412.1	2,419.9	2,426.1	2,458.4	2,452.2	ʳ2,466.9	ʳ2,481.8	ʳ2,501.6	ʳ2,518.0	2,532.5
Interest paid by persons	112.2	111.1	110.5	110.5	110.6	110.6	110.9	112.3	112.4	112.4	112.7	112.7	112.2	ʳ113.1	ʳ113.5	113.7
Personal transfer payments to rest of the world (net)	10.5	10.4	9.7	9.7	9.7	10.5	10.5	10.5	11.0	11.0	11.0	ʳ11.0	ʳ11.0	ʳ11.0	ʳ11.0	11.0
Equals: personal saving	201.5	238.7	224.1	225.3	209.5	231.5	211.5	396.2	156.4	156.8	220.4	ʳ228.4	ʳ215.4	ʳ182.3	ʳ144.8	194.5
Personal saving as percentage of disposable personal income †	4.8	5.3	5.1	4.9	4.9	4.8	6.0	5.5	5.1	3.9	4.4	ʳ4.7	ʳ4.4	ʳ3.9	3.7	....
Disposable personal income in constant (1987) dollars	3,529.0	3,632.5	3,613.4	3,628.4	3,632.8	3,666.8	3,656.9	3,829.1	3,630.7	3,636.5	3,660.4	ʳ3,694.2	ʳ3,697.7	ʳ3,691.2	ʳ3,673.6	3,717.7
Personal consumption expenditures in constant (1987) dollars	3,258.6	3,341.8	3,336.3	3,348.2	3,368.1	3,385.0	3,391.3	3,415.4	3,408.4	3,414.5	3,388.4	ʳ3,416.7	ʳ3,431.2	ʳ3,450.2	ʳ3,462.0	3,467.3
Durable goods	426.6	456.6	456.0	460.3	461.8	471.4	466.0	482.9	485.7	465.5	464.4	ʳ479.5	ʳ485.2	ʳ487.9	ʳ489.3	488.1
Nondurable goods	1,048.2	1,062.9	1,057.5	1,064.1	1,067.0	1,079.3	1,079.8	1,086.2	1,078.6	1,082.2	1,067.4	ʳ1,079.0	ʳ1,081.7	ʳ1,088.8	ʳ1,089.4	1,089.6
Services	1,783.8	1,822.3	1,823.8	1,823.9	1,839.3	1,834.3	1,845.5	1,846.3	1,844.3	1,866.9	1,856.6	ʳ1,858.3	ʳ1,864.3	ʳ1,873.6	ʳ1,883.2	1,889.6
Implicit price deflator for personal consumption expenditures, 1987=100	119.9	123.9	124.3	123.3	124.6	125.1	125.3	125.4	125.9	126.3	126.5	126.9	127.0	127.1	127.2	127.5
INDUSTRIAL PRODUCTION																
[1987=100]																
Not seasonally adjusted:																
Total index	104.1	106.5	105.7	109.1	108.9	109.2	108.0	107.1	107.6	109.4	109.4	108.3	108.8	ʳ112.5	ʳ109.9	114.2
By industry groups:																
Mining	100.4	97.6	96.1	97.1	97.2	99.0	100.4	98.8	98.4	97.3	95.4	95.7	ʳ95.6	ʳ96.5	ʳ94.9	96.3
Utilities	112.2	112.0	112.6	110.9	105.6	102.0	109.6	127.7	133.4	129.2	121.2	107.8	ʳ101.3	ʳ108.6	ʳ120.9	120.0
Manufacturing	103.7	106.9	106.0	110.1	110.3	110.9	108.0	106.0	106.1	108.8	109.6	109.6	ʳ110.8	ʳ114.4	ʳ110.3	115.3
Durable	103.8	108.1	105.6	110.3	110.5	112.3	110.9	109.2	109.1	113.0	114.2	113.5	115.0	ʳ117.9	ʳ112.3	118.1
Nondurable	103.5	105.4	106.4	109.8	110.2	109.1	105.7	102.0	102.4	104.0	104.8	104.9	ʳ105.5	ʳ110.1	ʳ107.8	112.0
Seasonally adjusted:																
Total index	104.1	106.6	106.8	106.6	106.2	107.5	108.4	108.9	109.3	109.9	110.1	110.4	110.2	ʳ110.4	ʳ110.9	111.1
By market groups:																
Products, total	103.2	105.7	105.7	105.9	105.3	107.1	107.8	108.2	108.5	109.2	109.5	109.6	ʳ109.3	ʳ109.3	ʳ109.9	110.0
Final products	105.4	108.3	108.1	108.9	108.1	110.1	111.0	111.5	111.9	112.4	112.7	112.8	112.5	ʳ112.6	ʳ112.9	113.1
Consumer goods	102.9	105.2	104.9	105.1	104.4	106.4	107.1	107.5	107.6	108.5	108.6	108.1	ʳ107.3	ʳ107.3	ʳ107.5	107.3

See footnotes at end of tables.

Class I Railroads
Travel
(2) Communication

I. *Chemicals and Allied Products*

(1) Chemicals
Inorganic Chemicals
Inorganic Fertilizer
Materials
Industrial Gases
Organic Chemicals

(2) Alcohol

(3) Plastics and Resin
Materials

(4) Paints, Varnishes, and
Lacquers

J. *Electric Power and Gas*

(1) Electric Power

(2) Gas

K. *Food and Kindred Products,
Tobacco*

(1) Alcoholic Beverages

(2) Dairy Products

(3) Grain and Grain Products

(4) Poultry and Eggs

(5) Livestock

(6) Meat

(7) Miscellaneous Food
Products

(8) Tobacco

L. *Leather and Products*

(1) Leather

(2) Leather Manufactures

M. *Lumber and Products*

(1) Lumber—All Types

(2) Softwoods

(3) Hardwood Flooring

N. *Metals and Manufactures*

(1) Iron and Steel
Iron and Steel Scrap
Ore

Pig Iron and Iron Products
Steel, Raw and Semi-
Finished
Steel Mill Products

(2) Nonferrous Metals and
Products

(3) Machinery and Equipment

(4) Electrical Equipment

(5) Gas Equipment

O. *Petroleum, Coal, and Products*

(1) Coal

(2) Coke

(3) Petroleum and Products

P. *Pulp, Paper, and Paper Products*

(1) Pulpwood

(2) Wastepaper

(3) Woodpulp

(4) Paper and Paper Products

Q. *Rubber and Rubber Products*

(1) Rubber

(2) Tires and Tubes

R. *Stone, Clay, and Glass Products*

(1) Portland Cement

(2) Clay Construction Products

(3) Glass and Glass Products

(4) Gypsum and Products

S. *Textile Products*

(1) Fabric

(2) Cotton and Manufactures

(3) Manmade Fiber and
Manufactures

(4) Wool and Manufactures

(5) Floor Coverings

(6) Apparel

T. *Transportation Equipment*

(1) Aerospace Vehicles

(2) Motor Vehicles (New)

(3) Railroad Equipment

THE FEDERAL RESERVE BULLETIN

This is the main source of data on money, banking, credit conditions, and other financial sector indicators in the United States. Published by the Board of Governors of the Federal Reserve System, the *Federal Reserve Bulletin* consists of three main sections:

1. The first section consists of articles on aspects of the financial economy or on monetary policy. For instance, the semi-annual reports to Congress by the Chairman of the Board of Governors on the conduct of monetary policy are reprinted in the *Bulletin*. More representative was an article in the November 1993 issue on "Recent Trends in the Mutual Fund Industry."

2. Legal notices of changes in banking regulations are also presented in the *Federal Reserve Bulletin*. The minutes of the Federal Open Market Committee meetings are included.

3. Monetary and financial indicator statistics are presented each month in tabular form in the back of the *Federal Reserve Bulletin*.

Federal Open Market Committee (FOMC) Minutes

The Minutes of the FOMC meetings (held eight times a year) are the principal record of monetary policy. The Minutes typically summarize recent economic and financial conditions and evaluate these in light of past monetary policy actions.

At the end of the Minutes, there appears a "Directive" to the manager of the Open Market Desk at the Federal Reserve Bank of New York. The sample on pages 252–253 (taken from the Minutes of the August 17, 1993 meeting, published in the November 1993 issue of the *Federal Reserve Bulletin*), instructs the manager of the Open Market Desk on the implementation of the monetary policy decisions made at the FOMC meeting.

Minutes of the Federal Open Market Committee Meeting of August 17, 1993

A meeting of the Federal Open Market Committee was held in the offices of the Board of Governors of the Federal Reserve System in Washington, D.C., on Tuesday, August 17, 1993, at 9:00 a.m.

Present:

Mr. Greenspan, Chairman
Mr. McDonough, Vice Chairman
Mr. Angell
Mr. Boehne
Mr. Keehn
Mr. Kelley
Mr. LaWare
Mr. Lindsey
Mr. McTeer
Mr. Mullins
Ms. Phillips
Mr. Stern

Messrs. Broaddus, Jordan, Forrestal, and Parry, Alternate Members of the Federal Open Market Committee

Messrs. Hoenig, Melzer, and Syron, Presidents of the Federal Reserve Banks of Kansas City, St. Louis, and Boston respectively

Mr. Kohn, Secretary and Economist
Mr. Bernard, Deputy Secretary
Mr. Coyne, Assistant Secretary
Mr. Gillum, Assistant Secretary
Mr. Mattingly, General Counsel
Mr. Patrikis, Deputy General Counsel
Mr. Prell, Economist

Messrs. R. Davis, Promisel, Rosenblum, Scheld, Siegman, Simpson, and Slifman, Associate Economists

Ms. Greene, Deputy Manager for Foreign Operations
Ms. Lovett, Deputy Manager for Domestic Operations

Mr. Ettin, Deputy Director, Division of Research and Statistics, Board of Governors

Mr. Madigan, Associate Director, Division of Monetary Affairs, Board of Governors
Mr. Stockton, Associate Director, Division of Research and Statistics, Board of Governors
Ms. Johnson, Assistant Director, Division of International Finance, Board of Governors
Ms. Low, Open Market Secretariat Assistant, Division of Monetary Affairs, Board of Governors

Messrs. Beebe, J. Davis, T. Davis, Dewald, Goodfriend, and Ms. Tschinkel, Senior Vice Presidents, Federal Reserve Banks of San Francisco, Cleveland, Kansas City, St. Louis, Richmond, and Atlanta respectively

Messrs. McNees, Meyer, and Miller, Vice Presidents, Federal Reserve Banks of Boston, Philadelphia, and Minneapolis respectively

Ms. Meulendyke, Manager, Open Market Operations, Federal Reserve Bank of New York

By unanimous vote, the minutes for the meeting of the Federal Open Market Committee held on July 6-7, 1993, were approved.

Secretary's Note: Advice had been received of the election of William J. McDonough by the Board of Directors of the Federal Reserve Bank of New York as a member of the Federal Open Market Committee for the period commencing July 19, 1993, and ending December 31, 1993, and that he had executed his oath of office.

By unanimous vote, the Committee elected William J. McDonough as Vice Chairman of the Committee to serve until the first meeting of the Committee after December 31, 1993.

The Deputy Manager for Foreign Operations reported on developments in foreign exchange markets during the period since the July meeting. There were no System open market transactions in reserve conditions contemplated at this meeting were expected to be consistent with modest growth in M2 and little net change in M3 over the balance of the third quarter.

At the conclusion of the meeting, the Federal Reserve Bank of New York was authorized and directed, until instructed otherwise by the Committee, to execute transactions in the System account in accordance with the following domestic policy directive:

The information reviewed at this meeting suggests that economic activity is expanding at a moderate pace. Total nonfarm payroll employment increased in July at a rate close to its average advance in earlier months of the year, and the civilian unemployment rate declined to 6.8 percent. Industrial production turned up in July after posting small declines in May and June. Retail sales edged higher in July following a sizable rise in the second quarter. Housing starts were down somewhat in July, but permits moved up. Available indicators point to continued expansion in business capital spending. The nominal U.S. merchandise trade deficit declined in May, but for April and May combined it was larger than its average rate in the first quarter. After rising at a faster rate in the early part of the year, consumer prices have changed little and producer prices have fallen in recent months.

Short- and intermediate-term interest rates have changed little since the Committee meeting on July 6–7, while yields on long-term Treasury and corporate bonds have declined somewhat. In foreign exchange markets, the trade-weighted value of the dollar in terms of the other G-10 currencies was about unchanged on balance over the intermeeting period.

After expanding appreciably over the second quarter, M2 increased slightly further in July and M3 declined. For the year through July, M2 is estimated to have grown at a rate close to the lower end of the Committee's range for the year, and M3 at a rate slightly below its range. Total domestic nonfinancial debt has expanded at a moderate rate in recent months, and for the year

through June it is estimated to have increased at a rate in the lower half of the Committee's monitoring range.

The Federal Open Market Committee seeks monetary and financial conditions that will foster price stability and promote sustainable growth in output. In furtherance of these objectives, the Committee at its meeting in July lowered the ranges it had established in February for growth of M2 and M3 to ranges of 1 to 5 percent and 0 to 4 percent respectively, measured from the fourth quarter of 1992 to the fourth quarter of 1993. The Committee anticipated that developments contributing to unusual velocity increases would persist over the balance of the year and that money growth within these lower ranges would be consistent with its broad policy objectives. The monitoring range for growth of total domestic nonfinancial debt also was lowered to 4 to 8 percent for the year. For 1994, the Committee agreed on tentative ranges for monetary growth, measured from the fourth quarter of 1993 to the fourth quarter of 1994, of 1 to 5 percent for M2 and 0 to 4 percent for M3. The Committee provisionally set the monitoring range for growth of total domestic nonfinancial debt at 4 to 8 percent for 1994. The behavior of the monetary aggregates will continue to be evaluated in the light of progress toward price level stability, movements in their velocities, and developments in the economy and financial markets.

In the implementation of policy for the immediate future, the Committee seeks to maintain the existing degree of pressure on reserve positions. In the context of the Committee's long-run objectives for price stability and sustainable economic growth, and giving careful consideration to economic, financial, and monetary developments, slightly greater reserve restraint or slightly lesser reserve restraint might be acceptable in the intermeeting period. The contemplated reserve conditions are expected to be consistent with modest growth in M2 and little net change in M3 over the balance of the third quarter.

Votes for this action: Messrs. Greenspan, McDonough, Angell, Boehne, Keehn, Kelley, LaWare, Lindsey, McTeer, Mullins, Ms. Phillips, and Mr. Stern. Votes against this action: None.

Monetary and Financial Statistics

The *Federal Reserve Bulletin* is the source of many of the monetary and financial statistics for the U.S. Economy. The data presented in these tables are quite extensive (consisting of some 80 pages of tables) and fall into three broad categories:

A. *Domestic Financial Statistics*
  (1) Money Stock and Bank Credit
  (2) Policy Instruments
  (3) Federal Reserve Banks (Condition, Maturity Distribution of Loan and Security Holdings)
  (4) Monetary and Credit Aggregates
  (5) Commercial Banking Institutions
  (6) Weekly Reporting Commercial Banks
  (7) Financial Markets
  (8) Federal Finance
  (9) Securities Markets and Corporate Finance
  (10) Real Estate
  (11) Consumer Installment Credit
  (12) Flow of Funds
B. *Domestic Nonfinancial Statistics*
C. *International Statistics*
  (1) Summary Statistics
  (2) Reported by Banks in the United States
  (3) Reported by Nonbanking Business Enterprises in the United States
  (4) Securities Holdings and Transactions
  (5) Interest and Exchange Rates

The following three pages provide samples showing:

The Main Monetary Aggregates
A Sample of Interest Rates
Finances Raised in U.S. Credit Markets

1.10   RESERVES, MONEY STOCK, LIQUID ASSETS, AND DEBT MEASURES

Percent annual rate of change, seasonally adjusted[1]

Monetary or credit aggregate	1992		1993		1993				
	Q3	Q4	Q1	Q2	Apr.	May	June	July	Aug.
Reserves of depository institutions[2]									
1 Total............................	9.3	25.8	9.3	10.8	.7	36.5	5.1	9.4	9.8
2 Required........................	9.9	25.3	8.7	12.4	3.3	39.5	7.0	5.7	12.8
3 Nonborrowed.....................	8.4	27.1	9.5	10.6	1.1	35.5	3.8	8.1	7.6
4 Monetary base[3]................	10.5	12.6	9.1	9.8	7.6	13.8	10.9	9.5	11.5
Concepts of money, liquid assets, and debt[4]									
5 M1.............................	11.7	16.8	6.6	10.5	8.9	27.4	7.2ʳ	13.8ʳ	10.5
6 M2.............................	.9	2.7	-1.8	2.2	.7ʳ	10.5	2.5ʳ	1.9ʳ	1.4
7 M3.............................	.1	-.1	-3.7	2.6	3.3ʳ	8.6ʳ	.0ʳ	-1.2ʳ	.3
8 L..............................	1.1	1.6	-2.4	3.5ʳ	4.1ʳ	10.0ʳ	1.3ʳ	-1.0	n.a.
9 Debt...........................	5.7ʳ	4.3	3.8ʳ	4.6ʳ	4.6ʳ	4.8ʳ	6.4	5.6	n.a.
Nontransaction components									
10 In M2[5].......................	-3.2	-2.7	-5.3	-1.3	-2.9	3.3	.4ʳ	-3.3ʳ	-2.6
11 In M3 only[6]..................	-3.5	-14.4	-13.1	4.4ʳ	17.3ʳ	-1.4ʳ	-13.0ʳ	-17.1ʳ	-6.3
Time and savings deposits									
Commercial banks									
12 Savings, including MMDAs.............	10.9	12.9	1.6	4.6	3.3	14.0	6.4	.8	7.0
13 Small time[7].................	-17.4	-17.2	-7.9	-8.0	-11.2	-10.6	-10.5	-12.5ʳ	-11.2
14 Large time[8,9]..............	-18.6	-18.4	-17.9	.5	21.7	3.0	-11.5	-20.7	2.2
Thrift institutions									
15 Savings, including MMDAs.............	9.2	8.7	-.2	.7	2.0	9.0	2.8	2.5	1.7
16 Small time[7].................	-18.6	-21.7	-17.9	-10.1	-7.2	-8.3	-11.5	-12.0ʳ	-9.2
17 Large time[8,9]..............	-14.9	-11.3	-17.3	-7.9	11.2	-14.7	-9.3	-1.9	-7.5
Money market mutual funds									
18 General purpose and broker–dealer...........	-7.4	-4.2	-10.1	-.4	-4.7	18.1	-1.1	-.7	-6.4
19 Institution-only...............	32.9	-19.4	-14.1	.5	-3.0	14.4	-27.8	-18.8	-10.5
Debt components[4]									
20 Federal........................	12.5ʳ	6.7ʳ	7.6ʳ	10.4ʳ	10.7ʳ	10.2ʳ	12.2ʳ	7.4	n.a.
21 Nonfederal.....................	3.4ʳ	3.5ʳ	2.5ʳ	2.5ʳ	2.4ʳ	2.9ʳ	4.3ʳ	5.0	n.a.

1. Unless otherwise noted, rates of change are calculated from average amounts outstanding during preceding month or quarter.
2. Figures incorporate adjustments for discontinuities, or "breaks," associated with regulatory changes in reserve requirements. (See also table 1.20.)
3. The seasonally adjusted, break-adjusted monetary base consists of (1) seasonally adjusted, break-adjusted total reserves (line 1), plus (2) the seasonally adjusted currency component of the money stock, plus (3) (for all quarterly reporters on the "Report of Transaction Accounts, Other Deposits, and Vault Cash" and for all weekly reporters whose vault cash exceeds their required reserves) the seasonally adjusted, break-adjusted difference between current vault cash and the amount applied to satisfy current reserve requirements.
4. Composition of the money stock measures and debt is as follows:
M1: (1) currency outside the U.S. Treasury, Federal Reserve Banks, and the vaults of depository institutions, (2) travelers checks of nonbank issuers, (3) demand deposits at all commercial banks other than those owed to depository institutions, the U.S. government, and foreign banks and official institutions, less cash items in the process of collection and Federal Reserve float, and (4) other checkable deposits (OCDs), consisting of negotiable order of withdrawal (NOW) and automatic transfer service (ATS) accounts at depository institutions, credit union share draft accounts, and demand deposits at thrift institutions. Seasonally adjusted M1 is computed by summing currency, travelers checks, demand deposits, and OCDs, each seasonally adjusted separately.
M2: M1 plus (1) overnight (and continuing-contract) repurchase agreements (RPs) issued by all depository institutions and overnight Eurodollars issued to U.S. residents by foreign branches of U.S. banks worldwide, (2) savings (including MMDAs) and small time deposits (time deposits—including retail RPs—in amounts of less than $100,000), and (3) balances in both taxable and tax-exempt general-purpose and broker–dealer money market funds. Excludes individual retirement accounts (IRAs) and Keogh balances at depository institutions and money market funds. Also excludes all balances held by U.S. commercial banks, money market funds (general purpose and broker–dealer), foreign governments and commercial banks, and the U.S. government. Seasonally adjusted M2 is computed by adjusting its non-M1 component as a whole and then adding this result to seasonally adjusted M1.
M3: M2 plus (1) large time deposits and term RP liabilities (in amounts of $100,000 or more) issued by all depository institutions, (2) term Eurodollars held by U.S. residents at foreign branches of U.S. banks worldwide and at all banking offices in the United Kingdom and Canada, and (3) balances in both taxable and

tax-exempt, institution-only money market funds. Excludes amounts held by depository institutions, the U.S. government, money market funds, and foreign banks and official institutions. Also excluded is the estimated amount of overnight RPs and Eurodollars held by institution-only money market funds. Seasonally adjusted M3 is computed by adjusting its non-M2 component as a whole and then adding this result to seasonally adjusted M2.
L: M3 plus the nonbank public holdings of U.S. savings bonds, short-term Treasury securities, commercial paper, and bankers acceptances, net of money market fund holdings of these assets. Seasonally adjusted L is computed by summing U.S. savings bonds, short-term Treasury securities, commercial paper, and bankers acceptances, each seasonally adjusted separately, and then adding this result to M3.
Debt: Debt of domestic nonfinancial sectors consists of outstanding credit market debt of the U.S. government, state and local governments, and private nonfinancial sectors. Private debt consists of corporate bonds, mortgages, consumer credit (including bank loans), other bank loans, commercial paper, bankers acceptances, and other debt instruments. Data are derived from the Federal Reserve Board's flow of funds accounts. Data on debt of domestic nonfinancial sectors are monthly averages, derived by averaging adjacent month-end levels. Growth rates for debt reflect adjustments for discontinuities over time in the levels of debt presented in other tables.
5. Sum of (1) overnight RPs and Eurodollars, (2) money market fund balances (general purpose and broker–dealer), (3) savings deposits (including MMDAs), and (4) small time deposits.
6. Sum of (1) large time deposits, (2) term RPs, (3) term Eurodollars of U.S. residents, and (4) money market fund balances (institution-only), less (5) a consolidation adjustment that represents the estimated amount of overnight RPs and Eurodollars held by institution-only money market funds. This sum is seasonally adjusted as a whole.
7. Small time deposits—including retail RPs—are those issued in amounts of less than $100,000. All IRA and Keogh account balances at commercial banks and thrift institutions are subtracted from small time deposits.
8. Large time deposits are those issued in amounts of $100,000 or more, excluding those booked at international banking facilities.
9. Large time deposits at commercial banks less those held by money market funds, depository institutions, U.S. government and foreign banks and official institutions.

1.35 INTEREST RATES Money and Capital Markets

Averages, percent per year; figures are averages of business day data unless otherwise noted

Item	1990	1991	1992	1993 May	June	July	Aug.	1993, week ending July 30	Aug. 6	Aug. 13	Aug. 20	Aug. 27
MONEY MARKET INSTRUMENTS												
1 Federal funds[1,2,3]	8.10	5.69	3.52	3.00	3.04	3.06	3.03	3.03	3.10	2.98	3.06	2.98
2 Discount window borrowing[4,5]	6.98	5.45	3.25	3.00	3.00	3.00	3.00	3.00	3.00	3.00	3.00	3.00
Commercial paper[3,5,6]												
3 1-month	8.15	5.89	3.71	3.11	3.19	3.15	3.14	3.15	3.16	3.15	3.15	3.11
4 3-month	8.06	5.87	3.75	3.14	3.25	3.20	3.18	3.22	3.22	3.20	3.17	3.14
5 6-month	7.95	5.85	3.80	3.20	3.38	3.35	3.33	3.39	3.39	3.37	3.30	3.27
Finance paper, directly placed[3,5,7]												
6 1-month	8.00	5.73	3.62	3.05	3.12	3.08	3.08	3.09	3.10	3.09	3.08	3.03
7 3-month	7.87	5.71	3.65	3.07	3.16	3.12	3.13	3.14	3.16	3.13	3.12	3.11
8 6-month	7.53	5.60	3.63	3.07	3.16	3.15	3.16	3.19	3.17	3.17	3.16	3.15
Bankers acceptances[3,5,8]												
9 3-month	7.93	5.70	3.62	3.06	3.16	3.12	3.10	3.13	3.12	3.10	3.09	3.08
10 6-month	7.80	5.67	3.67	3.13	3.28	3.26	3.23	3.29	3.27	3.24	3.22	3.20
Certificates of deposit, secondary market[3,9]												
11 1-month	8.15	5.82	3.64	3.07	3.13	3.10	3.09	3.10	3.10	3.09	3.09	3.09
12 3-month	8.15	5.83	3.68	3.10	3.21	3.16	3.14	3.17	3.17	3.15	3.13	3.14
13 6-month	8.17	5.91	3.76	3.20	3.36	3.34	3.32	3.39	3.37	3.34	3.30	3.27
14 Eurodollar deposits, 3-month[3,10]	8.16	5.86	3.70	3.12	3.21	3.17	3.14	3.19	3.18	3.13	3.13	3.13
U.S. Treasury bills Secondary market[3,5]												
15 3-month	7.50	5.38	3.43	2.96	3.07	3.04	3.02	3.06	3.06	3.02	3.00	3.00
16 6-month	7.46	5.44	3.54	3.07	3.20	3.16	3.14	3.21	3.21	3.14	3.11	3.10
17 1-year	7.35	5.52	3.71	3.23	3.39	3.33	3.30	3.43	3.40	3.33	3.26	3.24
Auction average[3,5,11]												
18 3-month	7.51	5.42	3.45	2.96	3.10	3.05	3.05	3.10	3.10	3.05	3.03	3.02
19 6-month	7.47	5.49	3.57	3.07	3.23	3.15	3.17	3.24	3.25	3.18	3.12	3.12
20 1-year	7.36	5.54	3.75	3.13	3.40	3.42	3.30	3.44	n.a.	n.a.	n.a.	3.30
U.S. TREASURY NOTES AND BONDS												
Constant maturities[12]												
21 1-year	7.89	5.86	3.89	3.36	3.54	3.47	3.44	3.57	3.55	3.48	3.41	3.37
22 2-year	8.16	6.49	4.77	3.98	4.16	4.07	4.00	4.19	4.15	4.06	3.97	3.88
23 3-year	8.26	6.82	5.30	4.40	4.53	4.43	4.36	4.54	4.53	4.44	4.34	4.22
24 5-year	8.37	7.37	6.19	5.20	5.22	5.09	5.03	5.21	5.19	5.12	5.02	4.87
25 7-year	8.52	7.68	6.63	5.66	5.61	5.48	5.35	5.56	5.53	5.46	5.34	5.18
26 10-year	8.55	7.86	7.01	6.04	5.96	5.81	5.68	5.88	5.85	5.78	5.66	5.51
27 30-year	8.61	8.14	7.67	6.92	6.81	6.63	6.32	6.63	6.54	6.42	6.26	6.16
Composite												
28 More than 10 years (long-term)	8.74	8.16	7.52	6.68	6.55	6.34	6.18	6.37	6.30	6.24	6.19	6.08
STATE AND LOCAL NOTES AND BONDS												
Moody's series[13]												
29 Aaa	6.96	6.56	6.09	5.47	5.35	5.27	5.37	5.34	5.38	5.40	5.37	5.33
30 Baa	7.29	6.99	6.48	5.88	5.80	5.74	5.84	5.80	5.85	5.87	5.84	5.82
31 Bond Buyer series[14]	7.27	6.92	6.44	5.73	5.63	5.57	5.45	5.65	5.61	5.45	5.40	5.35
CORPORATE BONDS												
32 Seasoned issues, all industries[15]	9.77	9.23	8.55	7.78	7.66	7.50	7.19	7.50	7.40	7.28	7.13	7.04
Rating group												
33 Aaa	9.32	8.77	8.14	7.43	7.33	7.17	6.85	7.14	7.04	6.92	6.79	6.71
34 Aa	9.56	9.05	8.46	7.61	7.51	7.35	7.06	7.37	7.28	7.15	6.99	6.91
35 A	9.82	9.30	8.62	7.85	7.74	7.53	7.25	7.54	7.45	7.34	7.18	7.11
36 Baa	10.36	9.80	8.98	8.21	8.07	7.93	7.60	7.95	7.82	7.69	7.53	7.43
37 A-rated, recently offered utility bonds[16]	10.01	9.32	8.52	7.75	7.59	7.43	7.16	7.37	7.31	7.17	7.09	6.97
MEMO *Dividend–price ratio*[17]												
38 Preferred stocks	8.96	8.17	7.46	6.65	6.97	6.89	6.83	6.89	6.83	6.84	6.81	6.85
39 Common stocks	3.61	3.24	2.99	2.77	2.81	2.81	2.76	2.80	2.79	2.78	2.75	2.73

1. The daily effective federal funds rate is a weighted average of rates on trades through New York brokers.
2. Weekly figures are averages of seven calendar days ending on Wednesday of the current week; monthly figures include each calendar day in the month.
3. Annualized using a 360-day year or bank interest.
4. Rate for the Federal Reserve Bank of New York.
5. Quoted on a discount basis.
6. An average of offering rates on commercial paper placed by several leading dealers for firms whose bond rating is AA or the equivalent.
7. An average of offering rates on paper directly placed by finance companies.
8. Representative closing yields for acceptances of the highest-rated money center banks.
9. An average of dealer offering rates on nationally traded certificates of deposit.
10. Bid rates for Eurodollar deposits at 11 a.m. London time. Data are for indication purposes only.
11. Auction date for daily data; weekly and monthly averages computed on an issue-date basis.

12. Yields on actively traded issues adjusted to constant maturities. Source: U.S. Treasury.
13. General obligations based on Thursday figures; Moody's Investors Service.
14. General obligations only, with twenty years to maturity, issued by twenty state and local governmental units of mixed quality. Based on figures for Thursday.
15. Daily figures from Moody's Investors Service. Based on yields to maturity on selected long-term bonds.
16. Compilation of the Federal Reserve. This series is an estimate of the yield on recently offered, A-rated utility bonds with a thirty-year maturity and five years of call protection. Weekly data are based on Friday quotations.
17. Standard & Poor's corporate series. Preferred stock ratio is based on a sample of ten issues: four public utilities, four industrials, one financial, and one transportation. Common stock ratio is based on the 500 stocks in the price index.
NOTE. Data in this table also appear in the Board's H.15 (519) weekly and G.13 (415) monthly statistical releases. For ordering address, see inside front cover.

1.57   FUNDS RAISED IN U.S. CREDIT MARKETS[1]

Billions of dollars; quarterly data at seasonally adjusted annual rates

Transaction category or sector	1988	1989[r]	1990[r]	1991[r]	1992[r]	1991[r] Q3	Q4	1992[r] Q1	Q2	Q3	Q4	1993[r] Q1
						Nonfinancial sectors						
1 Total net borrowing by domestic nonfinancial sectors ..	752.6[r]	723.0	631.0	475.5	581.5	500.0	411.4	603.0	584.6	611.3	526.9	400.2
By sector and instrument												
2 U.S. government...................	155.1	146.4	246.9	278.2	304.0	379.5	272.5	323.8	352.9	299.1	240.1	229.6
3 Treasury securities	137.7	144.7	238.7	292.0	303.8	408.2	268.7	335.0	352.5	290.1	237.4	226.4
4 Agency issues and mortgages	17.4	1.6	8.2	-13.8	.2	-28.8	3.8	-11.2	.4	9.0	2.7	3.2
5 Private	597.5[r]	576.6	384.1	197.3	277.5	120.5	138.9	279.2	231.8	312.1	286.8	170.7
By instrument												
6 Tax-exempt obligations	53.7	65.3	57.3	69.6	65.7	68.8	77.6	68.0	76.6	75.8	42.4	62.1
7 Corporate bonds	103.1	73.8	47.1	78.8	67.3	81.6	60.2	76.3	77.8	61.3	53.7	75.0
8 Mortgages	279.6[r]	269.1	188.7	165.1	120.0	72.3	145.2	183.2	71.0	135.0	90.9	95.8
9 Home mortgages	219.6[r]	212.5	177.2	166.0	176.0	160.1	176.5	216.5	111.6	203.3	172.7	126.2
10 Multifamily residential	16.1[r]	12.0	3.4	-2.5	-11.1	-34.2	.2	11.6	-16.3	-11.1	-28.5	-5.6
11 Commercial	48.5[r]	47.3	8.9	.9	-45.5	-55.6	-28.6	-46.9	-24.6	-57.6	-53.0	-26.0
12 Farm	-4.6[r]	-2.7	-.8	.7	.6	2.1	-2.9	2.0	.4	.4	-.3	1.1
13 Consumer credit	50.1	49.5	13.4	-13.1	9.3	-20.4	-10.7	-9.8	-14.7	13.5	48.2	20.0
14 Bank loans n.e.c.	44.7[r]	36.4	4.2	-46.8	-4.7	-44.0	-53.7	-43.6	27.3	-24.3	22.0	-36.1
15 Open market paper	11.9	21.4	9.7	-18.4	8.6	-26.9	-5.0	2.5	-2.6	9.3	25.4	-24.2
16 Other	54.3[r]	61.0	63.6	-37.8	11.2	-10.9	-74.9	2.6	-3.5	41.5	4.2	-21.9
By borrowing sector												
17 State and local government	48.9	63.5	54.5	62.3	59.4	52.8	74.0	62.1	66.9	73.5	35.1	70.9
18 Household	300.1[r]	276.7	207.7	168.4	215.9	154.5	193.8	202.9	176.1	217.6	267.0	139.7
19 Nonfinancial business	248.4[r]	236.3	121.9	-33.4	2.2	-86.8	-129.0	14.2	-11.2	21.1	-15.3	-39.9
20 Farm	-10.0[r]	.5	1.8	2.4	.6	4.3	-4.6	2.1	3.2	-.5	-2.5	-1.5
21 Nonfarm noncorporate	57.2[r]	49.4	19.4	-24.5	-39.5	-81.5	-57.9	-21.7	-47.7	-37.5	-50.9	-28.8
22 Corporate	201.3[r]	186.5	100.7	-11.3	41.0	-9.6	-66.5	33.7	33.3	59.1	38.0	-9.6
23 Foreign net borrowing in United States	6.4	10.2	23.9	13.9	24.2	23.8	34.3	1.9	57.7	37.8	-.6	50.3
24 Bonds	6.9	4.9	21.4	14.1	17.3	15.6	18.5	4.9	21.9	20.3	22.2	75.6
25 Bank loans n.e.c.	-1.8	-.1	-2.9	3.1	2.3	1.4	6.5	1.5	14.1	3.9	-10.3	1.6
26 Open market paper	8.7	13.1	12.3	6.4	5.2	16.0	14.9	-8.0	27.8	13.1	-12.1	-21.7
27 U.S. government loans	-7.5	-7.6	-7.0	-9.8	-.6	-9.2	-5.6	3.6	-6.1	.5	-.4	-5.3
28 Total domestic plus foreign	759.0[r]	733.1	654.9	489.4	605.7	523.7	445.6	604.9	642.3	649.1	526.3	450.5
						Financial sectors						
29 Total net borrowing by financial sectors	239.9[r]	213.7	193.5	150.4	209.8	173.7	190.5	167.6	204.6	294.8	172.2	148.7
By instrument												
30 U.S. government-related	119.8	149.5	167.4	145.7	155.8	161.7	150.4	126.8	195.2	169.3	131.8	165.8
31 Sponsored-credit-agency securities	44.9	25.2	17.1	9.2	40.3	20.6	32.6	11.5	48.3	67.7	33.6	32.2
32 Mortgage pool securities	74.9	124.3	150.3	136.6	115.6	141.1	117.9	115.3	146.9	101.6	98.4	133.6
33 Loans from U.S. government	.0	.0	-.1	.0	.0	.0	-.1	.0	.0	.0	-.1	.0
34 Private	120.1[r]	64.2	26.1	4.6	54.0	12.0	40.1	40.8	9.4	125.5	40.4	-17.1
35 Corporate bonds	49.0[r]	37.3	40.8	56.8	58.7	35.0	73.7	28.6	59.1	73.0	74.2	60.1
36 Mortgages	.3	.5	.4	.8	.0	1.3	1.2	-.4	-1.5	.0	2.0	.9
37 Bank loans n.e.c.	-3.8[r]	6.0	1.1	17.1	-4.8	26.0	3.8	22.0	-39.1	16.9	-19.2	-21.2
38 Open market paper	54.8	31.3	8.6	-32.0	-.7	-11.7	-9.9	1.1	-14.8	17.5	-6.5	-75.5
39 Loans from Federal Home Loan Banks	19.7	-11.0	-24.7	-38.0	.8	-38.6	-28.6	-10.4	5.8	18.1	-10.1	18.6
By borrowing sector												
40 Sponsored credit agencies	44.9	25.2	17.0	9.1	40.2	20.6	32.5	11.5	48.3	67.7	33.5	32.2
41 Mortgage pools	74.9	124.3	150.3	136.6	115.6	141.1	117.9	115.3	146.9	101.6	98.4	133.6
42 Private	120.1[r]	64.2	26.1	4.6	54.0	12.0	40.1	40.8	9.4	125.5	40.4	-17.1
43 Commercial banks	-3.0	-1.4	-.7	-11.7	8.8	-2.6	-9.5	3.2	5.5	12.1	14.5	5.4
44 Bank affiliates	5.2	6.2	-27.7	-2.5	2.3	-11.2	7.0	10.9	-9.2	6.6	.8	21.1
45 Savings and loan associations	19.9	-14.1	-29.9	-39.5	-4.7	-41.1	-25.1	-20.3	2.7	10.0	-11.2	10.0
46 Mutual savings banks	1.9	-1.4	-.5	-3.5	1.8	-5.5	-8.7	4.3	.3	8.3	-5.6	6.1
47 Finance companies	23.9[r]	27.4	24.0	18.6	-3.6	16.0	39.0	-35.6	-20.1	21.2	19.9	-33.1
48 Real estate investment trusts (REITs)	1.8[r]	1.3	1.0	1.6	.1	1.8	3.3	1.7	.3	.9	-2.7	-1.4
49 Securitized credit obligation (SCO) issuers	35.9[r]	20.0	35.4	43.7	42.8	47.4	38.6	27.5	45.6	58.2	40.0	45.8

THE ECONOMIC REPORT OF THE PRESIDENT

This annual publication, compiled by the Council of Economic Advisors, is an invaluable source of U.S. Economic information.

The *Report* consists of roughly 300 pages of analysis and discussion on the U.S. macroeconomy. In addition, there are over 100 pages of tables presenting annual data (and recent monthly/quarterly data) on a range of U.S. economic data for the post-World War II period. These tables are organized into 10 areas:

1. National Income or Expenditure.
2. Population, Employment, Wages, and Productivity.
3. Production and Business Activity.
4. Prices.
5. Money Stock, Credit, and Finance.
6. Government Finance.
7. Corporate Profits and Finance.
8. Agriculture.
9. International Statistics.
10. National Wealth.

National Income or Expenditures

The table on the facing page presents current dollar GDP data, total and by major component, for the years 1959–91. In addition, quarterly data from first quarter 1989 through third quarter 1992 (at publication time—February 1993—the latest available data) are presented.

TABLE B–1.—*Gross domestic product, 1959–92*

[Billions of dollars, except as noted; quarterly data at seasonally adjusted annual rates]

Year or quarter	Gross domestic product	Personal consumption expenditures				Gross private domestic investment						
		Total	Durable goods	Non-durable goods	Services	Total	Fixed investment					Change in business inventories
							Total	Nonresidential			Residential	
								Total	Structures	Producers' durable equipment		
1959	494.2	318.1	42.8	148.5	126.8	78.8	74.6	46.5	18.1	28.3	28.1	4.2
1960	513.4	332.4	43.5	153.1	135.9	78.7	75.5	49.2	19.6	29.7	26.3	3.2
1961	531.8	343.5	41.9	157.4	144.1	77.9	75.0	48.6	19.7	28.9	26.4	2.9
1962	571.6	364.4	47.0	163.8	153.6	87.9	81.8	52.8	20.8	32.1	29.0	6.1
1963	603.1	384.2	51.8	169.4	163.1	93.4	87.7	55.6	21.2	34.4	32.1	5.7
1964	648.0	412.5	56.8	179.7	175.9	101.7	96.7	62.4	23.7	38.7	34.3	5.0
1965	702.7	444.6	63.5	191.9	189.2	118.0	108.3	74.1	28.3	45.8	34.2	9.7
1966	769.8	481.6	68.5	208.5	204.6	130.4	116.7	84.4	31.3	53.0	32.3	13.8
1967	814.3	509.3	70.6	216.9	221.7	128.0	117.6	85.2	31.5	53.7	32.4	10.5
1968	889.3	559.1	81.0	235.0	243.1	139.9	130.8	92.1	33.6	58.5	38.7	9.1
1969	959.5	603.7	86.2	252.2	265.3	155.2	145.5	102.9	37.7	65.2	42.6	9.7
1991: I	5,585.8	3,821.7	439.5	1,245.0	2,137.2	705.4	733.9	551.4	190.0	361.4	182.6	−28.5
II	5,657.6	3,871.9	441.4	1,254.2	2,176.3	710.2	732.0	545.8	185.2	360.6	186.2	−21.8
III	5,713.1	3,914.2	453.0	1,255.3	2,205.9	732.8	732.6	538.4	175.6	362.8	194.2	.2
IV	5,753.3	3,942.9	450.4	1,251.4	2,241.1	736.1	726.9	528.7	169.7	358.9	198.2	9.2
1992: I	5,840.2	4,022.8	469.4	1,274.1	2,279.3	722.4	738.2	531.0	170.1	360.8	207.2	−15.8
II	5,902.2	4,057.1	470.6	1,277.5	2,309.0	773.2	765.1	550.3	170.3	380.0	214.8	8.1
III	5,978.5	4,108.7	482.5	1,292.8	2,333.3	781.6	766.6	549.6	166.1	383.5	217.0	15.0

See next page for continuation of table.

TABLE B–1.—*Gross domestic product, 1959–92*—Continued

[Billions of dollars, except as noted; quarterly data at seasonally adjusted annual rates]

Year or quarter	Net exports of goods and services [1]			Government purchases					Final sales of domestic product	Gross domestic purchases [2]	Addendum: Gross national product [3]	Percent change from preceding period	
	Net exports	Exports	Imports	Total	Federal			State and local				Gross domestic product	Gross domestic purchases [2]
					Total	National defense	Non-defense						
1959	−1.7	20.6	22.3	99.0	57.1	46.4	10.8	41.8	490.0	495.8	497.0	8.7	9.1
1960	2.4	25.3	22.8	99.8	55.3	45.3	10.0	44.5	510.1	510.9	516.6	3.9	3.0
1961	3.4	26.0	22.7	107.0	58.6	47.9	10.6	48.4	528.9	528.4	535.4	3.6	3.4
1962	2.4	27.4	25.0	116.8	65.4	52.1	13.3	51.4	565.5	569.2	575.8	7.5	7.7
1963	3.3	29.4	26.1	122.3	66.4	51.5	14.9	55.8	597.5	599.8	607.7	5.5	5.4
1964	5.5	33.6	28.1	128.3	67.5	50.4	17.0	60.9	643.0	642.5	653.0	7.4	7.1
1965	3.9	35.4	31.5	136.3	69.5	51.0	18.5	66.8	693.0	698.8	708.1	8.4	8.8
1966	1.9	38.9	37.1	155.9	81.3	62.0	19.3	74.6	756.0	767.9	774.9	9.5	9.9
1967	1.4	41.4	39.9	175.6	92.8	73.4	19.4	82.7	803.8	812.9	819.8	5.8	5.9
1968	−1.3	45.3	46.6	191.5	99.2	79.1	20.0	92.3	880.2	890.6	895.5	9.2	9.6
1969	−1.2	49.3	50.5	201.8	100.5	78.9	21.6	101.3	949.8	960.7	965.6	7.9	7.9
1991: I	−28.7	573.2	602.0	1,087.5	451.3	332.4	118.8	636.3	5,614.4	5,614.6	5,614.9	1.8	−1.0
II	−15.3	594.3	609.6	1,090.8	449.9	325.9	124.0	640.8	5,679.4	5,672.9	5,674.3	5.2	4.2
III	−27.1	602.3	629.5	1,093.3	447.2	321.9	125.3	646.0	5,712.9	5,740.3	5,726.4	4.0	4.8
IV	−16.0	622.9	638.9	1,090.3	440.8	314.7	126.1	649.5	5,744.2	5,769.3	5,764.1	2.8	2.0
1992: I	−8.1	628.1	636.2	1,103.1	445.0	313.6	131.4	658.0	5,855.9	5,848.3	5,859.8	6.2	5.6
II	−37.1	625.4	662.5	1,109.1	444.8	311.7	133.1	664.3	5,894.1	5,939.4	5,909.3	4.3	6.4
III	−36.0	639.0	675.0	1,124.2	455.2	319.6	135.7	669.0	5,963.5	6,014.5	5,992.0	5.3	5.2

[1] Excludes receipts and payments of factor income from or to rest of the world.
[2] Gross domestic product (GDP) less exports of goods and services plus imports of goods and services.
[3] GDP plus net receipts of factor income from rest of the world.

Source: Department of Commerce, Bureau of Economic Analysis.

Population and the Labor Force

The table on the facing page presents data for the Household Employment Survey (civilian noninstitutional population, labor force, employment, unemployment, and the unemployment rate) for the years from 1947 through 1992 (and selected years from 1929). These data are also provided on a monthly basis from January 1989 through December 1992.

This is representative of the presentation of monthly data series in the *Economic Report of the President*. As a single source, it is truly invaluable to any business manager.

[Monthly data seasonally adjusted, except as noted]

Year or month	Civilian noninstitutional population [1]	Resident Armed Forces [1]	Labor force including resident Armed Forces	Employment including resident Armed Forces	Civilian labor force					Unemployment rate		Civilian labor force participation rate [4]	Civilian employment/population ratio [5]
					Total	Employment			Unemployment	All workers [2]	Civilian workers [3]		
						Total	Agricultural	Nonagricultural					
	Thousands of persons 14 years of age and over									Percent			
1929					49,180	47,630	10,450	37,180	1,550		3.2		
1933					51,590	38,760	10,090	28,670	12,830		24.9		
1939					55,230	45,750	9,610	36,140	9,480		17.2		
1940	99,840				55,640	47,520	9,540	37,980	8,120		14.6	55.7	47.6
1941	99,900				55,910	50,350	9,100	41,250	5,560		9.9	56.0	50.4
1942	98,640				56,410	53,750	9,250	44,500	2,660		4.7	57.2	54.5
1943	94,640				55,540	54,470	9,080	45,390	1,070		1.9	58.7	57.6
1944	93,220				54,630	53,960	8,950	45,010	670		1.2	58.6	57.9
1945	94,090				53,860	52,820	8,580	44,240	1,040		1.9	57.2	56.1
1946	103,070				57,520	55,250	8,320	46,930	2,270		3.9	55.8	53.6
1947	106,018				60,168	57,812	8,256	49,557	2,356		3.9	56.8	54.5
	Thousands of persons 16 years of age and over												
1947	101,827				59,350	57,038	7,890	49,148	2,311		3.9	58.3	56.0
1948	103,068				60,621	58,343	7,629	50,714	2,276		3.8	58.8	56.6
1949	103,994				61,286	57,651	7,658	49,993	3,637		5.9	58.9	55.4
1950	104,995	1,169	63,377	60,087	62,208	58,918	7,160	51,758	3,288	5.2	5.3	59.2	56.1
1951	104,621	2,143	64,160	62,104	62,017	59,961	6,726	53,235	2,055	3.2	3.3	59.2	57.3
1952	105,231	2,386	64,524	62,636	62,138	60,250	6,500	53,749	1,883	2.9	3.0	59.0	57.3
1953 [6]	107,056	2,231	65,246	63,410	63,015	61,179	6,260	54,919	1,834	2.8	2.9	58.9	57.1
1954	108,321	2,142	65,785	62,251	63,643	60,109	6,205	53,904	3,532	5.4	5.5	58.8	55.5
1955	109,683	2,064	67,087	64,234	65,023	62,170	6,450	55,722	2,852	4.3	4.4	59.3	56.7
1956	110,954	1,965	68,517	65,764	66,552	63,799	6,283	57,514	2,750	4.0	4.1	60.0	57.5
1957	112,265	1,948	68,877	66,019	66,929	64,071	5,947	58,123	2,859	4.2	4.3	59.6	57.1
1958	113,727	1,847	69,486	64,883	67,639	63,036	5,586	57,450	4,602	6.6	6.8	59.5	55.4
1959	115,329	1,788	70,157	66,418	68,369	64,630	5,565	59,065	3,740	5.3	5.5	59.3	56.0
1960 [6]	117,245	1,861	71,489	67,639	69,628	65,778	5,458	60,318	3,852	5.4	5.5	59.4	56.1
1961	118,771	1,900	72,359	67,646	70,459	65,746	5,200	60,546	4,714	6.5	6.7	59.3	55.4
1962 [6]	120,153	2,061	72,675	68,763	70,614	66,702	4,944	61,759	3,911	5.4	5.5	58.8	55.5
1963	122,416	2,006	73,839	69,768	71,833	67,762	4,687	63,076	4,070	5.5	5.7	58.7	55.4
1964	124,485	2,018	75,109	71,323	73,091	69,305	4,523	64,782	3,786	5.0	5.2	58.7	55.7
1965	126,513	1,946	76,401	73,034	74,455	71,088	4,361	66,726	3,366	4.4	4.5	58.9	56.2
1966	128,058	2,122	77,892	75,017	75,770	72,895	3,979	68,915	2,875	3.7	3.8	59.2	56.9
1967	129,874	2,218	79,565	76,590	77,347	74,372	3,844	70,527	2,975	3.7	3.8	59.6	57.3
1968	132,028	2,253	80,990	78,173	78,737	75,920	3,817	72,103	2,817	3.5	3.6	59.6	57.5
1969	134,335	2,238	82,972	80,140	80,734	77,902	3,606	74,296	2,832	3.4	3.5	60.1	58.0
1970	137,085	2,118	84,889	80,796	82,771	78,678	3,463	75,215	4,093	4.8	4.9	60.4	57.4
1971	140,216	1,973	86,355	81,340	84,382	79,367	3,394	75,972	5,016	5.8	5.9	60.2	56.6
1972 [6]	144,126	1,813	88,847	83,966	87,034	82,153	3,484	78,669	4,882	5.5	5.6	60.4	57.0
1973 [6]	147,096	1,774	91,203	86,838	89,429	85,064	3,470	81,594	4,365	4.8	4.9	60.8	57.8
1974	150,120	1,721	93,670	88,515	91,949	86,794	3,515	83,279	5,156	5.5	5.6	61.3	57.8
1975	153,153	1,678	95,453	87,524	93,775	85,846	3,408	82,438	7,929	8.3	8.5	61.2	56.1
1976	156,150	1,668	97,826	90,420	96,158	88,752	3,331	85,421	7,406	7.6	7.7	61.6	56.8
1977	159,033	1,656	100,665	93,673	99,009	92,017	3,283	88,734	6,991	6.9	7.1	62.3	57.9
1978 [6]	161,910	1,631	103,882	97,679	102,251	96,048	3,387	92,661	6,202	6.0	6.1	63.2	59.3
1979	164,863	1,597	106,559	100,421	104,962	98,824	3,347	95,477	6,137	5.8	5.8	63.7	59.9
1980	167,745	1,604	108,544	100,907	106,940	99,303	3,364	95,938	7,637	7.0	7.1	63.8	59.2
1981	170,130	1,645	110,315	102,042	108,670	100,397	3,368	97,030	8,273	7.5	7.6	63.9	59.0
1982	172,271	1,668	111,872	101,194	110,204	99,526	3,401	96,125	10,678	9.5	9.7	64.0	57.8
1983	174,215	1,676	113,226	102,510	111,550	100,834	3,383	97,450	10,717	9.5	9.6	64.0	57.9
1984	176,383	1,697	115,241	106,702	113,544	105,005	3,321	101,685	8,539	7.4	7.5	64.4	59.5
1985	178,206	1,706	117,167	108,856	115,461	107,150	3,179	103,971	8,312	7.1	7.2	64.8	60.1
1986 [6]	180,587	1,706	119,540	111,303	117,834	109,597	3,163	106,434	8,237	6.9	7.0	65.3	60.7
1987	182,753	1,737	121,602	114,177	119,865	112,440	3,208	109,232	7,425	6.1	6.2	65.6	61.5
1988	184,613	1,709	123,378	116,677	121,669	114,968	3,169	111,800	6,701	5.4	5.5	65.9	62.3
1989	186,393	1,688	125,557	119,030	123,869	117,342	3,199	114,142	6,528	5.2	5.3	66.5	63.0
1990	188,049	1,637	126,424	119,550	124,787	117,914	3,186	114,728	6,874	5.4	5.5	66.4	62.7
1991	189,765	1,564	126,867	118,440	125,303	116,877	3,233	113,644	8,426	6.6	6.7	66.0	61.6
1992	191,576	1,566	128,548	119,164	126,982	117,598	3,207	114,391	9,384	7.3	7.4	66.3	61.4

[1] Not seasonally adjusted.
[2] Unemployed as percent of labor force including resident Armed Forces.
[3] Unemployed as percent of civilian labor force.
[4] Civilian labor force as percent of civilian noninstitutional population.
[5] Civilian employment as percent of civilian noninstitutional population.
See next page for continuation of table.

[Monthly data seasonally adjusted, except as noted]

Year or month	Civilian noninstitutional population [1]	Resident Armed Forces [1]	Labor force including resident Armed Forces	Employment including resident Armed Forces	Civilian labor force					Unemployment rate		Civilian labor force participation rate [4]	Civilian employment/population ratio [5]
					Total	Employment			Unemployment	All workers [2]	Civilian workers [3]		
						Total	Agricultural	Nonagricultural					
	Thousands of persons 16 years of age and over									Percent			
1989: Jan	185,644	1,696	125,071	118,387	123,375	116,691	3,291	113,400	6,684	5.3	5.4	66.5	62.9
Feb	185,777	1,684	124,816	118,461	123,132	116,777	3,231	113,546	6,355	5.1	5.2	66.3	62.9
Mar	185,897	1,684	124,902	118,698	123,218	117,014	3,196	113,818	6,204	5.0	5.0	66.3	62.9
Apr	186,024	1,684	125,230	118,755	123,546	117,071	3,159	113,912	6,475	5.2	5.2	66.4	62.9
May	186,181	1,673	125,158	118,788	123,485	117,115	3,125	113,990	6,370	5.1	5.2	66.3	62.9
June	186,329	1,666	125,646	119,079	123,980	117,413	3,075	114,338	6,567	5.2	5.3	66.5	63.0
July	186,483	1,666	125,631	119,133	123,965	117,467	3,223	114,244	6,498	5.2	5.2	66.5	63.0
Aug	186,598	1,688	125,840	119,339	124,152	117,651	3,275	114,376	6,501	5.2	5.2	66.5	63.1
Sept	186,726	1,702	125,641	119,045	123,939	117,343	3,217	114,126	6,596	5.2	5.3	66.4	62.8
Oct	186,871	1,709	125,946	119,291	124,237	117,582	3,212	114,370	6,655	5.3	5.4	66.5	62.9
Nov	187,017	1,704	126,393	119,669	124,689	117,965	3,147	114,818	6,724	5.3	5.4	66.7	63.1
Dec	187,165	1,700	126,236	119,569	124,536	117,869	3,197	114,672	6,667	5.3	5.4	66.5	63.0
1990: Jan	187,293	1,697	126,246	119,640	124,549	117,943	3,157	114,786	6,606	5.2	5.3	66.5	63.0
Feb	187,412	1,678	126,301	119,728	124,623	118,050	3,119	114,931	6,573	5.2	5.3	66.5	63.0
Mar	187,529	1,669	126,429	119,938	124,760	118,269	3,219	115,050	6,491	5.1	5.2	66.5	63.1
Apr	187,669	1,657	126,406	119,695	124,749	118,038	3,160	114,878	6,711	5.3	5.4	66.5	62.9
May	187,828	1,639	126,559	119,976	124,920	118,337	3,286	115,051	6,583	5.2	5.3	66.5	63.0
June	187,977	1,630	126,275	119,872	124,645	118,242	3,262	114,980	6,403	5.1	5.1	66.3	62.9
July	188,136	1,627	126,274	119,562	124,647	117,935	3,104	114,831	6,712	5.3	5.4	66.3	62.7
Aug	188,261	1,640	126,461	119,449	124,821	117,809	3,138	114,671	7,012	5.5	5.6	66.3	62.6
Sept	188,401	1,601	126,493	119,372	124,892	117,771	3,170	114,601	7,121	5.6	5.7	66.3	62.5
Oct	188,525	1,570	126,535	119,280	124,965	117,710	3,193	114,517	7,255	5.7	5.8	66.3	62.4
Nov	188,697	1,615	126,545	119,043	124,930	117,428	3,171	114,257	7,502	5.9	6.0	66.2	62.2
Dec	188,866	1,617	126,835	119,109	125,218	117,492	3,270	114,222	7,726	6.1	6.2	66.3	62.2
1991: Jan	188,977	1,615	126,315	118,509	124,700	116,894	3,177	113,717	7,806	6.2	6.3	66.0	61.9
Feb	189,115	1,602	126,621	118,498	125,019	116,896	3,223	113,673	8,123	6.4	6.5	66.1	61.8
Mar	189,243	1,460	126,718	118,256	125,258	116,796	3,124	113,672	8,462	6.7	6.8	66.2	61.7
Apr	189,380	1,456	127,069	118,763	125,613	117,307	3,183	114,124	8,306	6.5	6.6	66.3	61.9
May	189,522	1,458	126,644	118,137	125,186	116,679	3,265	113,414	8,507	6.7	6.8	66.1	61.6
June	189,668	1,505	126,876	118,389	125,371	116,884	3,283	113,601	8,487	6.7	6.8	66.1	61.6
July	189,839	1,604	126,693	118,315	125,089	116,711	3,250	113,461	8,378	6.6	6.7	65.9	61.5
Aug	189,973	1,616	126,598	118,138	124,982	116,522	3,258	113,264	8,460	6.7	6.8	65.8	61.3
Sept	190,122	1,624	127,211	118,732	125,587	117,108	3,277	113,831	8,479	6.7	6.8	66.1	61.6
Oct	190,289	1,614	127,289	118,594	125,675	116,980	3,219	113,761	8,695	6.8	6.9	66.0	61.5
Nov	190,452	1,605	127,207	118,537	125,602	116,932	3,289	113,643	8,670	6.8	6.9	65.9	61.4
Dec	190,605	1,604	127,340	118,356	125,736	116,752	3,169	113,583	8,984	7.1	7.1	66.0	61.3
1992: Jan	190,759	1,599	127,627	118,635	126,028	117,036	3,146	113,890	8,992	7.0	7.1	66.1	61.4
Feb	190,884	1,585	127,770	118,547	126,185	116,962	3,213	113,749	9,223	7.2	7.3	66.1	61.3
Mar	191,022	1,585	128,133	118,849	126,548	117,264	3,194	114,070	9,284	7.2	7.3	66.2	61.4
Apr	191,168	1,577	128,320	119,095	126,743	117,518	3,206	114,312	9,225	7.2	7.3	66.3	61.5
May	191,307	1,574	128,613	119,154	127,039	117,580	3,186	114,394	9,459	7.4	7.4	66.4	61.5
June	191,455	1,570	128,868	119,080	127,298	117,510	3,244	114,266	9,788	7.6	7.7	66.5	61.4
July	191,622	1,568	128,918	119,290	127,350	117,722	3,207	114,515	9,628	7.5	7.6	66.5	61.4
Aug	191,790	1,566	128,970	119,346	127,404	117,780	3,218	114,562	9,624	7.5	7.6	66.4	61.4
Sept	191,947	1,566	128,840	119,290	127,274	117,724	3,221	114,503	9,550	7.4	7.5	66.3	61.3
Oct	192,131	1,552	128,618	119,239	127,066	117,687	3,169	114,518	9,379	7.3	7.4	66.1	61.3
Nov	192,316	1,531	128,896	119,595	127,365	118,064	3,209	114,855	9,301	7.2	7.3	66.2	61.4
Dec	192,509	1,517	129,108	119,828	127,591	118,311	3,262	115,049	9,280	7.2	7.3	66.3	61.5

* Not strictly comparable with earlier data due to population adjustments as follows: Beginning 1953, introduction of 1950 census data added about 600,000 to population and 350,000 to labor force, total employment, and agricultural employment. Beginning 1960, inclusion of Alaska and Hawaii added about 500,000 to population, 300,000 to labor force, and 240,000 to nonagricultural employment. Beginning 1962, introduction of 1960 census data reduced population by about 50,000 and labor force and employment by 200,000. Beginning 1972, introduction of 1970 census data added 800,000 to civilian noninstitutional population and 333,000 to labor force and employment. A subsequent adjustment based on 1970 census in March 1973 added 60,000 to labor force and to employment. Beginning 1978, changes in sampling and estimation procedures introduced into the household survey added about 250,000 to labor force and to employment. Unemployment levels and rates were not significantly affected. Beginning 1986, the introduction of revised population controls added about 400,000 to the civilian population and labor force and 350,000 to civilian employment. Unemployment levels and rates were not significantly affected.

Note.—Labor force data in Tables B–30 through B–39 are based on household interviews and relate to the calendar week including the 12th of the month. For definitions of terms, area samples used, historical comparability of the data, comparability with other series, etc., see "Employment and Earnings."

Source: Department of Labor, Bureau of Labor Statistics.

GLOSSARY

AGGREGATE DEMAND: The components of GDP viewed from the demand side: consumption, investment, net exports, and government spending. These are the sum of the expenditures of households (personal consumption expenditures and residential investment), business (nonresidential investment including both fixed investment in structures and durable equipment and the change in business inventories), foreigners (exports less imports, or net exports), and by government entities on goods and services.

AGGREGATE SUPPLY: This represents the production of the goods and services that are demanded. It is an alternative way of viewing GDP, principally focusing on the factors of production—especially labor and capital—required to produce the GDP.

BASIS POINTS: Interest rates are expressed in percentage points and basis points, where each percentage point consists of 100 basis points. Thus, if a bond's yield changes from 6.25% to 6.00%, it can be said that it declined by 25 basis points.

BREAK-EVEN POINT: The amount that a company sells in order to earn a revenue just equal to its total cost of production. The break-even quantity can be computed using the following formula:

$$\text{Break-even quantity} = \frac{\text{Total fixed cost}}{\text{Price} - \text{Average variable cost}}$$

The denominator of this equation is the firm's contribution margin per unit of product sold. Thus, when a firm breaks even, its total contribution margin [Quantity × (Price − Average variable cost)] will be just equal to its Total fixed cost.

BUSINESS CYCLE: Economic activity typically does not grow steadily, but rather undergoes extended bouts of downturn (recession), recovery, and fresh expansions to new heights. A complete business cycle can be measured from peak to peak, including these three phases—recession, recovery, and expansion. Alternatively, a cycle can

263

be measured from trough to trough, including in succession: recovery, expansion, and recession.

CAPITAL STOCK: The accumulated investment of plant and equipment that is used to produce aggregate output. The capital stock changes as a result of investment (additions to the stock) net of depreciation (the amount of worn-out and obsolete capital that is subtracted from the capital stock).

COMMAND PROCESS: The use of a central authority, usually the government, to decide on the key elicitation questions faced by every economy: "What? How? and For whom?" Heavy reliance is placed on central planning and the administrative allocation of resources.

CONSUMER PRICE INDEX (CPI): This is a measure of the prices consumers pay for a representative "basket of goods and services." The measure is compiled monthly by the Bureau of Economic Analysis and expressed on an index basis (1982–84 = 100).

CONSUMPTION FUNCTION: One of the principal components of Aggregate Demand, which states that consumer spending rises as income rises, but less than by the full increase in income.

CONTRIBUTION MARGIN: The amount that a firm's revenue exceeds its variable cost of production. This amount can be considered as a "contribution" to the fixed cost that the firm would have incurred in the short run, regardless of its level of activity; hence its name.

COST-PLUS PRICING: A technique that helps managers to arrive at a product price by simply marking up the unit cost of production. Economists consider this to be a very imprecise way to find a firm's profit maximizing price because it does not take into explicit account the price elasticity of the consumers. However, the degree to which a firm can mark-up a product from its unit cost depends on price elasticity. Experienced managers who recognize this will be indirectly taking price elasticity into account by being aware of the limitations of their ability to mark up the price.

COST STRUCTURE: The relationship of a firm's fixed to variable cost. Firms with a relatively high fixed cost relative to its variable cost are said to have a high operating leverage. (See **Operating Leverage**.)

CROSS-PRICE ELASTICITY: The relationship between the quantity demanded of a good or service and the price of a substitute or a complementary product. A firm tries to minimize the cross-price elasticity of its product relative to the price of its competition through advertising, promotion. It may also try to promote the sale of a particular product that has a high cross-price elasticity with a complementary product. For example, a computer store reduces the price of its PCs in order to sell more software.

CURRENT ACCOUNT: The main measure of the international payments position of the United States, consisting of the flows of merchandise, services, and investment incomes between the United States and its trading partners.

DEMAND: The amount of a good or service that people are ready to buy at different prices, other factors besides the price (see Determinants of Demand) held constant.

DETERMINANTS OF DEMAND: In economic analysis, these are factors other than the price itself that affect the amount that people are willing to buy of a particular good or service. They are: (1) income, (2) tastes and preferences, (3) prices of complementary and substitute goods, (4) future expectations about market price, and (5) number of buyers. A change in any of these factors causes a change in demand (i.e., a shift in the demand line).

DETERMINANTS OF SUPPLY: In economic analysis, these are factors other than the price itself that affect the amount that people are willing to sell of a particular good or service. They are: (1) cost, (2) technology, (3) number of sellers, (4) prices of other products that the sellers could offer, (5) weather conditions, and (6) future expectations about market price. A change in any of these factors causes a change in supply (i.e., a shift in supply).

DISECONOMIES OF SCALE: An increase in the unit cost of production as a firm increases all of its factors of production (i.e., its "scale" of production). Among the factors causing diseconomies of scale are: (1) managerial inefficiencies (i.e., bureaucratic tie-ups) and (2) disproportionate increases in indirect labor and staff.

DISPOSABLE PERSONAL INCOME: Personal income exclusive of income taxes.

ECONOMIC PROFIT: The amount of profit that a firm earns above and beyond its opportunity cost of production. In economic analysis, this occurs whenever a firm is able to sell a product at a price that is greater than its average total cost. Because opportunity cost is included along with accounting cost in a firm's total cost, a price that is greater than its average total cost implies an amount of total revenue that exceeds both the opportunity and accounting costs that make up a firm's total cost.

ECONOMIES OF SCALE: The decrease in the unit cost of production as a firm increases its scale of production. In economic analysis, this means that a firm increases all of its factors of production. Therefore, scale economies are considered to be a "long-run" phenomenon. Some of the key factors causing economies of scale are: (1) discounts on raw materials and supplies from larger bulk purchases, (2) the ability to use more efficient machinery justifiable only at higher volumes of output, (3) increasing opportunities to use specialization and division of labor, and (4) managerial efficiencies whereby supervisory personnel are able to exercise larger spans of control.

ECONOMIES OF SCOPE: The ability of a company to reduce its unit costs by producing two or more goods or services that involve complementary skills, experience, or productive facilities. For example, a video rental store might achieve economies of scope by making use of certain unused floor space for selling compact discs, or for providing one-hour photo developing services. A soft drink company such as PepsiCo can achieve economies of scope by manufacturing snack foods using the same production skills and distribution channels involved in soft drinks for the snack food business.

EFFICIENCY: In economic analysis, there are two types of efficiency. "Economic efficiency" is the production of goods and services in the least costly way. "Allocative efficiency" is the production of goods and services in close accordance with consumer demand.

ESTABLISHMENT SURVEY OF (PAYROLL) EMPLOYMENT: The measure of employment conditions, compiled by the Bureau of Labor Statistics, which emphasizes: the number of nonfarm jobs, the hours worked per week by production workers, and hourly wages. The data are compiled from the unemployment insurance payments employers make for their employees. Thus, the data exclude the self-employed and other nonpayroll workers.

FEDERAL FUNDS RATE: The interest rate that banks with excess reserves (against the Federal Reserve's reserve requirements) charge for overnight loans to banks with inadequate reserves. This is the principal policy instrument of the Federal Reserve.

FEDERAL OPEN MARKET COMMITTEE (FOMC): The principal policy-making body of the Federal Reserve. It consists of the seven Governors of the Federal Reserve System and the twelve Federal Reserve District bank Presidents, although only five of the twelve are voting members (the President of the New York Federal Reserve Bank and four of the other eleven, on a rotating basis).

FEDERAL RESERVE SYSTEM: The central banking institution of the United States that has responsibility for the conduct of the nation's monetary policy. It consists of the Board of Governors in Washington and twelve regional District Banks.

FIXED COST: The cost incurred by a firm that does not change with the level of its output (for example, rent and staff salaries).

FOREIGN EXCHANGE RATES: The rate at which currencies exchange for one another.

GROSS DOMESTIC PRODUCT (GDP): The broadest measure of United States' economic activity, GDP measures output produced within the United States (including exports net of imports). GDP measures economic activity using two approaches: (1) the total *income* payments made to the factors of production, and (2) the value of goods and services *produced*.

GDP IMPLICIT PRICE DEFLATOR: A measure of the price component of the GDP, the implicit deflator is found by dividing the GDP, measured in current dollar terms, by GDP adjusted for inflation.

GUIDING FUNCTION OF PRICE (ALSO CALLED ALLOCATING FUNCTION): A movement of resources into or out of markets in response to changes in price. As price in one market increases (e.g., seafood) and another one (e.g., beef) falls, suppliers are provided with the incentive to increase their resources in seafood and to decrease their resources in beef. Moreover, new firms would enter the seafood market and original firms would leave the market for beef.

HOUSEHOLD SURVEY OF EMPLOYMENT: The measure of the employment status of the population, compiled by the Bureau of Labor Statistics, that differentiates the portion of the adult population between those who are employed and unemployed. These are the data from which the unemployment rate—the percentage of total employed and unemployed who are unemployed—is calculated.

HOUSING STARTS: The start of construction of a new housing unit. A start takes place when the foundation is begun. In the case of multi-family units, the start of the foundation is taken as the start of construction of all the units in the building.

INCOME ELASTICITY: The relationship between quantity demanded of a good or service and the incomes of those who purchase it, measured in terms of percentage changes. If there is a direct relationship between income and quantity demanded, a good is considered to be "normal." An inverse relationship indicates an "inferior" good. For example, as people's incomes go up, they may be inclined to buy less pork and beans or canned meats. From a business standpoint, selling an "inferior" good or at least one whose demand is hardly affected by changes in income may be desirable during recessions.

INCREMENTAL COST: The change in a firm's cost of production relative to some designated change in economic activity. For example, if a new plant is built, the incremental cost of this project would be the additional cost incurred to the firm in building this plant.

INDUSTRIAL PRODUCTION INDEX: The measure of the output of the "goods" producing sectors: manufacturing, mining, and utilities (electric and natural gas). The output is expressed as an index (1987 = 100) compiled by the Federal Reserve. The industrial production index, when divided by an index of productive capacity, yields the capacity utilization rate, which is a measure of capital use analogous to the unemployment rate as a measure of labor use.

INFLATION: Refers to a *general* rise in the price level (as opposed to occasional rises in specific prices). Inflation is a state of macroeconomic disequilibrium, usually associated with strong demand pressures. There is usually some inflation that is tolerated as a short-term market imperfection similar to the notion of "frictional" unemployment.

INTEREST RATES: Interest is the payment made by borrowers to lenders for the use of their funds. Interest rates reflect this payment expressed as a percentage of the amount lent. Interest rates are usually expressed in percentage points and basis points (there are one hundred basis points in a percentage point), such as 6.02%. Among the main factors affecting interest rates are: (1) a *liquidity* premium, which increases with the length of the loan, (2) a *default risk* premium, reflecting the credit quality of the loan, (3) an *inflation* premium, reflecting a payment for the expected inflation over the term of the loan; and, in some cases, and (4) a *tax treatment* premium.

INVENTORY CHANGE: That portion of investment that represents the change in raw materials, goods in progress, and final goods ready for sale. Inventories are necessary to have in order to meet customer demand, but it costs money to finance inventory holding. Thus, businesses aim at a particular level of inventories. Surprises on the demand side, however, can lead to an unplanned increase (if demand suddenly falters) or a decrease (if demand suddenly surges). As a result, the change in business inventories is one of the most volatile parts of GDP.

THE LAW OF DEMAND: States that "the amount of a good or service that people are willing to buy is inversely related to its price."

THE LAW OF DIMINISHING RETURNS: States that as additional units of a variable factor of production are combined with a fixed factor, at some point, the additional or marginal units of output will begin to diminish. This law has an impact on a firm's marginal cost because at the point at which it occurs, it will cost a firm *increasingly more* to produce additional units of output.

THE LAW OF SUPPLY: States that "the amount of a good or service that people are willing to sell is directly related to its price."

LEADING INDICATORS: This is a composite index of eleven economic indicators that have been found to lead business cycle turning points (peaks and troughs).

LONG-RUN TIME PERIOD: In economic analysis, this time period provides enough time for sellers already in the market to react to changes in market price by varying *all* of their productive factors. Furthermore, there is enough time for new sellers to enter the market or for original sellers to exit. From the standpoint of demand, the long-run time period provides enough time for consumers to change their tastes and preferences as a result of the change in market price.

MARGINAL COST: The change in a firm's cost of production relative to a unit change in its output.

MARKET: All potential buyers and sellers of a good or service.

MARKET EQUILIBRIUM: A situation that exists when the quantity of a good or service that people are ready to buy is equal to the quantity that other people are willing to sell. Graphically, it is depicted as the point where the demand and supply lines intersect. At this point, there is an "equilibrium price" and an "equilibrium quantity." In such a situation, there is neither a shortage nor a surplus and the market is said to be "cleared."

MARKET PROCESS: The use of supply, demand, and material incentive to answer an economy's allocation questions of what, how, and for whom?

MARKET STRUCTURE: The number and relative sizes of buyers and sellers in a market.

MERCHANDISE TRADE: Refers to the international trade in goods. Merchandise trade is reported monthly, with the data compiled from customs receipts (in the case of imports) and other shipping and insurance records (in the case of exports). Merchandise trade is also reported quarterly on a Balance of Payments basis as part of the current account.

MONOPOLISTIC COMPETITION: This type of market is similar to perfect competition because it has a large number of relatively small buyers and sellers, entry and exit are fairly easy, and there is complete information about market price. The key difference is that each firm can exercise a certain degree of market power by differentiating its product from the competition. Small retail establishments provide a good example of this type of market (e.g., restaurants, dry cleaners, florists, duplicating centers, produce stores).

MONOPOLY: There is only one seller in this market and it therefore exercises a considerable amount of market power. However, this power is often kept in check by regulatory commissions. Public utilities provide the best examples of this type of market. However, there have been significant changes in the telecommunications industry, starting with the break-up of AT&T in 1982. In the 1990s, an increasing number of local telephone monopolies have been experiencing competition from new entrants. Companies also exercise monopolies by having their products under government patent protection. Companies in the pharmaceutical industry make extensive use of this source of monopoly power.

MR = MC RULE: The rule in economic theory that states that a firm wishing to maximize its short-run profit or minimize its short-run loss should produce up to the point at which the marginal revenue earned by selling the last unit of product is just equal to the marginal cost of producing that unit. In perfect competition, a firm is a price taker and therefore its marginal revenue is in fact the going market price (P). Thus, in economic analysis, this rule is often expressed as $P = MC$.

MUTUAL INTERDEPENDENCE: This occurs in oligopolistic markets when each firm sets its price with the explicit consideration of the reactions by its competitors. Because each firm watches the prices of the others so closely, the competitors often end up charging the same or very similar prices.

NONRESIDENTIAL FIXED INVESTMENT: Consists of spending for nonresidential structures and producers' durable equipment. This is the closest concept to the change in capital contained in the GDP data. Nonresidential fixed investment is sometimes called business fixed investment, which is slightly inaccurate. Nonprofit, nonbusiness investment is also included.

OLIGOPOLY: This market has a relatively small number of large sellers that dominate the market. In this market, the price is established through the "mutual interdependence" (see definition above) of each of the large, competing firms. In general, a change in price is initiated by a price leader, usually the firm with the greatest market share. Oligopolies are typically found in the manufacturing sector. Some oligopolies make standardized products (e.g., steel, oil, industrial chemicals). Others manufacture differentiated products (e.g., breakfast cereals, soap, toothpaste and detergents, large home appliances, mainframe computers).

OPERATING LEVERAGE: The relationship between a firm's fixed and variable cost. A firm that has a relatively high fixed cost and a relatively low variable cost has a "high" operating leverage. It therefore needs to sell a relatively larger volume of output in order to break even than a firm that has a "low" operating leverage. But once it breaks even, it will be earning relatively higher profits than the firm with low operating leverage. Nonetheless, high leverage firms that do not reach their break-even points stand to lose proportionately more than low leverage firms in the same situation. Thus, a high-leverage operation is said to involve greater risk.

OPPORTUNITY COST: The amount that is sacrificed or foregone by choosing one activity over the next best alternative. From the standpoint of a country, opportunity cost can be seen in a country's decisions about allocating its resources to national defense or to various peacetime activities. For example, the opportunity cost of defense spending might be the healthcare that a country could have paid for with the same amount of government funding. From the standpoint of a company, a good example of opportunity cost is the "hurdle rate" that the chief financial officer often applies to a capital budgeting decision. This is the interest rate that a company would forego by using its funds in a particular project rather than simply making a particular financial investment (e.g., buying a government bond). Projects whose estimated rate of return is higher than the hurdle rate are considered to have financial benefits greater than their opportunity cost to the company.

PERFECT COMPETITION: A market in which buyers and sellers have no market power and act strictly as price takers. Price is determined by the interactive forces of supply and demand. This type of market is characterized by: (1) a very large number of relatively small buyers and sellers, (2) a standardized product (no product differentiation), (3) free entry into and exit out of the market, and (4) complete information about the going market price. Examples of this type of market can be found in the agricultural sector (e.g., corn, wheat, soybeans, pork bellies).

PERSONAL INCOME: This concept refers to the income received by persons from all sources. Personal income mainly consists of: wage and salary payments and other labor income, rent, dividends, and personal interest receipts. In addition to these factor payments, however, personal income also contains transfer payments (pensions, social security benefits, unemployment insurance benefits, and welfare payments) with which no current production is associated.

PRICE DISCRIMINATION: A practice exemplified by a firm selling the same product in different markets at different prices.

PRICE ELASTICITY: The responsiveness of buyers to changes in product price, measured in terms of percentage changes. If the percentage change in quantity demanded is greater than the percentage change in price, this response is deemed "elastic." If it is less, then it is considered "inelastic." A "unitary elastic" demand is one in which the percentage changes in quantity demanded and price are equal. The degree of elasticity determines whether total revenue increases or decreases as a result of an increase or decrease in price.

PRICE LEADERSHIP: In an oligopolistic market, mutual interdependence tends to result in each firm setting the same price. The price leader in this type of market is the one that breaks out of the common price point with the implicit understanding that the others will eventually follow. However, short of the illegal practice of price fixing, there is no guarantee that the others will indeed follow.

PRICE SKIMMING: A pricing technique in which a firm that is the first to enter the market charges a higher price for a product due to the absence of competition. The idea is to "skim" as much of the profits as possible before other entrants reduce the ability of the firm to charge the higher price.

PRODUCER PRICE INDEX (PPI): This is a measure of the prices of all goods produced in the United States. Unlike the "basket of goods" concept of the CPI, the PPI is comprehensive including all goods produced, but excluding imports. The PPI is organized into three sub-indices: crude goods (such as wheat or raw steel), intermediate goods (such as flour or sheet steel), and finished goods (such as bread and passenger cars). Generally, the finished goods index is emphasized.

RATIONING FUNCTION OF PRICE: The increase or decrease in price to clear the market of any shortage or surplus. Typically, this function operates when changes in the market cause supply or demand (or both) to change. The resulting shortage or surplus then triggers the "rationing function of price" by causing the price to either rise or fall.

RELEVANT COST: The cost that is considered to be relevant to a particular business decision. In economic analysis, variable cost, marginal cost, and incremental cost are relevant costs. In certain cases, opportunity cost may also be relevant.

RETAIL SALES: The sales of durable and nondurable goods directly to consumers at retail outlets. The main categories are: hardware and building supply stores, auto dealers, furniture and appliance stores, general merchandise (including department stores) stores, food stores, gasoline service stations, apparel stores, eating and drinking places, and drug stores.

SHORT-RUN TIME PERIOD: In economic analysis, this is an amount of time that gives only those sellers already in the market to react to changes in market price by changing the amount of certain productive factors deemed to be "variable" (e.g., labor hours and raw materials). In this short-run time period, consumers have only time enough to react by buying more or less because the price has changed. A full understanding of this concept is provided by comparing it to the **Long-Run Time Period** (see glossary entry).

SHUT-DOWN POINT: In the perfectly competitive model of the firm, this occurs when the going market price is just equal to the lowest point on the firm's average variable cost curve. At this point, the firm would just as well shut down its operations because its loss would just equal its total fixed cost. Any price below this level would definitely cause the firm to shut down.

SUNK COST: A previously incurred cost that is not affected by a current decision. Another way of understanding this type of cost is to consider it as a cost that cannot be avoided, no matter what a business decides to do. For example, mid-way through a software development project, a firm decides to reconsider the desirability of this activity. All the costs incurred up to that point would be considered sunk, because it will not change whether the firm continues or stops the project.

SUPPLY: The amount of a good or service that people are ready to sell at different prices, other factors besides the price (see **Determinants of Supply**) held constant.

TRADITIONAL PROCESS: The use of customs and traditions to answer an economy's allocations questions of what, how, and for whom.

UNEMPLOYMENT RATE: The main measure of labor force utilization. The unemployment rate is equal to the number of unemployed as a percentage of the labor force.

VARIABLE COST: The cost incurred as the level of output changes (for example, the cost of direct labor, raw materials, and energy).

NOTES

CHAPTER 2

1. John Maynard Keynes, *The General Theory of Employment Interest and Money,* (Londons MacMillan Press Ltd., 1936 reissued 1973).

2. In December 1993, General Motors and Ford Motor Company announced they would no longer announce "10-day" sales (which had begun in the 1930s), but only monthly sales.

CHAPTER 3

1. John Maynard Keynes, *The General Theory of Employment Interest and Money,* (Londons MacMillan Press Ltd., 1936 reissued 1973).

2. The trade deficit can be presented in a variety of ways. The merchandise trade deficit discussed in Chapter 2 was a narrower concept that excluded trade in services. A wider concept is the current account trade balance, which views the balance of trade in goods and services on a balance of payments (BoP) basis. This is similar to but slightly different from the national income accounts (NIA) basis included in GDP. The BoP approach focuses on the flow of *monetary payments,* whereas the NIA approach focuses on *resource use.*

CHAPTER 4

1. This concept was explained in *The Survey of Current Business,* December 1983 (pp. 20–21). The U.S. Commerce Department last updated the concept in *The*

Survey of Current Business, March 1989. Michael Webb, an economist at the U.S. Department of Commerce, has made the basic data available to the authors. We have extended the concept through 1992 and applied it to real GDP as the basic measure of U.S. output.

CHAPTER 5

1. When unemployment or inflation is high, the overall economy—as measured by GDP—may be in equilibrium, but the labor market or the goods market is experiencing some degree of disequilibrium.

2. The energy component is shown only for the years after 1974. Although these are domestic prices, the effect of the OPEC embargo and price increases in 1973–1974 was quite dramatic on U.S. domestic oil and other energy prices. Before that time, energy prices showed greater stability than other prices.

3. There is an even narrower concept, CPI-W, reflecting urban wage earners—clerical workers, sales workers, craft workers, operatives, service workers, or laborers—who are paid hourly wages rather than salaries. The index is being phased out but is still used as the basis for some labor negotiations.

4. Only private business sector productivity is measured. An assumption is made that there is zero productivity in the government and nonprofit sectors. (This may strike some readers as a plausible result of bureaucratic inefficiencies. In fact, the assumption stems from the difficulty of measuring output in these sectors and may well be untrue.) In addition, the Labor Department compiles two measures of multifactor productivity: One measures the productivity of labor and capital inputs for the private business sector; the other measures the productivity of labor, capital, energy, materials, and purchased service inputs for the manufacturing sector. These measures are only compiled on an annual basis and are less often noted by business managers than the more conventional labor productivity measure.

5. A number of statistical methods are followed for seasonal adjustment ranging from quite simple, but effective, moving average methods to complex ARIMA (autoregressive integrated moving average) methods.

6. A. W. Phillips, "The Relation between Unemployment and the Rate of Change of Money Wage Rates in the United Kingdom, 1861–1957," *Economica,* Vol. 25 (November 1958), pp. 283–299.

7. Milton Friedman, "The Role of Monetary Policy," *American Economic Review,* Vol. 58 (1968), pp. 1–17.

8. Edmund S. Phelps, *Microeconomic Foundations of Employment and Inflation Theory* (New York: Norton, 1970).

9. Published in Arthur M. Okun and George L. Perry, *Curing Cronic Inflation* (Washington, D.C.: The Brookings Institution, 1978).

CHAPTER 6

1. Only the *nonfinancial* sectors are analyzed because the *financial* sectors play a role as intermediaries, by raising credit from one sector to make it available to a

different entity in the same or a different sector. Very little of the credit raised by the financial sector is raised for its own use.

2. Debt is the accumulated borrowing, or deficits. Some of the debt is held by the Social Security trust fund and other government trust funds, rather than by the public. The borrowing shown in Table 6–1 is *net* of these amounts.

3. The interest earned on U.S. Treasury securities is exempt from state and local taxation but is subject to federal income tax.

4. That is, 5 percent compounded over 5 years is 27.6 percent. Dividing this into the principal means that $10,000 loaned at the start of the period now has purchasing power equal to $7,835.

5. One-year bills are instruments with less than a 1-year maturity because they become due in 364 days.

6. Money market mutual funds owned by institutions are included in M3, but not in M2.

7. When a governor resigns before the end of a term, the successor is appointed for the duration of the unexpired term. Thus, the sequence of the terms is maintained.

CHAPTER 7

1. This system resulted from the International Monetary and Financial Conference of the United and Associated Nations, held at Bretton Woods, New Hampshire, in July 1944. This conference resulted in the creation of the International Monetary Fund (IMF) and World Bank, which oversaw the international payments system for the next quarter century.

2. The United States has had a deficit—net outflow—in its balance on unilateral transfers in each of the post-World War II years except 1991. The surplus in that year represented payments by our allies in the combined Desert Shield-Desert Storm operations.

3. The trade balance, exports, and imports referred to are actually the flows of goods *and services* in the GDP data. However, exports and imports of goods dominate here as well, so there is very little, if any, difference in the trends that result.

4. The trade accounts in Table 7–1 are in current dollars, but the ones in Figure 7–1 are in constant dollars. The former reflects the actual call on *financial* resources, while the latter reflects the use of *real* resources.

5. Special drawing rights (SDRs) are "paper gold," reserves created by the International Monetary Fund for settling balance of payments imbalances.

CHAPTER 9

1. For example, Paul Keat and Philip Young, *Managerial Economics: Economic Tools for Today's Decision Makers* (Macmillan, 1992), and John McAuley, *Economic Forecasting for Business* (Prentice-Hall, 1986).

CHAPTER 10

1. Chicago Fed letter, March 1993, Number 67.

2. Michael E. Porter, *Competitive Advantage* (New York: Free Press, 1985).

3. "Procter & Gamble Hits Back," *Business Week,* July 19, 1993, p. 21.

4. For further information on cost and strategy, see John K. Shank and Vijay Govindarajan, *Strategic Cost Management* (New York: Free Press, 1993).

CHAPTER 11

1. The extreme case of marginal analysis is to consider infinitesimally small changes around some given point. In so doing, calculus can be employed to analyze a firm's pricing and output decision. Readers interested in learning more about how calculus is used in economic analysis are encouraged to refer to any microeconomics or managerial economics textbook.

2. Interested readers should consult a textbook in microeconomic theory or managerial economics for more information about this topic. For example, see Keat and Young, *Managerial Economics* (Macmillan, 1992), and Pindyck and Rubinfeld, *Microeconomics* (Macmillan, 1992).

3. Shortly after "Marlboro Friday," full-page ads for Philip Morris's brand-name cigarettes began to appear with the slogan "Premium Quality at Lower Prices."

4. Even with complete information about cost, multiproduct companies may still have a problem correctly allocating overhead costs across the different product lines. In recent years, a new method of cost allocation called "activity-based costing" has been touted as the best method to deal with this problem.

5. In mid-1993, Kodak charged Fuji with "dumping" (selling below cost) its photographic paper in U.S. markets and demanded that tariffs of up to 235 percent be imposed on Fuji's product to restore the competitive balance.

INDEX